BEST of the BEST
from
VIRGINIA
COOKBOOK

—◆◆—

Selected Recipes from Virginia's
FAVORITE COOKBOOKS

BEST of the BEST
from
VIRGINIA
COOKBOOK

Selected Recipes from Virginia's
FAVORITE COOKBOOKS

Edited by
Gwen McKee
and
Barbara Moseley

Illustrated by Tupper England

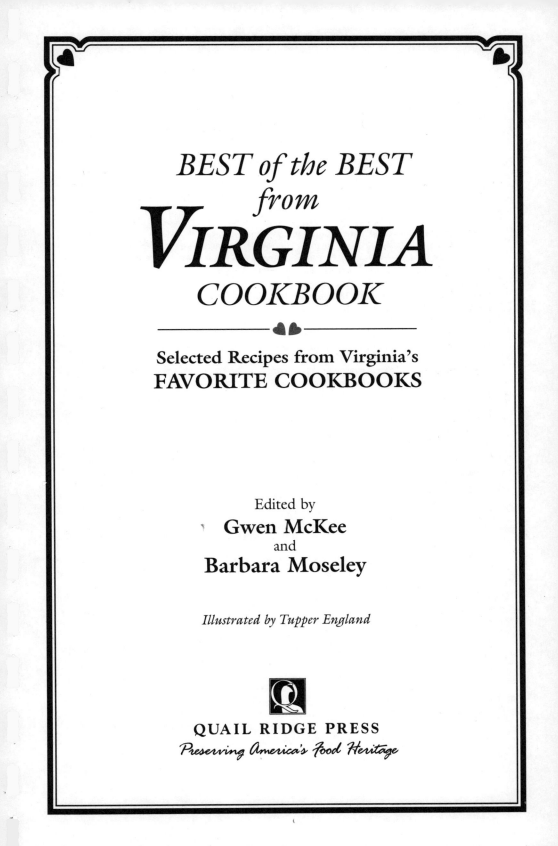

QUAIL RIDGE PRESS
Preserving America's Food Heritage

Library of Congress Cataloging-in-Publication Data

Best of the best from Virginia cookbook : selected recipes from Virginia's favorite cookbooks / edited by Gwen
McKee and Barbara Moseley ; illustrated by Tupper England.
    p. cm.
Includes index.
ISBN-13: 978-0-937552-41-4
ISBN-10: 0-937552-41-0
    1. Cookery—Virginia. 2. Cookery, American—Southern style. I. McKee, Gwen. II. Moseley, Barbara.
    TX715.B48565 1991
    641.59755--dc20   91-23169
                                                                                        CIP

ISBN-13: 978-0-937552-41-4 • ISBN-10: 0-937552-41-0

First printing, October 1991 • Second, March 1992 • Third, November 1992
Fourth, November 1993 • Fifth, November 1994 • Sixth, April 1997
Seventh, August 1998 • Eighth, January 200° • Ninth, August 200°
Tenth, July 2001 • Eleventh, January 2004 • Twelfth, January 2008
Printed by Tara TPS in South Korea

Design by Barney and Gwen McKee

Cover photo: George Washington's Mount Vernon,
courtesy of Virginia Tourism Corporation.

Back cover photo by Greg Campbell

QUAIL RIDGE PRESS • 1-800-343-1583
email: info@quailridge.com • www.quailridge.com

The Governor's Palace at Williamsburg once housed Patrick Henry and Thomas Jefferson as the first two governors of the Commonwealth.

Contents

*Editors Barbara Moseley and Gwen McKee
on the Blue Ridge Parkway.*

Preface

Virginia is for lovers—for lovers of nature, history, mountains, beaches . . . and most definitely, for lovers of good food.

We found Virginia to be fascinating from the moment we entered the southwestern tip, and our fascination never waned throughout the beautiful Shenandoah Valley, atop the Blue Ridge Mountains, across the hunt country fields and meadows, up to the quaint areas of Old Alexandria, then down to historic Williamsburg, and along the soothing seashore. The history throughout "The Old Dominion" is so well preserved that one seems to walk around with an almost overwhelming pride that here is where our country began. This is the land that our forefathers lived on, planted on, fought on, and died on. And in the meantime, our foremothers were feeding, clothing, birthing, and generally doing whatever needed to be done. Though their cuisine had European, African, and Indian origins, the land was so fertile and the sea so bountiful that they soon found new ways to prepare the abundant variety of foods available to them.

Martha Washington's "To Make A Frykecy" is presented with hearthside instructions (as well as modern ones) to make this timeless chicken fricasee. The simple "Kiss Froth" came from Thomas Jefferson's Monticello. The "Farmer's Spoon Bread" and "Sally Lunn" are as popular now as they were when they were served in the taverns of Williamsburg. In contrast, try the "Lazy Person's Complete Breakfast" done quickly in your microwave, or make a "Dirt Cake" in a flower pot to fool and delight your friends. "Baked Virginia Ham," "Chesapeake Bay Clam Chowder," "Tidewater Mushrooms," "Brandied Cranberries," "Silver Bowl Macaroons," . . . the list goes on and on of recipes that invite you to Virginia's table.

The seventy cookbooks within these pages are all special to us. Our correspondence with the authors, editors, committee chairpersons, and publishers enabled us to get to know a little about the people behind the recipes (no wonder they're so good), and we thank them all sincerely for their cooperation in making this book possible. There's a wealth of Virginia cuisine and history within these books, so valuable to cooks and collectors. We invite you to order their individual books directly from them (see catalog section in the back of the book). And please forgive us if we inadvertently overlooked any book that might have been included.

Tupper England is without a doubt the "Best" artist, and we thank her for providing such flavorful Virginia artwork. We are indebted to the many newspaper food editors and home economists all across the state who helped us with our research. We particularly want to thank our devoted readers who, like collectors Lemma Nite, Arlene Luskin and Myrtis Reavis, enthusiastically send us suggestions and even lists of cookbooks to contact. They along with the many book and gift store managers who answer our questions and lend us their knowledge, are much appreciated. We also thank the Virginia Division of Tourism for their use of pictures and information.

It was a joy to travel through Virginia, not only for the sheer physical beauty of the state, but for the wonderful people we met along the way. Though they differ from one region to another, all the Virginians we asked were proud to share their food and cookbook knowledge. Thank you Barbara in Bristol, young man with sleeping baby in Marion, Marine wife on Quantico Base, sweet Mennonite Martha in Waynesboro, helpful Hood at the Lyceum in Alexandria, lovely Janet in Warrenton, Chris and Annette in Middleburg, several mechanics who helped us get our van well, and all the people whose names we missed, but whose spirit we remember. We are excited to share these treasured recipes of beautiful Virginia with you.

Gwen McKee and Barbara Moseley

Contributing Cookbooks

Apron Strings
The Belle Grove Plantation Cookbook
The Best of the Bushel
The Boar's Head Cookbook
The Candy Cookbook Plus
Cardinal Cuisine
Chesapeake Bay Country
Children's Party Book
Command Performances
Cooking with Class
Cooking with Heart in Hand
Could I Have Your Recipe?
Culinary Contentment
Dan River Family Cookbook
Delectable Cookery of Alexandria
Dining at the Homestead
The Enlightened Titan
Favorite Meals from Williamsburg
The Foxcroft Cook Book
From Ham to Jam
Gourmet by the Bay
Granny's Kitchen
The Great Chefs of Virginia Cookbook
The Great Taste of Virginia Seafood Cookbook
The Ham Book
Happy Times with Home Cooking
Hearthside Cooking
A Heritage of Good Tastes
Historic Lexington Cooks
Holiday Treats from Granny's Kitchen
The Hunt Country Cook Book
Keeping the Feast
Kitchen Keys
Mennonite Community Cookbook
Mennonite County-Style Recipes & Kitchen Secrets
The Microwave Affair

Contributing Cookbooks

More Delectable Cookery of Alexandria
More Richmond Receipts
More Than a Cookbook
The Mount Vernon Cookbook
A Neapolitan Peasant's Cookbook
The New Life Cookbook
Of Pots and Pipkins
The Old Virginia Cook Book
The Other Side of the House
The Rappahannock Seafood Cookbook
Recipes from Jeffersonville Woman's Club
Richmond Receipts
The Smithfield Cookbook
Smyth County Extension Homemakers Cookbook
A Southern Lady's Spirit
Spotsylvania Favorites Cookbook
The Stuffed Cougar
Taste of Goodness
Think Healthy
Thomas Jefferson's Cookbook
Tidewater on the Half Shell
The Trellis Cookbook
The VIP Cookbook: A Potpourri of Virginia Cooking
Virginia Hospitality
The Virginia House-wife
The Virginia Presidential Homes Cookbook
Virginia Seasons
Virginia Wine Country
Virginia's Historical Restaurants and Their Recipes
THE What in the World Are We Going to Have for Dinner? COOKBOOK
The Williamsburg Cookbook
The Words Worth Eating Cookbook
WYVE's Bicentennial Cookbook
WYVE's Cookbook/Photo Album

Beverages and Appetizers

Quaint old row houses on cobblestone streets near the Potomac River in historic Alexandria.

Irish Coffee Glow
(Microwave)

½ cup water
¼ cup Irish whiskey
2 teaspoons sugar
2 teaspoons instant coffee

½ cup whipped cream
1 teaspoon crème de menthe
  (optional)

Add water to a 1-cup measuring glass. Microwave on HIGH (100%) 1¼–2 minutes until very hot, or microwave to 180° using the temperature probe.

    Measure whiskey and sugar in a 6-ounce serving glass. Add hot water and instant coffee. Stir. Top with whipped cream. If desired, drizzle with crème de menthe over top of whipped cream. Serve with a straw.

The Microwave Affair

Mary Todd Lincoln Punch

1 (6-ounce) package frozen
  raspberries, slightly thawed
Juice of 3 or 4 lemons
½ gallon Sauterne wine

1 cup brandy
1½ cups orange curaçao
2 bottles champagne
2 (24-ounce) bottles club soda

The day before serving, put slightly thawed raspberries in a loaf pan; fill with water and freeze.

    Mix lemon juice with wine in a punch bowl. Add brandy and curaçao; stir lightly. When ready to serve, add champagne and soda and slide in the raspberry ice block. Serves 25.

A Heritage of Good Tastes

Orgeat

A necessary refreshment at all parties.

Boil two quarts of milk with a stick of cinnamon, and let it stand to be quite cold, first taking out the cinnamon; blanch four ounces of the best sweet almonds, then pound them in a marble mortar with a little rose-water; mix them well with the milk, sweeten it to your taste, and let it boil a few minutes only, lest the almonds should be oily; strain it through a very fine sieve, till quite smooth and free from the almonds; serve it up either cold or lukewarm in glasses with handles.

The Virginia House-wife

Frozen Banana Punch

4 cups sugar
6 cups water
1 (46-ounce) can pineapple
 juice
1 (12-ounce) can frozen
 lemonade, thawed
2 (12-ounce) cans frozen
 orange juice, thawed

3 small cans crushed
 pineapple
6–7 ripe bananas, mashed
 (use blender)
6 (28-ounce) bottles ginger ale

Dissolve sugar in water. Add juices, pineapple, and mashed bananas. Freeze in 6 equal portions in freezer containers. Take out of freezer about 2 hours before serving time. Mix 1 portion with 1 ginger ale. Punch will be best at a slushy stage. Makes 72 punch cup servings.

Note: This punch is very pretty tinted a light green, too.

Recipes from Jeffersonville Woman's Club

Wedding Punch
(Pink)

5 cups sugar
5 cups water
2 small packages strawberry
 Kool-Aid
1 (6-ounce) can frozen
 orange juice concentrate

1 (6-ounce) can frozen
 lemonade concentrate
1 (46-ounce) can pineapple
 juice
2 quarts ginger ale

Combine sugar and water in saucepan. Heat to boiling, stirring until sugar is dissolved.

Add Kool-Aid to mixture while hot. Then cool. Add remaining ingredients along with enough water and ice to make 3 gallons.

Mennonite Country-Style Recipes

Frozen Fruit Slush

This mixture is delightfully refreshing on a hot day. It is a good item for lunches if weather isn't too hot. Cover top of insulated foam cup with plastic wrap fastened with a rubber band. It should be half thawed by dinner time, and just right to eat!

1 quart canned peaches, or 4 cups sliced fresh peaches
1½–2 cups sugar (use less if peaches are sweetened)
3 cups water and reserved juice

1 (6-ounce) can frozen orange juice with water added
1 (20-ounce) can crushed pineapple, undrained
7 or 8 bananas, diced

If using canned peaches, drain and reserve juice. Mash slightly with potato masher, just so they aren't chunky. Add enough water to juice to make 3 cups and dissolve sugar in it. Mix all together and freeze until slushy. Or fill foam cups and freeze firm. Partially thaw to serve. Yields approximately 18–20 (7-ounce) cups.

Note: I like to keep a shallow foil-lined cardboard box filled with fruit cups in the freezer for quick use. Tear a sheet of plastic wrap to cover the whole box. They keep indefinitely, and are so handy to have ready for quick use. Just set a cup in the microwave for 1 minute to make almost instant slush! Allow a couple of hours for thawing in the refrigerator.

Mennonite Country-Style Recipes

"Carlton" Punch

1 fifth cognac
1 fifth light (white) rum
½ pint peach brandy
½ pint apricot brandy
¼ cup Myers dark rum

¼ cup sugar syrup
¾ cup fresh lemon juice
1½ quarts green tea
1 quart unchlorinated water

Bottle and let stand for at least 60 days. It achieves its full flavor after 12 months. To increase strength, add only cognac. Pour over large piece of ice in punch bowl. Yields 6 fifths.

More Than a Cookbook

Julie's Mint Tea

2 family-size tea bags (4 regular)
Fresh mint
2 quarts boiling water

1⅓ cups sugar
½ cup lemon juice
¾ cup orange juice
2 cups ginger ale

Put tea bags and mint in a large container. Pour over two quarts boiling water. Cool. Add remaining ingredients and serve over ice. Makes about three quarts.

From Ham to Jam

Bourbon Slush

4 tea bags
2 cups boiling water
2 cups sugar
7 cups water
1 (12-ounce) frozen orange juice concentrate

1 (6-ounce) frozen lemonade concentrate
1 cup bourbon

Steep tea bags in boiling water for 2–3 minutes. Remove tea bags and stir in sugar until melted. Add all remaining ingredients and stir well. Pour into 2–3 freezing cartons. Remove from mold and thaw 20–30 minutes before serving from punch bowl. Yields 20 (5-ounce) servings.

The Enlightened Titan

Clifton Sunset

As pretty as a sunset. A pretty way to start off a romantic meal.

1 (413) can cranberry juice
1 (12-ounce) can frozen limeade
  concentrate
12 ounces Southern Comfort

3 lemons, sliced or halved
3 limes, sliced or halved
3 oranges, sliced or halved

Combine above liquids. Add fruits that have been halved or sliced and muddled (mashed with spoon) to extract juices. Pour into pitcher or container. Stays refrigerated for a long time. When serving, garnish each glass with a fresh slice of lemon, lime, and orange, and a sprig of mint.

Cooking with Heart in Hand

Raspberry Cordial

To each quart of ripe red raspberries, put one quart of best French brandy, let it remain about a week, then strain it through a sieve or bag, pressing out all the liquid; when you have got as much as you want, reduce the strength to your taste with water, and put a pound of powdered loaf sugar to each gallon; let it stand till refined. Strawberry cordial is made the same way. It destroys the flavor of these fruits to put them on the fire.

The Virginia House-wife

Old Virginia Mint Julep

Steep fresh mint in best brandy; make a syrup of sugar and water (use this sparingly); fill a tumbler (cut-glass) to one-third of brandy; put in three teaspoonfuls of syrup; fill the glass with pounded ice; stick five or six sprigs of mint on top and two or three strawberries. If old whiskey is used instead of brandy, more is required to make it strong enough. For an extra fillip, dash the julep with rum.

Chesapeake Bay Country

Hot Buttered Rum

1 pound butter, softened
1 (16-ounce) package light
  brown sugar
1 (16-ounce) package
  powdered sugar
2 teaspoons ground cinnamon

2 teaspoons ground nutmeg
1 quart vanilla ice cream,
  softened
Light rum
Whipping cream
Cinnamon sticks

Combine butter, sugars, spices; beat until light and fluffy. Add ice cream, stirring until well blended. Spoon mixture into 2-quart freezer container; freeze.

To serve, thaw slightly. Place 3 tablespoons butter mixture and 1 jigger rum in a large mug; fill with boiling water. Stir well. (Unused butter mixture can be refrozen.) Top with whipped cream; serve with cinnamon stick stirrers. Yields 25 (8-ounce) servings.

Taste of Goodness

Hot Crabmeat Dip

1 (8-ounce) package cream
  cheese, softened
7 (7-ounce) can King
  crabmeat, or fresh
¼ cup mayonnaise
1 teaspoon grated onion

1 teaspoon mustard
1 teaspoon powdered sugar
Pinch of salt
2 tablespoons white wine or
  dry Vermouth
1 garlic clove

Put all ingredients in chafing dish except garlic clove. Put garlic clove through a press over other ingredients. Mix everything together well (hard job) and heat. Keep hot over boiling water, not direct flame. Delicious—hard to judge amount it feeds as it is always eaten up by any number.

The Foxcroft Cook Book

Crab Dip

1 can crabmeat
1 can cream of celery soup
½ cup chopped celery

¾ cup mayonnaise
6 green onions, chopped
1 packet Knox gelatine

Drain crabmeat well. Heat soup on low; add gelatine. Add rest of ingredients. Mold in lobster mold, approximately 3 hours.

Smyth County Extension Homemakers Cookbook

Hot Mushroom Dip

4 slices bacon
½ pound fresh mushrooms,
  sliced
1 medium onion, chopped
1 garlic clove, minced
2 tablespoons flour
¼ teaspoon salt
⅛ teaspoon pepper

1 (8-ounce) package cream
  cheese, cut into small pieces
2 teaspoons Worcestershire
  sauce
2 teaspoons soy sauce
½ cup sour cream
Crackers or bread sticks

Fry bacon until crisp, drain, crumble and set aside. Add mushrooms, onion, and garlic to pan and cook until tender; drain. Add remaining ingredients to pan, except sour cream and bacon. Heat on low and stir until cheese melts. Stir in sour cream and bacon; heat thoroughly. Serve warm with crackers or breadsticks. Yields 2½–3 cups.

Keeping the Feast

Shrimp Ball

Shrimply delightful! A very popular appetizer.

2 (6- or 8-ounce) packages
  small frozen, cooked shrimp
2 (8-ounce) packages cream
  cheese, softened
1 teaspoon minced onion
¼ teaspoon garlic salt

½–1 teaspoon hot sauce, to
  taste
Mayonnaise to moisten (about
  2 tablespoons)
Salt to taste
Chopped parsley, dried or fresh

Thaw and drain shrimp well (I press in paper towels to remove all water). Combine cream cheese, onion, garlic salt, hot sauce, mayonnaise, and salt, if needed. Add shrimp and mix well. Form into a ball; wrap in plastic wrap. Chill until ready to serve. Sprinkle with chopped parsley. Serve with assorted crackers. Makes 1 ball (serves approximately 50).

Hint: Make a day ahead so flavors will blend. Tips for garnish: Instead of sprinkling with chopped parsley, top ball with shrimp and garnish base with fresh parsley. For Christmas, sprinkle ball with parsley and paprika.

Granny's Kitchen

Shrimp Mold

Big hit on a cocktail table!

1 package unflavored gelatin
¼ cup water
1 cup mayonnaise
1 (8-ounce) package cream
  cheese, softened
Juice of ½ lemon
Dash of Worcestershire sauce

1 pound cooked shrimp, cut
  in small pieces
1 cup finely chopped celery
1 small onion, minced
1 very small bottle of olives
½ cup chopped green pepper

Dissolve gelatin in water. Whip mayonnaise, cream cheese, lemon juice and Worcestershire until creamy. Add dissolved gelatin and rest of the ingredients, mixing well. Pour into lightly greased mold. If using a fish-shaped mold, save 1 olive slice to make an eye.

The Smithfield Cookbook

Marinated Shrimp

Prepare one day before serving.

2½ pounds fresh shrimp
  (in shells)
½ cup chopped celery

½ cup pickling spices
1 large onion, sliced
7 bay leaves

SAUCE:

1½ cups vegetable oil
¾ cup white vinegar
1½ teaspoons salt

2½ teaspoons celery seed
2 dashes Tabasco sauce

In large pan, add enough water to cover shrimp. Add celery and pickling spices. Boil until shrimp turns pink (approximately 3 minutes). Drain shrimp and rinse off celery and pickling spices. In a large bowl, alternate shrimp and onion. Place bay leaves on top. In a separate bowl, prepare sauce and mix well. Pour over shrimp, cover and store for 24 hours. Drain sauce and serve.

Note: Do not shell shrimp. Shrimp are to be peeled when eating.

The Rappahannock Seafood Cookbook

Marinated Shrimp in Avocado

This is one of my favorite appetizers. It also is good for a brown bag lunch if you wrap it all in Saran Wrap. Much more elegant than a sandwich.

½ cup salad oil
½ cup lime or lemon juice
2 tablespoons vinegar
1½ teaspoons salt
½ teaspoon each dill seed
  and dry mustard
Dash of cayenne

2 teaspoons capers
1 pound shrimp, cooked,
  shelled and cleaned
3 or 4 avocados, halved and
  peeled
Boston lettuce

Combine for marinade: oil, lime juice, vinegar, seasonings and capers. Toss with shrimp and chill several hours, stirring occasionally.

Brush avocado halves with some of marinade. Arrange on lettuce and fill with shrimp. Serve with remaining marinade. Makes 6–8 servings.

Could I Have Your Recipe?

Crab-Swiss Bites

1 (7½-ounce) can crabmeat, drained and flaked
1 tablespoon sliced green onion
4 ounces (1 cup) processed shredded Swiss cheese
½ cup mayonnaise
1 teaspoon lemon juice
¼ teaspoon curry powder
12 flaky-style refrigerator rolls
1 (5-ounce) can water chestnuts, sliced

Combine crabmeat, green onion, Swiss cheese, mayonnaise, lemon juice, curry powder.

Separate each roll into 3 layers. Place on ungreased baking sheet. Spoon on crabmeat mixture. Top with water chestnut slices. Bake at 400° for 8 minutes.

Command Performances

Cheezy Crab Hors D'Oeuvres

1 (8-ounce) package cream cheese, softened
1 teaspoon milk
1 tablespoon instant minced onion
¼ cup Parmesan cheese
½ teaspoon horseradish
1 cup (8 ounces) crabmeat
Salt and pepper to taste
1 (2-ounce) package slivered almonds (optional)

Blend together cream cheese, milk, onion, Parmesan cheese and horseradish. Gently mix in crabmeat. Add salt and pepper. Put in shallow 1-quart baking dish; sprinkle almonds over top. Bake at 350° until lightly browned on top, about 20 minutes. Serve hot on crackers or as a dip.

Note: Can be served without cooking. Simply add milk to proper consistency for use as a spread or dip. Keep refrigerated until served.

The Rappahannock Seafood Cookbook

Newport News is known as the largest shipbuilding city in the world. It was named for Captain Christopher Newport, whose "news" was that more settlers were coming.

Iris' Meatballs

MEATBALLS:

1½ pounds ground beef
¾ cup rolled oats
1 can water chestnuts
  (drained and chopped)
½ cup milk
1 egg, beaten

1 tablespoon soy sauce
1 tablespoon Ac'cent
½ teaspoon onion powder
½ teaspoon garlic salt
¼ teaspoon salt
Dash of Tabasco

Mix well. Form into small balls. Brown and drain.

SAUCE:

1 (8½-ounce) can crushed
  pineapple
1 cup brown sugar
2 tablespoons cornstarch
1 cup beef bouillon

½ cup red wine vinegar or
  lemon juice
2 tablespoons soy sauce
⅓ cup chopped green pepper

Drain pineapple. Put pineapple juice, sugar, and cornstarch in pan and gradually add other liquids. Cook, stirring until thick. Add pineapple and green pepper. Simmer meatballs in sauce 30 minutes. Yields approximately 8 dozen.

The Stuffed Cougar

Piccalilli

2½ pounds round steak,
  ground
1 pound lean pork, ground
3 large onions, chopped fine
5–6 cloves garlic, chopped fine
5–6 extra large ripe tomatoes,
  skinned and diced
1 package almonds, chopped

¾ large box seedless raisins
1 small jar jalapeño peppers,
  diced
3 teaspoons oregano
Salt to taste
Cracked pepper to taste
½ cup flour

Cook meat until brown. Sauté onions with meat but do not let them brown. Add garlic, tomatoes, almonds, raisins, jalapeño peppers, oregano, salt, and pepper. Simmer until tomatoes are done. Sprinkle with flour and stir until thick enough to dip. Do not use any water. Serve hot in a chafing dish and dip with Doritos or Fritos.

Of Pots and Pipkins

Brandied Meat Balls

"I've had raves for this recipe each time I've served it."

2 pounds ground beef	2 drops hot sauce
¾ cup milk	2 tablespoons hot cooking oil
½ cup bread crumbs	Brandied Peach Sauce
1 tablespoon Worcestershire sauce	1 tablespoon cornstarch (if needed)
1½ teaspoons salt	1 tablespoon cold water (if needed)
1 teaspoon garlic powder	1 (20-ounce) can sliced peaches, drained
¼ teaspoon nutmeg	
¼ teaspoon ginger	
¼ teaspoon pepper	

Blend first 10 ingredients together in a bowl. Shape mixture into 1 to 1½-inch balls. In a large heavy skillet, brown meat balls in hot oil. Remove with a slotted spoon, set aside and keep warm. Reduce heat, blend Brandied Peach Sauce into meat drippings, and simmer for 10 minutes. Add meat balls to sauce and coat thoroughly. Cover and simmer for 45 minutes to 1 hour. If necessary, blend cornstarch with cold water until smooth; add to sauce, stirring constantly, and cook on low heat until thickened. Transfer to a chafing dish for buffet service. Garnish with canned sliced peaches. About 40 meat balls.

BRANDIED PEACH SAUCE:

1 (18-ounce) jar peach preserves	½ cup brandy
¾ cup light brown sugar, firmly packed	½ cup peach brandy
	¼ teaspoon nutmeg

Combine ingredients in a bowl, blending well. About 3 cups.

Apron Strings

Curry Puffs

2 tablespoons butter
1 medium yellow onion,
  chopped very fine
2 cloves garlic, chopped very fine
2 tablespoons curry powder
½ teaspoon ground coriander

½ teaspoon ground cumin
1 pound ground beef
2 medium-size boiled potatoes,
  cut in tiny pieces
Vienna Pastry
Salt and pepper to taste

In a skillet melt butter and add onion; cook until soft. Then add garlic. Cook a few minutes. Then add curry powder and coriander and cumin. Stir constantly so it does not burn. Cook for 3 minutes.

Add ground beef and cook 5 minutes; mix well with the curry powder and other ingredients. Lastly add potatoes, salt and pepper to taste. Set aside and prepare pastry. Any good pastry recipe may be used.

VIENNA PASTRY:
1 (3-ounce) package cream
  cheese, softened

¼ pound butter, softened
1 cup flour

Mix together and chill. When ready to put the Curry Puffs together, roll out pastry to ⅛-inch thickness; cut with a 3-inch cutter. Place 1 teaspoon of beef mixture in center of round and fold over. Moisten edge with a little water and pinch around the half circle of pastry. Bake in oven set at 400° for 15–20 minutes, or until slightly brown. Serve warm. Yields about 75 puffs.

The Hunt County Cookbook

Florentine Cheddar Squares

This is a great appetizer, especially served warm from the oven for an open house, tea, or pre-dinner hors d'oeuvre. It freezes well, too.

1 cup flour
1 teaspoon baking powder
1 cup milk
1 stick margarine, melted
2 eggs, beaten
1 cup minced onion

10 ounces Cheddar cheese,
  shredded
1 package frozen chopped
  spinach, cooked and squeezed
  dry

Mix all ingredients together in order given. Bake at 350° in a 9-inch square greased pan for 30 minutes. Cut into squares to serve (36 squares).

Taste of Goodness

Almond Puffs with Chicken

1 cup whole-wheat flour
Dash of salt
¾ cup butter
1 cup chicken stock
4 eggs

1 cup chopped chicken
4 tablespoons chopped toasted
    almonds
Dash of paprika

Preheat oven to 450°. Do not sift flour; add salt to flour. Combine butter and chicken stock in a medium saucepan; keep over low heat until butter is melted. Add flour all at once and stir until mixture leaves sides of pan. Remove from heat and beat eggs in one at a time; continue beating until a thick dough is formed. Stir in chicken, almonds, and paprika. Drop by teaspoonfuls on greased cookie sheet. Bake 10 minutes at 450°, reduce heat to 350°, and bake 5–10 minutes until golden brown.

The New Life Cookbook

Hospitable Grapes 'n Cheese Spread

16 ounces cream cheese,
    softened
3 tablespoons Brandy
⅓ cup finely chopped
    chutney
¼ cup finely chopped green
    onions

¼ cup chopped toasted
    almonds
¼ teaspoon curry powder
1 cup green grapes, halved
    and seeded
Green onion tops
Grapes in clusters

In large bowl, mix first 6 ingredients until well blended. Chill. When firm, mound in oval shape on serving tray, covering surface with grape halves, cut side down, to resemble a pineapple. Insert green onion tops at top of cheese mound. Surround with grape clusters and serve with crisp crackers. Yields 2½ cups.

Note: After cheese has been mounded, it can be refrigerated for up to 2 days before completing.

Tidewater on the Half Shell

Virginia Beach is the longest resort-beach city in the world.

Curried Cheese Mousse

2 envelopes (tablespoons)
 unflavored gelatin
1½ cups beef broth
1 garlic clove, peeled and
 minced
¼–½ teaspoon curry powder
4 (3-ounce) packages cream
 cheese, at room temperature

Salt and pepper to taste
Thinly sliced pitted black
 olives, drained
Parsley or watercress sprigs
 for garnish
Melba toast rounds

In a small heavy saucepan, soften gelatin in beef broth; allow to stand for 2–3 minutes. Simmer over low heat, stirring to dissolve gelatin thoroughly. In a blender container, combine broth mixture, garlic, and curry powder; cover and blend at medium speed for 30 seconds. With blender motor running, gradually add cream cheese, one third at a time, until mixture is smooth. Add salt and pepper and beat at high speed for 30 seconds. Adjust seasoning, if desired. Spoon into a lightly oiled 3-cup mold or loaf pan. Chill in refrigerator for several hours or until firm. Unmold onto a chilled serving plate and garnish with thin olive slices and parsley or watercress sprigs. Serve with melba toast rounds.

Variation: After unmolding, omit olive garnish and spoon ½–1 cup of finely chopped chutney over top of mousse, being careful not to allow chutney to drip over sides of mousse.

Richmond Receipts

Hot Cheese Puffs

1 loaf firm white unsliced
  bread
3 ounces cream cheese
¼ pound sharp Cheddar
  cheese, grated

½ cup butter
2 egg whites, stiffly beaten

Trim bread and cut in 1-inch cubes. In the top of a double boiler, melt cheeses and butter, cool, and fold in stiffly beaten egg whites. With a fork, pick up bread cubes and dip them, one at a time, into the cheese mixture. Ease off fork with knife onto cookie sheet. Refrigerate overnight, or freeze. Bake at 400° until fluffy and brown. If frozen, no need to thaw before baking. May be doubled. Makes about 100 small puffs.

The Belle Grove Plantation Cookbook

Cheese Puff

2 cups Hellmann's mayonnaise
2 cups grated sharp Cheddar
  cheese

1 small onion, grated

Mix above and put in fairly deep casserole dish. Bake at 350° about 30 minutes or until hot, brown, and bubbly. Serve with rye melba, toast points, your favorite crackers, or Wheat Sticks, below.

You may increase amount prepared—just use the same amount of mayonnaise and cheese.

WHEAT STICKS:

Trim crusts from one loaf of whole-wheat bread. Cut trimmed slices into 8 sticks each. Place sticks on ungreased baking sheet, and bake for 2 hours at 200°. Serve with party dips. Ideal dipper with Cheese Puff recipe. Store any remaining sticks in air-tight container. Will keep for several weeks. Dice leftover sticks and sprinkle with garlic salt for ideal salad croutons.

A Southern Lady's Spirit

Herbal Sticks

This recipe is used on "Wine and Cheese" night at the Marshall's. It's a very special treat. Serve with aged Cheddar cheese.

3 cups all-purpose flour
6 tablespoons Royal baking
  powder
2 teaspoons salt
4 tablespoons raw sugar
1½ cups cornmeal

1 tablespoon each: marjoram,
  thyme, sweet basil
3 eggs
2½ cups milk
1 pound butter, melted

Sift flour with baking powder, salt, and sugar. Stir in cornmeal and herbs.

In another bowl, beat eggs; stir in milk and melted butter. Add dry ingredients and stir just until moist. Spoon into corn stick pans and bake in a hot oven at 400° until golden. Makes approximately 65 sticks.

The New Life Cookbook

Olive Cheese Nuggets

¼ pound Cheddar cheese,
grated
¼ cup butter or margarine
¾ cup sifted flour

⅛ teaspoon salt
½ teaspoon paprika
36–40 medium stuffed olives

Blend butter and cheese. Add flour, salt, and paprika. Mix well to form dough. Using about 1 teaspoon dough, flatten out in palm and wrap around olive. Place on ungreased cookie sheet and bake at 400° for 12–15 minutes until light brown. These may be made in advance and refrigerated, or frozen baked or unbaked. Yields 36–40.

The Stuffed Cougar

Sylvia's Cheese

1 pound Cheddar cheese
(medium or sharp),
shredded

1 pound Monterey Jack with
jalapeño peppers, grated
8 eggs

Grease 8x12-inch Pyrex pan. Spread Cheddar on bottom. Top with a layer of Monterey Jack. Beat 8 eggs and pour on top. Cook at 350° 20–30 minutes or until set.

Serve hot. Dip or spread on Triscuits or other crackers. Can be halved easily. Place in 8-inch square Pyrex pan. Feeds a lot.

Keeping the Feast

Curry Almond Spread

2 (8-ounce) bars cream
cheese, softened
1 cup chutney, chopped
2 teaspoons curry powder
½ teaspoon dry mustard

⅓ cup chopped spring onions
(plus 2 teaspoons for garnish)
¾ cup chopped almonds,
toasted

Combine cheese, ½ cup chutney, curry, mustard, onions, and ½ cup chopped almonds. Refrigerate 2 hours in shallow dish. Cover with remaining chutney and almonds. Sprinkle 2 teaspoons spring onions on top. Yields 4 cups.

Attractive spread with interesting texture. Serve with crackers or sliced apple and celery sticks.

The Enlightened Titan

Vegetable Pizza

2 cans crescent rolls
2 (8-ounce) packages
  cream cheese, softened
1 cup sour cream
2 teaspoon dill weed
¼ teaspoon garlic powder

Variety of grated vegetables
  such as: cauliflower pieces,
  carrots, broccoli flowers, green
  pepper, celery slices, tomato
  pieces, radish shreds, etc.
Grated Cheddar cheese

Press and seal seams of rolls on a cookie sheet. Prick so it won't puff up. Bake according to directions. Cool. Combine cream cheese, sour cream, dill, and garlic powder. Spread crust with cream cheese mixture. Top with veggies and cheese last of all. Slice when serving. Serves 12.

Think Healthy

Bucky Sutherland's Vegetable Sandwiches

1 envelope unflavored gelatin
¼ cup water
1 cup diced celery
1 cup diced onion

2 small carrots, diced
½ green pepper, diced
1 teaspoon salt
2 cups mayonnaise

Soak gelatin in ¼ cup water and melt over hot water. Mix all ingredients and add to gelatin. It makes several dozen small sandwiches. Filling can be kept in refrigerator for days.

Historic Lexington Cooks

Stuffed Beets

Whole pickled beets
Eggs

Salt and pepper
Mustard

Cut centers out of small whole pickled beets. Hard boil eggs; mash whole peeled eggs and season with salt, pepper and mustard to taste. Stuff beets, chill, and serve.

Kitchen Keys

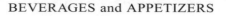

Sweet Potato and Peanut Chips

Nice appetizer or accompaniment to ribs or chicken.

½ cup honey roasted peanuts　　**Salt to taste**
2 large sweet potatoes, peeled　　**½ cup unsalted butter, melted**

Preheat oven to 475°. Line 2 large baking sheets with foil. Lightly butter the foil. Process the peanuts in a food processor fitted with steel blade until finely chopped but not powdered. Transfer to a bowl. Slice potatoes to ⅛-inch thickness and dip in melted butter to coat both sides. Arrange slices on baking sheets. Sprinkle top with peanuts. Bake chips until the tops are lightly browned and potatoes are tender (15–20 minutes). Watch carefully to prevent burning. Transfer to paper towels and drain. Let cool 5 minutes. Salt to taste. Yields 4 dozen.

The Enlightened Titan

Asparagus Canapés

1 loaf Pepperidge Farm
  thin-sliced bread
8 ounces Roquefort cheese, at
  room temperature
1 (8-ounce) package cream
  cheese, at room temperature

1 tablespoon mayonnaise
1 egg, beaten
1 (15-ounce) can asparagus
Melted butter

Cut crust from bread. Roll bread flat and spread with mixture of both cheeses, mayonnaise and egg combination. Roll one stalk of asparagus in each bread slice. Secure with pick. Dip each bread roll in melted butter. Place in freezer for a short time. Cut each roll into thirds. Bake at 350° for 15 minutes. Yields 36 canapés.

Note: These can be made ahead and frozen until you want to serve.

A Heritage of Good Taste

Asparagus Ham Rolls

16 asparagus stalks, cooked
4 thin slices of boiled ham
½ cup grated sharp Cheddar
  cheese

1 cup medium white sauce
  (2 tablespoons butter,
  2 tablespoons flour, 1 cup
  milk and salt and pepper)

Put 4 asparagus stalks on each ham slice. Roll up and fasten with a toothpick. Broil for 5 minutes on each side. Add cheese to heated sauce. Stir till melted and pour over ham rolls. Broil to golden brown. Garnish with toast points.

Dan River Family Cookbook

The first seven astronauts were trained at the NASA Langley Space Center at Hampton.

Stuffed Snow Peas

1 (3-ounce) package cream
  cheese, softened
⅓ cup finely chopped
  walnuts
3 tablespoons finely chopped
  green pepper
2 tablespoons finely chopped
  onion

1½ tablespoons chopped
  pimiento, drained
1½ tablespoons ketchup
¼ teaspoon salt
¼ teaspoon pepper
2½ dozen tender snow peas
Cherry tomatoes
Fresh parsley

Combine first 8 ingredients, mixing well. Chill in a covered container for at least 1 hour. String snow peas and blanch in boiling water for 30 seconds. Plunge into cold water and drain. With a small knife, slit open the straight side of each snow pea. Spread about 1½ teaspoons filling into each snow pea. Arrange on a platter with cherry tomatoes and parsley in the center. Yields 30 snow peas.

Cardinal Cuisine

Cucumber Whimsies

½ pound crabmeat
1 scallion, minced
2 tablespoons chopped dill
1 teaspoon grated lemon zest
1 small tomato, chopped
¼ cup mayonnaise
⅛ teaspoon cayenne pepper

Salt and pepper
1 (10- to 12-inch) English
  cucumber
Lemon pepper
Dill sprigs or fresh parsley
  for garnish

Drain crabmeat. In mixing bowl, place crabmeat, scallion, chopped dill, lemon zest, tomato, mayonnaise, cayenne, salt and pepper. Chill for at least 1 hour to allow flavors to marry. Score cucumber with tines of a fork, being careful to score evenly for pretty slices. Cut cucumber into ¼-inch slices and sprinkle with lemon pepper. Mound 1½ teaspoons of crabmeat on each cucumber slice and garnish with sprig of dill or parsley. Light, refreshing, and very elegant.

Gourmet by the Bay

Chinese Fried Walnuts

6 cups water
4 cups California walnuts
½ cup sugar

Salad oil
Salt

In 4-quart saucepan over high heat, heat water to boiling; add walnuts and heat to boiling; cook 1 minute. Rinse walnuts under running hot water; drain. Wash saucepan and dry well.

In large bowl with rubber spatula, gently stir warm walnuts with sugar until sugar is dissolved. (If necessary, stand 5 minutes to dissolve sugar.) Meanwhile, in same saucepan over medium heat, heat about 1 inch salad oil to 350° on deep-fat thermometer (or heat oil according to manufacturer's directions in deep-fat fryer set at 350°). With slotted spoon, add about half of walnuts to oil; fry 5 minutes or until golden, stirring often. With slotted spoon, place walnuts in coarse sieve over bowl to drain; sprinkle very lightly with salt; toss lightly to keep walnuts from sticking together. Transfer to paper towels to cool. Fry remaining walnuts. Store in tightly covered container. Makes 4 cups.

Dan River Family Cookbook

Cranberry Chutney

2 cups fresh cranberries
2 large pears
2 cups golden raisins
2½ cups light brown sugar
   (firmly packed)
1½ cups vinegar

2 teaspoons salt
1 tablespoon mixed pickling
   spices
10–12 whole allspice
4–5 whole cloves

Rinse cranberries. Peel, core, and slice pears. Combine fruits in large saucepan with raisins, brown sugar, vinegar, and salt. Place spices in a 6-inch square cheese cloth or a teaball. Add to fruit mixture and bring to a boil over high heat. Reduce to medium heat and cook for 20 minutes, stirring. Remove spice bag, put in jars, and seal with paraffin. Serve over a block of cream cheese with crackers.

A Southern Lady's Spirit

Bread and Breakfast

Along the Blue Ridge Parkway south of Roanoke, Mabry Mill still grinds corn and buckwheat as it did long ago.

Garlic Casserole Bread

1 cup milk, scalded	2 packages yeast
3 tablespoons sugar	1 cup warm water
2 teaspoons garlic salt	4 cups unsifted flour
2 tablespoons butter	

Mix the milk, sugar, garlic salt, and butter in a bowl and cool to luke-warm. Dissolve the yeast in warm water, then stir into milk mixture. Add the flour and beat until blended. Cover and let rise in a warm place for about 1–1½ hours or until doubled in bulk. Stir down and beat for about 30 seconds with a wooden spoon. Turn into a greased 1½-quart casserole. Bake at 375° for about 1 hour, or until done.

Happy Times with Home Cooking

French Bread

1 rounded tablespoon butter	⅔ cup lukewarm water
1 rounded tablespoon salt	6 cups flour
1 rounded teaspoon sugar	Yellow cornmeal
2 cups boiling water	
1 tablespoon dry yeast*	
(I use 1½ envelopes)	

Combine butter, salt, and sugar in a large bowl. Add 2 cups boiling water and stir until dissolved. Cool to lukewarm. In separate bowl, I sprinkle yeast over ⅔ cup lukewarm water to soften. Stir then pour into butter mixture and mix. Stir in flour. Knead until smooth and elastic. Place dough in covered bowl and put in cold oven to rise for 1½ hours. Punch dough down and let it rise again about 1 hour.

Butter a large baking sheet and sprinkle lightly with cornmeal. Divide into 3 parts and roll each part into a rectangle 8x14 inches. Roll the long side of the rectangle towards you in a tight neat roll. Place the 3 long rolls, seam-sides-down, on prepared baking sheet, and let rise until double in size.

Brush tops with cold water and make 3 or 4 diagonal slashes across each loaf. Bake in 400° oven for 30 minutes, brushing tops with cold water every 15–20 minutes.

*A shallow pan of hot water in the oven while loaves are baking will give the good crisp crust of real French bread.

Culinary Contentment

Granny's Best Dinner Rolls

Real light with a soft texture—old fashioned goodness made so easy with instant potatoes and no kneading.

2 cups milk	½ cup lukewarm water
½ cup margarine	2 teaspoons sugar (to feed yeast)
½ cup sugar	2 eggs, beaten
¼ cup instant potato flakes	5½–6 cups all-purpose flour
1 tablespoon salt	
2 packages dry yeast	
(2 tablespoons)	

Scald milk; add margarine, sugar, potato flakes, and salt. Cool to lukewarm. Soften yeast in lukewarm water with 2 teaspoons sugar (let set until foamy, about 8 minutes). Add yeast to milk mixture with eggs and 3 cups flour. Beat with electric mixer until smooth and light (about 5 minutes).

Stir in enough flour to make a soft dough, just until dough leaves side of bowl. (Do not get too stiff; dough will be sticky, but will stiffen in refrigerator.) Cover and let rise about 30 minutes. Punch down and refrigerate until cold, or overnight. When needed, shape into rolls as desired (I make mine Parker House style). Place into greased pans, let rise until double in bulk (about 1½ hours). Bake at 400° for 15 minutes or until golden brown. Brush tops with melted butter or margarine as removed from oven (to give a pretty "glow"). Serve hot. Makes 4–5 dozen delicious rolls.

Variation: To make whole-wheat Dinner Rolls, substitute brown sugar for sugar and half of whole-wheat flour for half of the all-purpose flour.

Tip: I bake extra rolls, cool and roll in foil. Freeze. When ready to serve, then I heat in a 325° oven (leave in foil) for about 15 minutes (longer if rolls are still frozen). They taste like fresh baked rolls. Great to have in the freezer.

Note: Homemade rolls will give your guests double pleasure, the aroma while baking and the delicious taste. As my grandchildren hit the door, I hear them say—mmmmmm, it smells like Granny's kitchen.

Holiday Treats

Farmer's Spoon Bread

*A fluffy and moist bread that is spooned from the dish from which it is baked.
My favorite spoon bread.*

1 cup cornmeal	1 teaspoon salt
1½ cups boiling water	1 teaspoon sugar
1 tablespoon softened butter	1 teaspoon baking powder
3 egg yolks	¼ teaspoon baking soda
1 cup buttermilk	3 egg whites

In large bowl, stir boiling water into cornmeal. Blend in butter and egg
yolks. Stir in buttermilk, salt, sugar, baking powder, and baking soda.
Beat egg whites until soft peaks form; fold into batter. Pour into a
greased 2-quart casserole. Bake at 375° for 45–50 minutes. Serve piping hot with butter.

Granny's Kitchen

Potato Yeast Rolls

2 cakes yeast (or 2 packages dry yeast)	½ cup sugar
½ cup lukewarm water	¾ cup vegetable shortening
1 cup hot water	1 cup mashed potatoes
3 teaspoons salt	2 eggs, lightly beaten
	6–7 cups flour

Dissolve yeast in lukewarm water and set aside. In a large bowl, pour
hot water over salt, ¼ cup sugar, shortening and potatoes. Cool, and
add yeast mixture, eggs and 1½ cups flour. Let rise 1½ hours, covered. Add remainder of flour and sugar. Knead well. Let rise about 2
hours. Form into rolls and let rise 2 more hours. Bake at 350° for 30
minutes, until brown. Makes 40 large rolls. May be doubled; may be
made several days ahead; freezes well after baking.

Note: When 40 rolls are more than you need, you may use part of the dough
the day of mixing, refrigerating the rest until ready to use. Several days later,
you may make any leftover dough into a loaf of bread. I have been using this
southern Virginia recipe for 50 years.

The Belle Grove Plantation Cookbook I

Sally Lunn

According to tradition, Sally Lunn is named after a young girl who in the eighteenth century "cried" the sweet yeast bread that bears her name in the streets of England's fashionable spa, Bath. Some now doubt whether Sally Lunn really ly existed and suggest other sources for the name. Who knows? But Sally Lunn does have a place in the Oxford English Dictionary, and hers was a household name in the southern colonies as it was in England.

1 cup milk	**⅓ cup sugar**
½ cup shortening	**2 teaspoons salt**
¼ cup water	**2 packages active dry yeast**
4 cups sifted all-purpose flour, divided	**3 eggs**

Preheat the oven to 350° 10 minutes before the Sally Lunn is ready to be baked. Grease a 10-inch tube cake pan or a Bundt pan. Heat the milk, shortening, and ¼ cup of water until very warm—about 120°. The shortening does not need to melt.

Blend 1⅓ cups of flour with the sugar, salt, and dry yeast in a large mixing bowl. Blend the warm liquids into the flour mixture. Beat with an electric mixer at medium speed for about 2 minutes, scraping the sides of the bowl occasionally. Gradually add ⅔ cup of the remaining flour and the eggs and beat at high speed for 2 minutes. Add the remaining flour and mix well. The batter will be thick but not stiff. Cover and let the dough rise in a warm, draft-free place (about 85°) until it doubles in bulk—about 1 hour and 15 minutes.

Beat the dough down with a spatula or at the lowest speed on an electric mixer and turn into the prepared pan. Cover and let rise in a warm, draft-free place until it has increased in bulk ⅓–½—about 30 minutes.

Bake for 40–50 minutes at 350°. Run a knife around the center and outer edges of the bread and turn it onto a plate to cool.

The Williamsburg Cookbook

Williamsburg was founded in 1699. It was the colonial capital of Virginia and is now America's largest restored 18th-century town.

Salt Rising Bread

1½ tablespoons salt
2 tablespoons cornmeal
2½ cups potatoes, sliced
1 quart boiling water
1 teaspoon baking soda

1½ teaspoons sugar
11 cups flour
1 cup warm milk
1 tablespoon shortening, melted

Sprinkle 1 tablespoon salt and the cornmeal over potatoes. Add boiling water and stir until salt has dissolved. Cover and keep warm from noon to the following morning. Then drain off liquid. Add to it the soda, 1½ teaspoons sugar, and 5 cups flour. Stir until ingredients are well blended; this sponge should be the consistency of cake batter.

Set mixture in a warm place and let rise until light and full of bubbles. This requires about 1½ hours. Scald milk and cool to lukewarm; add shortening. Add milk and remaining flour to sponge. Knead for 10–12 minutes and shape into loaves. Makes 3 medium-sized loaves. Let rise until light, about 1½ hours. Bake at 350° for 1 hour. Delicious!

Mennonite Community Cookbook

Cracklin Corn Bread

1 tablespoon lard
1 cup self-rising cornmeal
1 cup self-rising flour
1 tablespoon sugar

2 eggs
1½ cups milk (use either sweet
   or buttermilk)
½ cup cracklins

Put lard in a 6x12-inch pan and let it melt. Mix all other ingredients together well. Pour the batter into the pan and bake in 425° oven for 20–25 minutes.

Dan River Family Cookbook

Bacon Scallion Cornbread

½ pound bacon (sliced)
1 bunch scallions
1½ cups cornmeal (white
  or yellow)
¾ cup flour

2 teaspoons baking powder
1 teaspoon salt
1½ cups buttermilk
½ cup sour cream
2 medium eggs

Preheat the oven to 350°. Cook the bacon for 8–10 minutes or until crisp. Drain the fat, reserving one tablespoon. Crumble the bacon. This should yield about ½ cup. Clean the scallions by removing the root end and then washing. Slice the scallions on an angle. Combine the cornmeal, the flour, the baking powder, and the scallions. To this mixture add the buttermilk, sour cream and eggs.

Put the one tablespoon of bacon fat in a 9-inch cast-iron skillet and heat the skillet in the oven for 5 minutes. Mix the dry ingredients thoroughly with the wet ingredients. Add the batter to the hot skillet and bake for 20–25 minutes or until golden brown and firm. Cut the bread into 8 wedges.

The Great Chefs of Virginia Cookbook

Clara's Smithfield Inn Cornbread Cakes

Clara Ford Williams has presided over the Smithfield Inn's kitchen for more than 26 years. Her cornbread cakes are a specialty of the house.

1½ cups cornmeal
1 tablespoon flour
1 teaspoon sugar (or more)
1½ teaspoons baking powder

½ teaspoon salt
2 eggs, beaten
1½ cups buttermilk

Mix all ingredients together. Drop by large spoonfuls in shallow hot fat. Fry until brown on both sides.

The Smithfield Cookbook

In colonial times, the taverns were meeting places to talk and eat. But if the cook wasn't good, the tavern didn't survive.

Oatmeal Bread

2 cups steel-cut oatmeal
1 quart boiling water
1 cup black molasses
1 tablespoon salt
1 large tablespoon shortening

1 yeast cake or 1 package
  granulated yeast
1 cup lukewarm water
1 tablespoon sugar
Flour

Mix together first 5 ingredients and let cool. Add yeast dissolved in 1 cup lukewarm water with 1 tablespoon of sugar added. Add enough white flour so dough won't stick to hands when kneading. Cover with towels and let rise until doubled. Place in 3 greased loaf pans. Cover with towel and let rise about 2 hours. Bake 45 minutes at 350°.

The Foxcroft Cook Book

Apricot Nut Bread

2½ cups Gold Medal flour*
1 cup sugar
3½ teaspoons baking powder
1 teaspoon salt
1 tablespoon plus 1 teaspoon
  grated orange peel

3 tablespoons salad oil
½ cup milk
¾ cup orange juice
1 egg
1 cup finely chopped nuts
1 cup finely cut-up dried apricots

Heat oven to 350°. Grease and flour 1 (9x5x3-inch) loaf pan, or 2 (8½x4½x2½-inch) loaf pans. Measure all ingredients into large mixer bowl; beat on medium speed ½ minute. Pour into pan(s). Bake 55–65 minutes or until wooden pick inserted in center comes out clean. Remove from pan(s); cool thoroughly before slicing.

*If using self-rising flour, omit baking powder and salt.

WYVE's Cookbook/Photo Album

Thanksgiving, exclusively an American holiday, was first celebrated in Berkeley in 1619, almost two years before the pilgrims landed at Plymouth Rock.

Zucchini Bread

3 cups flour
2 teaspoons baking soda
1 teaspoon salt
½ teaspoon baking powder
1½ teaspoons cinnamon
¾ cup chopped walnuts
3 eggs
2 cups sugar
1 cup oil
2 teaspoons vanilla
2 cups coarsely shredded
  zucchini
1 (8-ounce) can crushed
  pineapple, well drained

Combine flour, soda, salt, baking powder, cinnamon, and nuts. Set aside. Beat eggs lightly in a large bowl; add sugar, oil and vanilla. Beat until creamy. Stir in zucchini and pineapple. Add dry ingredients stirring only until ingredients are moistened. Spoon batter into 2 well-greased and floured 9x5x3-inch loaf pans. Bake at 350° for 1 hour. Cool 10 minutes before removing from pans.

More Than a Cookbook

Blueberry Bread

1½ cups sugar
½ cup brown sugar
½ cup butter, melted
1¾ cups orange juice
2 eggs, beaten
4 cups flour
1 tablespoon baking powder
1 teaspoon salt
1 teaspoon baking soda
2 cups nuts, chopped
1 cup oats
2 cups blueberries, fresh or
  frozen
½ cup orange marmalade

Combine sugars, butter, orange juice, and eggs. Sift together flour, baking powder, salt, and soda. Add nuts and oats to dry ingredients and blend. Combine dry ingredients with orange juice mixture. Stir in blueberries and orange marmalade. Pour into 2 greased and floured loaf pans and allow to stand 20 minutes before baking. Bake at 350° for 1 hour and 15 minutes. Cool 10 minutes before removing from pan. Preparation: 30 minutes. Yields 2 loaves.

Virginia Seasons

"The Best" Pumpkin Bread

A very moist, tasty bread—the best I have ever eaten.

2½ cups flour
2 teaspoons baking soda
1 teaspoon salt
1 teaspoon cinnamon
½ teaspoon nutmeg
¼ teaspoon ginger
1 (3½-ounce) package
  butterscotch instant pudding

1 (3½-ounce) package
  lemon instant pudding
5 eggs
1½ cups sugar
1½ cups cooking oil
1 (1-pound) can pumpkin (2 cups)
3 teaspoons vanilla
1 cup chopped pecans, optional

Sift first 8 ingredients together in large bowl. Beat eggs; add sugar, oil, pumpkin and vanilla. Stir into dry ingredients and mix well. Stir in nuts, if desired. Pour into 2 greased 8½ x 4½-inch loaf pans. Bake at 350° for 1 hour or until tests done (tester should come out clean), but do not bake too brown. Cool in pan 10 minutes; carefully turn out onto cake rack to cool.

Tip: Make pumpkin-wiches by spreading softened cream cheese between pumpkin bread slices.

Holiday Treats

Almost Bloomies Bran Muffins

I developed this recipe trying to duplicate the bran muffins sold at Bloomingdale's.

1 cup whole-wheat flour
1 cup unprocessed bran
1¼ teaspoons baking soda
½ teaspoon salt
½ teaspoon cardamom
2 eggs

6 tablespoons honey
2 tablespoons molasses
¾ cup milk
¼ cup oil
1 cup grated carrots

Put the dry ingredients into a bowl. Make a well. Mix liquid ingredients together with a wisk and pour into the well. Stir with fork or wisk till the dry ingredients are moistened. Pour into greased or paper-lined muffin tins. Bake 20–25 minutes at 350°. Makes 1 dozen.

Could I Have Your Recipe?

Sweet Potato Muffins

Begin with all ingredients at room temperature.

1 stick butter (no margarine)
1¼ cups granulated sugar
1¼ cups mashed sweet potatoes
  (cooked fresh or canned)
2 eggs
1½ cups all-purpose flour
2 teaspoons baking powder

1 teaspoon cinnamon
¼ teaspoon salt
¼ teaspoon nutmeg
1 cup milk
½ cup chopped black walnuts
  (or pecans, if preferred)
½ cup chopped raisins

Cream butter, sugar, and sweet potatoes until smooth. Add eggs and blend well. Sift flour, baking powder and spices. Add alternately with milk to the egg batter, being careful not to overmix. Fold in nuts and raisins last. Sprinkle a little cinnamon-sugar on top before baking. Bake in greased muffin tins at 400° for about 25 minutes or until muffins test done. Makes 2½ dozen regular-sized muffins, 5 dozen small. May be frozen and reheated.

A Southern Lady's Spirit

Banana Chocolate Chip Muffins

1½ cups sifted flour
¼ teaspoon nutmeg
¼ teaspoon salt
¾ cup semi-sweet chocolate
  pieces
¾ cup English walnuts or
  pecans
½ cup butter or margarine,
  at room temperature

½ cup sugar
1 tablespoon hot water
1 teaspoon baking soda
1 egg, lightly beaten
1 cup mashed peeled ripe
  bananas (about 2–3 medium)

In a small bowl, sift together the first 3 ingredients; add chocolate pieces and nuts, coating each well with the flour mixture. In a medium bowl, cream butter until smooth. Gradually add sugar, beating well. In a 1-cup measure, blend hot water and baking soda together. In a small bowl, combine egg, mashed bananas, and soda-water, mixing well; stir into butter mixture. Add flour mixture, mixing just until dry ingredients are thoroughly moistened. Fill greased muffin pans (2¾ inches in diameter) two-thirds full. Bake in a moderate oven (375°) for 20 minutes or until done. Yields 12 muffins.

More Richmond Receipts

Buttermilk Muffins

1 cup buttermilk	1 cup self-rising flour
¼ teaspoon baking soda	1 egg, beaten

Combine buttermilk and soda. Add flour, stirring until smooth. Stir in egg. Spoon into greased muffin tins. Bake at 425° for 30–40 minutes.

*THE What in the World Are We Going
to Have for Dinner? COOKBOOK*

Colonial Buttermilk Biscuits

2 cups all-purpose flour	½ cup butter
2 cups cake flour	2 egg yolks
½ teaspoon salt	1¼ cups buttermilk
4 teaspoons baking powder	Melted butter (optional)
2 tablespoons sugar	

Preheat the oven to 450°. Lightly grease a baking sheet. Sift the flours, salt, baking powder, and sugar together. Cut in the butter with knives or a pastry blender until the mixture is mealy.

Beat the egg yolks and buttermilk together until well blended. Make a well in the center of the flour mixture. Add the egg yolks and buttermilk. Mix just long enough to moisten completely.

Knead the dough on a lightly floured surface for about 30 seconds. Roll the dough ½ inch thick. Cut the dough with a 1½-inch biscuit cutter. Brush the tops of the biscuits with melted butter if desired. Place the biscuits on the prepared baking sheet. Bake at 450° for 12 minutes. Makes 4 dozen.

Favorite Meals from Williamsburg

Virginia Ground-Ham Biscuits

2 cups flour
3 teaspoons baking powder
½ cup ground cooked
   Virginia or country ham

3 tablespoons shortening
¾ cup milk

Preheat oven to 450°. Sift dry ingredients together. Combine with ground ham. Cut shortening in with knife till it is like meal. Add milk. Roll out ¼ inch thick on a floured board. Cut out with a biscuit cutter. Place on an ungreased baking sheet. Bake 12–15 minutes or until brown. Makes about 20.

The Ham Book

Virginia Ham and Shiitake Mushroom Biscuits

1 teaspoon shallots (minced)
1 cup (2 sticks) butter,
   divided
½ cup finely diced Virginia
   ham
½ cup finely diced shiitake
   mushrooms

3 cups flour
1¼ tablespoons baking
   powder
½ teaspoon salt
½ teaspoon baking soda
1 cup buttermilk

Preheat the oven to 325°. Heat the shallots in 2 tablespoons butter, until transparent. Add the ham and the mushrooms. Sauté for about 3 minutes. Set aside to cool completely.

Mix the flour, the baking powder, the salt, and the soda. Cut in the remaining butter until the mixture is mealy. Add the cooled ham and mushroom mixture and mix completely. Make a well in the center and add the buttermilk all at once. Stir only until the ingredients cling together. Roll out the dough to a thickness of ¾ inch and cut into desired shapes. Bake the biscuits on a cookie sheet for 25–30 minutes or until done. Yields 2 dozen.

The Great Chefs of Virginia Cookbook

Aunt Mary's Beaten Biscuits

These can be kept in tins indefinitely and are delicious with cured ham. These are hard biscuits.

1 quart flour
1 teaspoon sugar
2 teaspoons salt

1 rounded kitchen spoon of lard
Cold water

Make very stiff dough and work until it is blistered all over. Roll to about ¼ inch and cut into small biscuits. Take fork tines and prick three times on top. Bake in moderate oven until lightly browned.

The Virginia Presidential Homes Cookbook

Geba's Famous Biscuits

My mother, Geneva Winningham, "Geba" to the grandchildren, makes "melt in your mouth" tiny biscuits. Customers of her antiques business, friends, and family from all over the world expect these flaky, delicious morsels whenever they visit and no one has been disappointed yet!

3 cups self-rising flour
¾ cup lard or shortening

1 full cup buttermilk

Preheat the oven to 475°. Put flour in bowl; add shortening in small pieces. Work with fingers until mixture resembles coarse cornmeal. Make a well in center of dry mixture. Add buttermilk, work in with fingers. Do not overwork dough. Turn dough out onto lightly floured pastry board and "turn over or knead" quickly. Roll out ½ inch thick and cut with 1-inch cutter. Place on greased baking sheet with sides of biscuits touching each other. Bake 8–10 minutes until lightly brown and serve immediately. Makes 36 bite-size biscuits.

Note: Use the grease that country ham has been fried in to grease the pan. You can also take a spoon and lightly brush the tops of the biscuits with the ham-flavored grease. I've also used melted clarified butter to do the job.
    Dip biscuit cutter into flour to keep the dough from sticking.

Cooking with Heart in Hand

Stollen

Wonderful to give as a Christmas gift.

1½ cups margarine
1 cup milk
2 packages yeast
1 teaspoon sugar
¾ cup warm water
1 cup flour
2 eggs
¾ cup sugar
Grated peel of ½ lemon

Pinch of cardamom
4½–5½ cups all-purpose flour
1 pound raisins
½ pound diced candied fruit
4 ounces sliced almonds
Butter
2 tablespoons rum
Granulated sugar

Melt margarine in milk. Set aside to cool. Make a sponge mixture by dissolving the yeast and sugar in warm water; add 1 cup flour and mix well in medium-size bowl. Cover bowl and let rise in a warm place, then fall (about 20 minutes).

In extra large bowl mix eggs, sugar, lemon peel, and cardamom. Beat well, then add sponge mixture and cooled milk/margarine mixture. Beat well. Add enough flour to make a soft dough, raisins, candied fruit, and almonds. Mix well. Let rest for 20 minutes.

Pat dough out on floured board until it measures approximately 9x18 inches. Fold ends in about 1 inch, then fold dough in half lengthwise. Put carefully and quickly on buttered cookie sheet. Let rest for a few minutes. Bake at 325° for 45–60 minutes. Test middle for doneness. Remove from oven and while still hot, brush with melted butter to which has been added 2 tablespoons rum. Sprinkle with granulated sugar. Serves 20.

The Best of the Bushel

Popovers Fontaine

If you have never had the thrill of seeing a "runny" batter bloom into a large golden cloud, try this recipe. Popovers are definitely a Sunday morning breakfast treat. Serve with fried ham and scrambled eggs. Butter generously and top with honey or syrup.

3 eggs
1 cup milk
3 tablespoons salad oil or
** melted butter**

1 cup flour
½ teaspoon salt

Preheat oven to 400°. Lightly grease 8 (5-ounce) custard cups or an old-fashioned popover pan. In a medium bowl, with a rotary beater, beat until well combined the eggs, milk and oil. Sift flour and salt into egg mixture. Beat just until smooth. Pour batter into greased custard cups, filling each half full. Place cups on a baking sheet and bake 45–50 minutes, until golden brown. Serve at once. Makes 8.

The Ham Book

Popovers Patrick Henry

No popovers we have tasted equal those in flavor and simplicity. A special treat any time.

3 eggs
1 cup milk

1 cup flour
¾ teaspoon salt

Have milk and eggs at room temperature. Mix all ingredients in bowl together and beat hard for 2 minutes. Grease 11–12 cups of muffin tin with vegetable shortening or lard. Pour batter from pitcher, filling each cup half to three-fourths full. Place in cold oven and set temperature for 450°. Bake for 25 minutes. Expect them to fall when removed, for that is the nature of popovers. Butter heavily (with the real dairy product) and serve.

More Delectable Cookery of Alexandria

Patrick Henry was the first commander-in-chief of the Virginia forces. One year after delivering his stirring "Give me liberty or give me death" speech at Richmond in 1775, Virginia declared itself an independent commonwealth. Henry became the first governor of Virginia.

French Breakfast Puffs

⅓ cup soft shortening
½ cup sugar
1 egg
1½ cups flour
1½ teaspoons baking powder
½ teaspoon salt

¼ teaspoon nutmeg
½ cup milk
6 tablespoons melted margarine
  or butter
½ cup sugar
1 teaspoon ground cinnamon

Mix together shortening, ½ cup sugar, 1 egg in large mixing bowl. Set aside. Sift together flour, baking powder, salt and nutmeg. Stir into shortening mixture alternately with milk. Fill greased muffin cups two-thirds full. Bake at 350° for 20–25 minutes or golden brown. Remove from oven; roll immediately in melted butter, then in sugar and cinnamon mixture. Serve warm. Makes 12.

Think Healthy

Egg Casserole

Great for a brunch.

¼ cup butter
¼ cup flour
1 teaspoon salt
1 cup cream
1 cup milk
¼ teaspoon thyme
¼ teaspoon basil
¼ teaspoon marjoram
¼ teaspoon chervil

1 pound sharp Cheddar cheese,
  grated
1½ dozen hard-boiled eggs,
  sliced
1 pound bacon, sautéed and
  crumbled
¼ cup finely chopped parsley
Buttered bread crumbs

Melt butter and make cream sauce using flour, salt, cream and milk. Add herbs. Stir cheese into cream sauce until melted. Place a layer of sliced eggs in 3-quart casserole. Sprinkle bacon over eggs, and garnish with parsley. Add layer of cheese sauce over all and repeat two more layers. Top with buttered bread crumbs. Bake uncovered at 350° for 30 minutes. Serves 10–12.

The Stuffed Cougar

Anne Jefferson's Crazy Cheese Pie

This luncheon dish looks like over-liquid pancake dough before it is cooked and like a soufflé when it has baked. Putting the cheese over the middle causes it to settle down in the middle and look like a pie with a puffy crust.

1 egg	**⅛ teaspoon pepper**
1 cup milk	**4 ounces shredded Muenster**
¾ cup flour	**cheese (1 cup)**
½ teaspoon salt	

In a bowl, combine egg, ½ cup milk, flour, salt, and pepper, beating until smooth. Add remaining ½ cup milk and beat until well blended. Stir in half of the cheese. Pour into a greased 8-inch pie plate. Bake in a hot oven (425°) for 30 minutes. Sprinkle remaining cheese over top and bake additional 2–3 minutes or until cheese is melted. Serve immediately. Makes 4 servings.

Apron Strings

Fabulous Cheese Casserole

9 slices bread (not fresh)
Salt and pepper
1½ tablespoons instant
   minced white onion
1½ tablespoons instant
   minced green onion

1 pound Cheddar cheese
4 eggs
3 cups milk
1 teaspoon dry mustard
1 teaspoon Worcestershire
   sauce

Cut 3 slices of the bread in 3 strips each and fit tightly on the bottom of a very lightly greased 2-quart casserole. Sprinkle with salt and pepper and a third of the white and green onion. Grate a third of the cheese over this, even it out and press down.

Make two more layers the same way. Beat eggs slightly and add milk, mustard, and the Worcestershire sauce. Pour over bread layers. Let stand for at least 8 hours, preferably overnight in the refrigerator. Remove from the refrigerator 2 hours ahead of serving time to allow the casserole to come to room temperature. Bake uncovered at 325° for 50–60 minutes or until firm in center. Yields 4–6 generous servings.

Note: To double recipe, double all the ingredients but use only 5 cups of milk.

The Foxcroft Cook Book

Sausage Casserole

6 eggs
2 cups milk
1 teaspoon salt
1 teaspoon dry mustard

3 slices bread, toasted and cubed
1 pound sausage, browned and
   drained
1 cup grated cheese

Spray dish with Pam. Place bread cubes in casserole dish. Sprinkle sausage over bread cubes. Sprinkle cheese over sausage. Mix together eggs, milk, salt, and dry mustard. Pour over sausage and cheese. Bake 1 hour at 350°.

Cooking with Class

Swiss Omelet Roll

½ cup mayonnaise
2 tablespoons flour
1 cup milk
12 eggs, separated
½ teaspoon salt

⅛ teaspoon white pepper
1½ cups chopped ham
1 cup shredded Swiss cheese
¼ cup chopped green onion

In a heavy saucepan combine mayonnaise and flour. Gradually add milk and beaten egg yolks. Cook over low heat stirring constantly until thickened. Remove from heat and cool 15 minutes.

Beat egg whites until stiff. Fold mayonnaise mixture and seasonings into egg whites. Line a jellyroll pan with greased waxed paper. Pour in omelet and bake at 425° for 20 minutes. Remove omelet from oven and invert on a towel. Carefully remove waxed paper. Cover evenly with ham, cheese and green onion. Roll from narrow end, lifting towel while rolling. (May freeze at this point.) Serve seam-side-down on a platter. Top with mustard sauce. Arrange fresh vegetables around omelet: cocktail tomatoes, broccoli flowerettes, whole mushrooms. Garnish with parsley or watercress.

MUSTARD SAUCE:

1 cup mayonnaise
2 tablespoons prepared
  mustard

2 tablespoons chopped green
  onion

Mix and refrigerate.

*THE What in the World Are We Going
to Have for Dinner? COOKBOOK*

Four of the first five American presidents were from Virginia: George Washington, Thomas Jefferson, James Madison, and James Monroe. Later, four other Virginia-born men also were elected to the Presidency: William Henry Harrison, John Tyler, Zachary Taylor, and Woodrow Wilson.

Christiana Campbell's Tavern
Shad Roe Omelet

3 ounces shad roe	¼ cup light cream
Salt and pepper to taste	¼ cup fine bread crumbs
2 eggs	2 tablespoons butter

Drop the shad roe into boiling salted water to cover and cook until the roe is firm (about 6 minutes). Drain the roe, chop it coarsely, and season with the salt and pepper.

Beat the eggs, cream, and bread crumbs together until the mixture is light and foamy. Add salt and pepper to taste.

Heat the butter in an omelet pan over high heat; remove the pan from the heat. Add the eggs and return to the heat. When the eggs begin to set, lift the edges with a fork or spatula so that any uncooked egg will run to the bottom of the pan. Shake the pan occasionally to prevent sticking. When the egg mixture is completely set, add the shad roe, fold the omelet over, roll it onto a warm plate, and serve at once. Serves 1–2.

The Williamsburg Cookbook

The Williamsburg Inn's Fantasio Omelet

1 medium apple
1 slice stale bread
¼ cup butter, divided
2 ounces sausage
1 teaspoon chopped walnuts
  or pecans

3 eggs
1 tablespoon light cream
Salt and pepper to taste
¼ cup shredded Cheddar
  cheese

Peel and dice the apple. Trim the bread and cut into croutons. Fry the croutons until brown and crisp in 1 tablespoon of butter, turning to brown all sides; reserve. Crumble the sausage and sauté until cooked through; drain and reserve. Sauté the apple in the sausage drippings and, when it is almost done, add the chopped nuts. Combine the croutons, sausage, apple and nuts; set aside. Beat the eggs and cream together until the mixture is light and foamy. Add salt and pepper to taste. Heat the remaining butter in an omelet pan over high heat; remove the pan from heat. Add the eggs and return to heat. When the eggs begin to set, lift the edges with a fork or spatula so that any uncooked egg will run to the bottom of the pan. Shake the pan occasionally to prevent sticking. When eggs are set, mound the apple mixture and the cheese on half of the omelet; fold it, and roll it around onto a plate. Serves 2–3.

Virginia's Historic Restaurants and Their Recipes

Dame Witty's Welsh Rarebit

¼ cup butter
½ cup flour
3 cups milk
1 pound very sharp Cheddar
  cheese (broken into pieces)
¾ teaspoon mustard
  (prepared)

½ tablespoon Worcestershire
  sauce
1 teaspoon Tabasco sauce
½ teaspoon salt
½ bottle beer (most children
  prefer this dish made
  without beer)

Melt butter, then add flour and stir until smooth. Pour in milk; continue stirring for 5 minutes in double boiler. Add cheese and seasonings and continue cooking until smooth. Finally add beer (if desired) and serve over crackers or toast triangles with a strip of bacon. Serves 6.

Delectable Cookery of Alexandria

Lazy Person's Complete Breakfast
(Microwave)

1 slice bread, cubed
1 egg
¼ cup milk
¼ cup chopped ham
Dash of Worcestershire sauce

2 tablespoons shredded
   Cheddar cheese
¼ teaspoon dry mustard
⅛ teaspoon salt

Combine all ingredients in a 6-inch serving bowl. Mix well. Cover tightly with plastic wrap. Vent.

Microwave on MEDIUM HIGH (80%) for 4½–5½ minutes. Halfway through the cooking time, turn the dish (so that the back is now facing the front of the oven.) Let stand, covered, 30–60 seconds to finish cooking. Serve with fresh fruit or fruit juice for a complete, nutritional breakfast.

You may wish to fix this the night before and refrigerate for a quick meal in the morning. Be sure to lengthen cooking times since ingredients are at a lower starting temperature.

The Microwave Affair

Edinburg Mill Restaurant's Sausage Gravy

1 pound mild sausage
4 tablespoons finely chopped
   onion
2 tablespoons sugar
1 teaspoon salt
½ teaspoon pepper

2 tablespoons Worcestershire
   sauce
¼ cup plain flour
½ cup water
½ cup milk
Dash of Kitchen Bouquet

Brown sausage in a skillet, adding one tablespoon at a time to prevent sticking. When sausage is browned, add onions, sugar, salt, pepper and Worcestershire sauce and simmer for 2 minutes. Add flour; sprinkling evenly on top of sausage. Add water and milk gradually until the right consistency is achieved. Add a dash of Kitchen Bouquet for color. Simmer for 10–15 minutes. Serves 6–8.

Virginia's Historic Restaurants and Their Recipes

Luncheon Pumpernickel Loaf

1 round loaf pumpernickel
bread, unsliced

¼ pound butter, softened

HAM FILLING:

10 ounces country cured ham,
ground

1 stalk celery, minced

1 tablespoon horseradish

2 tablespoons mayonnaise

CRABMEAT FILLING:

1 cup crabmeat, picked over

2 tablespoons butter,
softened

1 tablespoon lemon juice

1 green onion, chopped

EGG FILLING:

4 hard-boiled eggs, chopped

2 tablespoons mayonnaise

2 teaspoons prepared mustard

1 teaspoon dried dill weed

1 teaspoon salt

¼ teaspoon pepper

Combine ingredients for the fillings individually. Slice pumpernickel horizontally into 5 slices and butter both sides of each slice plus tops and bottoms. To assemble, spread half the ham filling on the bottom slice, top with the next slice and spread with all the crabmeat filling; top with the next slice and all the egg filling, and the next slice, with the remaining ham filling. Put a top slice on the entire loaf, wrap tightly in foil or plastic wrap, and refrigerate 3–4 hours. (Do not freeze.) May be doubled. To serve cut into wedges with a very sharp serrated knife, garnish with carrot sticks, cucumber slices and olives, and eat with a fork. This dresses up a tailgate picnic—but bring along sturdy plates!

The Belle Grove Plantation Cookbook

Fresh Blueberry Coffee Cake

Perfect for a summer breakfast!

¾ cup sugar

¼ cup shortening,
softened

1 egg

½ cup milk

2 cups presifted flour

2 teaspoons baking powder

½ teaspoon salt

1 pint blueberries

Preheat oven to 350°. Mix sugar and shortening with an electric mixer; add egg and milk. Mix in flour, baking powder and salt. Gently fold in berries and pour into a greased 8- or 9-inch square glass baking dish.

CONTINUED

Combine topping ingredients and spread over batter. Bake 45–50 minutes. Serve warm with butter for a delicious breakfast treat! Serves 6–8.

TOPPING:

½ teaspoon cinnamon
¼ cup dark brown sugar
¼ cup sugar
¼ cup margarine, softened
⅓ cup flour

Note: When blueberries are in season, freeze some to have on hand when they aren't readily available.

Words Worth Eating

Sour Cream Pumpkin Coffee Cake

½ cup butter or margarine, softened
¾ cup sugar
1 teaspoon vaniila
3 eggs
2 cups all-purpose flour
1 teaspoon baking powder
1 teaspoon baking soda
1 cup sour cream
1 (16-ounce) can pumpkin
1 egg, beaten
⅓ cup sugar
1 teaspoon pumpkin pie spice

STREUSEL:

1 cup brown sugar
⅓ cup butter or margarine
2 teaspoons cinnamon
1 cup chopped nuts

Cream butter, ¾ cup sugar and vanilla; add 3 eggs, beating well. Sift together flour, baking powder, and soda. Add dry ingredients to butter mixture, alternating with sour cream. Set aside.

Combine pumpkin, egg, ⅓ cup sugar, and spice. Set aside. For streusel, cut butter into brown sugar and cinnamon; when well blended, add nuts. Spoon half of sour cream batter into 13x9x2-inch greased baking pan; spread to corners. Sprinkle half of streusel over batter. Spread pumpkin mixture next. Carefully spread remaining batter. Sprinkle remaining streusel on top. Bake in a preheated 325° oven for 50–60 minutes or until done.

Recipes from Jeffersonville Woman's Club

Basic Buttermilk Pancakes

2 cups unbleached white flour
1 teaspoon Royal baking
  powder
½ teaspoon salt
1½ cups buttermilk

½ cup honey
½ cup sour cream
2 eggs
½ cup butter, melted

Stir dry ingredients together. Beat all wet ingredients with eggs. Add dry ingredients a little at a time to egg mixture, until smooth. Be sure not to overbeat. For each pancake pour about ¼ cup of batter on a lightly buttered hot griddle or skillet and cook until top is covered with bubbles and bottom is golden. Turn and cook until bottom is golden. Serve hot with natural maple syrup or honey.

NINE VARIATIONS:

¾ cup fresh or drained blueberries
¾ cup wheat germ plus ½ cup additional liquid
¾ cup chopped dried dates, figs, or peaches
½ cup carob powder plus ¼ cup additional liquid
½ cup grated fresh coconut plus ¼ cup additional liquid
¾ cup granola plus ½ cup additional liquid (these will be crunchy)
½ cup chopped pecans plus 2 eggs plus ¼ cup water
Indian Harvest: ¾ cup cut sweet fresh corn
½ cup brewers yeast plus ¼ cup additional liquid

The New Life Cookbook

The largest canyon east of the Mississippi River, Breaks Interstate Park on the Virginia-Kentucky border, is called "The Grand Canyon of the South."

Soups

PHOTO COURTESY OF VIRGINIA TOURISM CORPORATION

The State Capitol, designed by Thomas Jefferson, is beautiful in its winter coat.

Cold Avocado Soup

1 ripe avocado
1 can chilled chicken broth
2 tablespoons rum

½ teaspoon curry powder
½ teaspoon salt
1 cup light cream

Blend all ingredients in blender until frothy. Serve at once in chilled bowls garnished with a lime or avocado slice. Season with freshly ground pepper if desired. Preparation: 10 minutes. Serves 4.

Note: Buy the dark pebbly avocados in summer and let ripen on your windowsill. The big smooth ones are watery and have little taste.

Virginia Seasons

Dixie's Summer Tomato Soup

2 pounds tomatoes
1 tablespoon sugar
2 teaspoons salt
½ teaspoon onion juice
Juice and grated rind of ½
  lemon

8 tablespoons half-and-half
2 slices ham, diced (any type,
  but Smithfield is best)
½ cucumber, diced
Fresh parsley, finely
  chopped

Purée tomatoes with seasonings and lemon in a blender. Chill in refrigerator; then add the cream, ham, and cucumber. Stir. Garnish with parsley and serve. If your cucumber has hard seeds, scrape them off before dicing. Makes 4 servings.

From Ham to Jam

Shrimp Gazpacho Soup

This is a cold soup, but is also delicious served hot with melted Cheddar cheese on top.

½ cucumber, diced
1 stalk celery, diced
1 carrot, diced
1 medium onion, diced
1 green pepper, diced
1 (46-ounce) can V8 juice
1 teaspoon salt
1 teaspoon pepper
Tabasco
Worcestershire sauce

2 tablespoons chives
2 tablespoons parsley
1 tablespoon basil
1 tablespoon tarragon
1 tablespoon chervil
1 tablespoon paprika
1 tablespoon sugar
⅛ cup lemon juice
1 pound boiled shrimp,
   shelled

Combine all vegetables with V8 juice. Add spices and shrimp. Chill for 3–4 hours.

Gourmet by the Bay

Jellied Mushroom Soup

1 pound mushrooms, chopped
3½ cups strong chicken stock
2 tablespoons dry sherry
Salt and pepper to taste
1–2 tablespoons lemon juice

1 envelope unflavored gelatin
¼ cup cold water
Sour cream
Watercress, parsley or chives

Simmer mushrooms in stock for 3 minutes. Place in blender for 30 seconds. Add additional stock if necessary to make 3¾ cups. Add sherry, salt, pepper and lemon juice. Soften gelatin in cold water. Bring soup to boiling point, add gelatin and stir until dissolved. Chill. Serve with dollop of sour cream and snipped watercress, parsley or chives. Serves 6–8.

The Mount Vernon Cookbook

King's Arms Tavern Cream of Peanut Soup

Brazil is the native home of the peanut, the "ground nut" that sailed with Portuguese explorers to Africa and back to the Americas with the Negro. In 1794, Thomas Jefferson recorded the yield of sixty-five peanut hills at Monticello. The cultivation of peanuts increased in the South in the nineteenth century, but it was not until after the Civil War that they gained national acceptance.

Peanut soup is comparatively new, but it is much in demand in the King's Arms Tavern.

1 medium onion, chopped	2 quarts chicken stock, or
2 ribs of celery, chopped	canned chicken broth
¼ cup butter	2 cups smooth peanut butter
3 tablespoons all-purpose	1¾ cups light cream
flour	Peanuts, chopped

Sauté the onion and the celery in butter until soft, but not brown. Stir in the flour until well blended. Add the chicken stock, stirring constantly, and bring to a boil.

Remove from the heat and purée in a food processor or a blender. Add the peanut butter and cream, stirring to blend thoroughly. Return to low heat and heat until just hot, but do not boil. Serve, garnished with peanuts. Serves 10–12.

Note: This soup is also good served ice cold.

The Williamsburg Cookbook

Three ships, named *Discovery, Godspeed,* and *Susan Constant,* brought the first colonists to Jamestown in 1607. "James Towne," the first permanent English settlement, was named in honor of King James I of England. It is one of the very few tangible traces of 17th-century America in existence.

Peanut Soup

A light soup that is quick to prepare.

1 packet dry onion soup mix	**1 quart chicken stock**
2 ribs celery, chopped, or 4	**½ tablespoon flour**
teaspoons parsley flakes	**½ cup peanut butter**
2 tablespoons butter	**1 cup milk**

Mix first 4 ingredients and heat to boiling, then add ½ tablespoon flour which has been mixed with cooled stock to the mixture. Pour this all through a strainer and then add the peanut butter and milk. Cook at low heat—do not boil—until warmed and blended. Serve garnished with additional crushed peanuts.

Note: I usually use low-fat milk and some powdered milk to thicken to my own liking. Regular milk will do fine, or cream for a very full-bodied soup.

The Smithfield Cookbook

Cream of Spinach Soup

½ cup chopped onion
2 tablespoons butter or
  margarine
1 tablespoon flour
  (all-purpose)
1 (10-ounce) package frozen
  chopped spinach, thawed and
  drained
1 (14-ounce) can chicken broth

⅛ teaspoon ground nutmeg
1 cup heavy cream (half-and-
  half may be used, but the soup
  will not be quite as thick and
  creamy)
Salt to taste
White pepper to taste
Croutons (optional)

Sauté onion lightly in the butter or margarine; stir in flour. Add spinach, chicken broth, and nutmeg. Heat to boiling; reduce heat, cover and cook 5 minutes. Purée until smooth in blender or food processor.

Return spinach mixture to pan; add cream. Heat thoroughly but do not boil. Add salt and pepper to taste. Optional: serve with croutons. Yields 4 servings. Recipe can easily be doubled.

CROUTONS:

Trim crusts from 1 slice bread and cut into small cubes. Melt 1 tablespoon butter with a dash or 2 of paprika. Add bread and sauté over low heat until browned and crisp. Stir frequently. Yields about ½ cup croutons.

Keeping the Feast

Shirley Plantation Mushroom Soup

Original recipe from the Shirley Plantation Collection:

½ lb. fresh mushrooms, peel & put the caps & stems chopped fine in a saucepan with 2 tablespoons of butter. Cover, heat slowly & simmer 20 minutes. Stir in 2 tablespoons of flour, add slowly 5 cups of hot milk, stir until smooth & thickened, season with salt & cayenne. May be served in cups with very stiff whipped cream on top at the last minute. Serves 6–8.

1 pound fresh mushrooms	3 cups milk
6 tablespoons butter	1½ teaspoons salt
5 tablespoons flour	¼ scant teaspoon cayenne
3 cups cream	pepper

HEARTH:

1. Rinse, trim, and finely chop mushrooms.
2. While the mushrooms are being prepared, place a pan with butter on a trivet on the hearth, near but not in the fire. Allow butter to melt slowly.
3. Stir in mushrooms. Cover pan and shovel a few coals under the trivet. Allow mushrooms to simmer slowly, stirring occasionally, until done, about 15–20 minutes.
4. Stir in flour and continue cooking mushroom mixture, stirring occasionally, until liquid is absorbed and flour is cooked. Replenish coals if necessary, but keep the mixture at a simmer.
5. In the meantime, combine cream and milk in a separate pan and heat over flames to scalding. When mushroom mixture is ready, slowly add hot liquid, salt, and cayenne pepper, stirring constantly. Continue to let soup cook for a few minutes while stirring, until slightly thickened. Do not let soup boil. Correct seasoning and serve immediately.

MODERN:

Follow hearth direction 1.

2. Slowly melt butter in saucepan over low heat. Stir in mushrooms and cover pan. Allow mushrooms to cook 15–20 minutes until done, stirring occasionally.
3. Stir in flour and continue to cook mixture at a gentle simmer. Do not allow liquid to boil.

Follow hearth directions 4 through 5. Serves 6–8.

Hearthside Cooking

Martha Washington's Porridge of Green Peas

This soup is from Mrs. Washington's collection of recipes—the flavor is very light and I have found that it is most pleasing when a wine is not served, as one does not want to diminish the delicacy of the flavor.

2 cups young green peas	**2 cups milk**
2 cups boiling water	**1 tablespoon flour**
1 teaspoon sugar	**2 tablespoons butter**
1 teaspoon salt	**Black pepper**
Sprig of mint	

Drop peas into boiling water. Add sugar, salt, and mint. Cook slowly until peas are tender. Rub through a sieve. Add milk and bring to boil. Mix the flour and butter, and thicken soup with this. Add more salt, if necessary, and freshly ground black pepper to taste.

The Virginia Presidential Homes Cookbook

Luscious Lentil Soup

This is the only way my kids will eat lentils. In fact, they love it so much, I always double the recipe.

2 tablespoons olive oil	**1½ cups dried lentils,**
2 cups chopped raw onion	**picked over and rinsed**
4 raw carrots, coarsely grated	**6 ounces dry red wine**
1 teaspoon crumbled marjoram	**Salt and pepper to taste**
1 teaspoon crumbled thyme	**⅓ cup chopped fresh parsley**
1 (28-ounce) can tomatoes	**4 ounces Cheddar cheese,**
with juice, coarsely chopped	**grated**
7 cups broth (beef, chicken	
or vegetable)	

Heat oil in large saucepan and sauté the onions, carrots, marjoram, and thyme, stirring the vegetables for about 5 minutes. Add tomatoes, broth and lentils. Bring soup to a boil, reduce the heat, cover pan and simmer for about 1 hour or until the lentils are tender. Add the salt, pepper, wine, and parsley and simmer the soup for a few minutes. Serve with cheese sprinkled on top. This also freezes quite well. Serves 18.

Think Healthy

Golden Glow Corn Chowder

This is wonderful when you're out of everything else!

6 slices bacon, cut into
  1-inch pieces
2 small onions, peeled and
  chopped
½ green medium pepper,
  seeded, cored and chopped
4 medium potatoes, peeled
  and cubed and seeded

2 cups water
1 (16-ounce) can whole-kernel
  corn, drained
1 cup evaporated milk or
  half-and-half
1 (2-ounce) jar chopped
  pimento, drained
Salt and pepper, to taste

In a heavy skillet, pan-fry bacon over medium heat until crisp. Remove and drain on absorbent paper. Sauté onions and green pepper in bacon drippings over moderate heat until tender but not browned. Drain off excess drippings. In a heavy 2- to 3-quart saucepan, cook potatoes in water over moderate heat until tender. Add onions, green pepper, corn, milk, pimento, salt and pepper to taste. Heat through. Garnish each serving with crisp bacon pieces. Makes 4–6 servings.

Apron Strings

Hearty Cheddar Cheese Chowder

3 cups chicken stock
4 medium potatoes, peeled
   and diced
1 medium onion, sliced
1 cup thinly sliced carrots
½ cup diced green pepper

⅓ cup butter
⅓ cup flour
3½ cups milk
4 cups (1 pound) shredded sharp
   Cheddar cheese

In a large Dutch oven bring chicken stock to boil. Add vegetables. Cover and simmer 10 minutes or until vegetables are tender. Melt butter in a heavy saucepan. Blend in flour and cook 1 minute. Gradually add milk. Stirring constantly, cook over medium heat until thickened. Add cheese to white sauce and stir until melted. Stir cheese sauce into vegetable mixture. Cook over low heat until thoroughly heated. Do not boil. Makes 8–10 servings.

Taste of Goodness

Onion Soup

Chop up twelve large onions, boil them in three quarts of milk and water equally mixed, put in a bit of veal or fowl, and a piece of bacon, with pepper and salt. When the onions are boiled to pulp, thicken it with a large spoonful of butter mixed with one of flour. Take out the meat, and serve it up with toasted bread cut in small pieces in the soup.

The Virginia House-wife

Crème St. Jacques
Cream of Scallop Soup

1½ quarts water
1 pound potatoes
(3–4 medium)
2 medium onions, coarsely
chopped
½ bay leaf
¼ teaspoon thyme

Salt and freshly ground
black pepper to taste
1 cup sea scallops, coarsely
chopped
¼ teaspoon garlic salt
2 egg yolks
½ cup heavy cream

Bring the water to a boil and add the potatoes, onions, bay leaves, thyme, salt and pepper.

Simmer 50 minutes. Add the scallops and cook 5 minutes longer. Add the garlic salt. Remove bay leaves and put the soup through electric blender until smooth. Return the soup to the heat and bring to boil. Turn off heat and stir in the egg yolks blended with the cream. Serve very hot, but do not allow to return to boil after cream and yolks are added. Serves 8.

Dan River Family Cookbook

Soup à la Julienne

Take carrots, turnips and potatoes and cut them in strips about ¾ of an inch long and 1½ of an inch wide. There should be ¾ cupful of each. Melt 2 tablespoonfuls of butter; add the vegetables and fry gently, stirring carefully, until they begin to shrivel. Then put them in the soup. When it boils, add ¼ cup of sorrel, and ½ cup of spinach, which should first have been scalded with boiling water to take the sharpness out, then drain and chop fine. Add to your Julienne also 3 stalks of celery and 2 beets cut up like turnips and carrots. Also ½ cup of green peas, when they are in season.

This soup should be made with beef broth, about 2½ quarts, or if water is used 3 spoonfuls of dried beans that have been soaked should be put in.

It should cook for two hours. Before serving cut 3 slices of bread in small cubes and brown in butter. Add to soup.

Thomas Jefferson's Cook Book

Broccoli Clam Soup

¼ pound butter
1 bunch fresh or 1 package
   frozen broccoli
1 medium onion, chopped
2 cloves garlic, minced
½ cup flour

1 teaspoon dry mustard
1 teaspoon salt
3 cups milk
2 cups chicken broth
1½ cups grated cheese
1 small can clams

Melt butter in 3-quart pan. Cut broccoli in bite-size pieces. Sauté broccoli, onion, and garlic until crisp-tender. Blend in flour, mustard and salt. Gradually add milk and broth and cook over medium heat, stirring constantly until thickened. Reduce heat and blend in cheese and clams, stirring until smooth. Do not let boil after adding cheese and clams. Makes 1½ quarts.

Spotsylvania Favorites

Captain Rasmussen's Clam Chowder

12 chowder clams
4 cups water
¼ cup butter
1 cup chopped onion
¾ cup diced celery
¾ cup diced carrot
½ cup diced green pepper
1 clove garlic, pressed

½ cup chopped plum tomatoes
¼ cup tomato purée
1 cup cubed potatoes
⅛ teaspoon rosemary
⅛ teaspoon thyme
½ teaspoon salt
⅛ teaspoon white pepper
¼ teaspoon pepper

Scrub the clams well. Steam them in 4 cups of water. Remove the clams from their shells. Chop the clams finely. Reserve. Strain the clam broth. Reserve.

Melt the butter in a large saucepan. Add the onion, celery, carrot, and green pepper and sauté over medium heat until the vegetables are tender. Do not brown. Add the garlic, tomatoes, tomato purée, potatoes, rosemary, thyme, salt, white and black peppers, and clam broth. Bring to a boil, reduce the heat, and simmer, covered, for 20 minutes. Taste for seasoning. Add the chopped clams. Heat almost to the boiling point. Serves 8.

Note: If fresh clams are not available, 1 (8-ounce) bottle clam juice and 2 (6½-ounce) cans minced clams and their liquid may be substituted.

Favorite Meals from Williamsburg

Chesapeake Bay Clam Chowder

18 chowder clams
2 quarts plus 1 tablespoon
  cold water
1 tablespoon vegetable oil
4 stalks celery, diced
2 medium leeks, white part
  only, diced

1 medium onion, diced
Salt and pepper to season
2 pounds potatoes, peeled, diced,
  and covered with cold water
2 bay leaves
2 tablespoons chopped fresh
  thyme (or 2 teaspoons dried)

Wash and scrub the clams under cold running water. Place in a 5-quart saucepan and cover with 2 quarts cold water. Place the saucepan over medium heat. Bring the water to a boil, lower the heat, and simmer until the clams begin to open, about 20 minutes. Remove the saucepan from the heat. Strain and reserve 6 cups clam stock. Shuck the clams, removing and discarding the tough side muscle. Slice the clams into thin strips. Cover with film wrap and refrigerate until needed.

Heat the vegetable oil with 1 tablespoon water in a 5-quart saucepan over medium heat. When hot, add the diced celery, leeks, and onion. Season with salt and pepper and sauté 5 minutes. Add the reserved clam stock to the sautéed vegetables.

Drain and rinse the diced potatoes under cold running water. Add the potatoes to the stock and vegetables and bring to a simmer over medium heat. Tie the bay leaves and thyme in a small piece of cheese-cloth and add to the simmering chowder.

Simmer until the potatoes are cooked, about 30 minutes. Add the clams and simmer for 2 minutes. Remove from the heat. Salt and pepper. Cool the chowder properly, then cover and refrigerator for 24 hours before serving. Heat the chowder slowly over low heat, stirring frequently so that the potatoes do not stick to the bottom of the pot. When hot, adjust the seasoning and serve immediately.

The Trellis Cookbook

The name *Chowder* is derived from the French *Chaudiere* which was the kettle in which stews and soups were cooked.

Crab Bisque

5 or 6 scallions
4 tablespoons unsalted
  butter
¼ cup all-purpose flour
3 cups milk
1½ cups heavy cream

2 teaspoons salt
½ teaspoon ground mace
½ teaspoon paprika
Tabasco
1 pound crabmeat

Chop scallions, white and green parts, crosswise into fine pieces. Cut butter into small pieces. In a large kettle sauté the scallions in the melted butter until softened. Blend in the flour and cook over low heat for 5 minutes. Stir in milk and cream. Cook just until warm. Stir in spices and Tabasco to taste, blending well. Add the crabmeat, but do not stir or the crabmeat may break into small pieces. Heat gently (do not boil) and serve.

Cooking with Class

Crab Soup

1 stick butter or margarine
1 tablespoon flour
1 pound crabmeat
2 teaspoons onion juice
1¼ cups chicken broth
1 quart half-and-half

½ teaspoon Worcestershire
  sauce
1 hard-boiled egg, chopped
Salt and pepper to taste
4 tablespoons dry sherry

Melt butter and blend flour in. Add all other ingredients except sherry. Cook slowly over hot water for 20 minutes. Add ½ tablespoon sherry to individual bowls. Add soup and serve piping hot.

A Southern Lady's Spirit

Holiday Seafood Bisque

1 tablespoon minced shallots
¼ cup butter or margarine, melted
½ cup flour
4 cups Shrimp Stock
¼ cup chopped green pepper
¼ cup chopped sweet red pepper

4 ounces crabmeat, shell and cartilage removed
8 ounces peeled deveined raw shrimp, cut into ¼-inch pieces
¼ cup heavy cream, at room temperature
¼ cup dry sherry
Salt and pepper to taste

In a large heavy saucepan, sauté shallots in butter over moderate heat until tender but not browned. Reduce heat; with a wire whisk, blend in flour and cook, whisking constantly, for 5 minutes. Gradually whisk in Shrimp Stock, being careful that lumps do not form. Increase heat and bring to a boil. Reduce heat; add peppers and simmer for 15–20 minutes (see note). Add crab and shrimp and continue to cook for 3–5 minutes or until shrimp are done (light pink in color). In a small heavy saucepan, boil sherry over moderate heat until liquid is reduced in half. Add cream and continue to cook until mixture is reduced by one-third. Blend cream-sherry mixture into shrimp mixture. Season to taste with salt and pepper. Serve immediately.

Note: At this point, bisque may be cooled, covered, and refrigerated until ready to serve.

SHRIMP STOCK:

Shells from 8 ounces raw shrimp
2–3 ribs celery, cut in 2-inch pieces
1 large onion, peeled and quartered
1 large carrot, peeled and quartered

Water
1 sprig parsley
½ bay leaf
¾ teaspoon whole black peppercorns

Spread shrimp shells evenly across the bottom of a small roaster pan. Arrange celery, onion, and carrot pieces over shells. Bake, uncovered, in a moderate oven (350°) for 10–15 minutes, until shrimp shells turn red. Transfer pan to range top, add water to cover, and bring to a rolling boil. Reduce heat, add parsley, bay leaf, and peppercorns. Cook until mixture is reduced by one-third. Strain, pressing out the liquid in the vegetables and shells with the back of a wooden spoon.

Richmond Receipts

Flounder Chowder Fulgham

3 pounds whole flounder
2 cups water
2 medium onions
Bacon drippings as needed
½ pound fresh mushrooms
¾ cup (1½ sticks) butter
7 medium potatoes
2 teaspoons salt
½ teaspoons white pepper
1 pint heavy cream
⅛ cup sherry
1 tablespoon sugar

Clean and filet flounder. Retain head, tail, and backbone and boil in 2 cups of water for 30 minutes. Strain and retain the broth. Dice onion and sauté slowly in bacon drippings. Dice mushrooms and sauté in one stick of butter. Dice potatoes and put into broth along with the fish and simmer together for one hour. Add mushrooms, onions, salt, and pepper. Simmer for ½ hour. Cool for one hour. Add cream, sherry, sugar, and remaining butter. Heat slowly. Do not boil! Yields 8 servings.

The Great Taste of Virginia Seafood Cookbook

Chickahominy River Fish Stew

2 tablespoons olive oil
1 clove garlic, minced
1 onion, diced
½ cup diced celery
3 tomatoes, seeded and
    chopped
1 tablespoon sugar
6 catfish fillets (may use
    flounder, cod, orange roughy,
    grouper, etc.)
1 cup Knorr fish stock
½ cup dry white wine
Squeeze of lemon
Chopped parsley
Chopped basil
Salt and pepper
Tabasco

In olive oil sauté garlic, onion, and celery. Add chopped tomatoes and sugar. Simmer until soft. Poach fish in stock and white wine and juice of 1 lemon until fish is just flaky. Remove fish and break into bite-size pieces. Add fish stock to vegetable mixture. Add seasonings to taste and fold in fish pieces. Heat through. Serve over rice in flat soup bowls. Crusty French bread is good to sop up juices. Serves 4.

The Enlightened Titan

Sinfully Rich Oyster Stew

4–6 tablespoons butter
1 cup milk
2 cups heavy cream
1½ pints oysters and liquor

Salt, fresh ground pepper
  to taste
Cayenne pepper to taste
Chopped parsley or paprika

Heat bowls and add 1 tablespoon butter to each. Keep bowls hot. Heat milk, cream and oyster liquor to the boiling point. Add the oysters and again bring to boiling point. Season with salt, pepper and cayenne. Ladle into hot bowls and garnish with a little chopped parsley or paprika. Serves 4–6.

The Rappahannock Seafood Cookbook

"Quintnoke" Oyster Stew

1 quart oysters
1 pound country sausage

Salt
Pepper

Carefully clean fresh oysters; reserve clean oyster liquid. Form thin sausage patties and fry until well done. Into an iron skillet, add 3 tablespoons of sausage fat, cooked sausage broken into bite-size pieces, oysters and reserved oyster liquid with enough water to make 1 quart. Cook until oyster edges begin to curl. Season with salt and pepper to taste. Serves 6–8.

Note: Toasted sharp cheese sandwiches go well with this stew. This was a Great Depression recipe because oysters and sausage were plentiful in the country.

The Rappahannock Seafood Cookbook

Hunt Breakfast Kidney Stew

4 pairs lamb kidneys
1 small onion, diced
2 tablespoons butter
2 tablespoons flour,
    approximately
1 tablespoon chili sauce
Juice of ½ lemon

½ teaspoon poultry
    seasoning
½ teaspoon Worcestershire
    sauce
Salt and pepper to taste
1 teaspoon sherry

Slice kidneys into ½-inch pieces, discarding core. Soak 1 hour or more in cold water, drain. Dice onion and sauté over low heat in butter until almost brown. Add kidneys, stirring occasionally until red color disappears—about 10 minutes. Sprinkle on flour, stirring to a thick brown paste. Add a cup or so of warm water and stir until you have the proper consistency. Season with remaining ingredients and serve over toast or waffles. Serves 4.

Delectable Cookery of Alexandria

Chowning's Tavern Brunswick Stew

By all accounts, every place named Brunswick from Canada to the Carolinas has tried to claim this stew as its own. There have also been many arguments about what precisely went into the original pot, and what should go in now.

All in all, Brunswick County, Virginia, has the best claim to being the birthplace of this popular dish, which in its heyday was served at all of Virginia's tobacco-curings and public gatherings. The story goes that a hunting party in Brunswick County, well provisioned with tomatoes, onions, cabbage, butter beans, red pepper, bacon, salt, and corn, left one man behind to mind the commissary and to have dinner ready at day's end. Disgruntled, he shot a squirrel, the only thing he could find within range of the camp, and threw it into the pot along with the vegetables. When it was served, everybody agreed that squirrel, one of the finest and tenderest of all wild meats, was what made the new stew just right. Chicken is now substituted.

1 stewing hen (6 pounds), or 2 broiler-fryers (3 pounds each)	**2 cups lima beans**
	3 medium potatoes, diced
	4 cups corn cut from cob or 2 (1-pound) cans corn
2 large onions, sliced	
2 cups okra, cut (optional)	**3 teaspoons salt**
4 cups fresh or 2 (1-pound) cans tomatoes	**1 teaspoon pepper**
	1 tablespoon sugar

Cut the chicken in pieces and simmer it in 3 quarts of water for a thin stew, or 2 quarts for a thick stew, until meat can easily be removed from the bones, about 2¼ hours. Add the raw vegetables to the broth and simmer, uncovered, until the beans and potatoes are tender. Stir occasionally to prevent scorching. Add the chicken, boned and diced if desired, and the seasonings. Serves 8–10.

Note: If canned vegetables are used, include their juices and reduce water to 2 quarts for a thin stew, 1 quart for a thick stew.

Also note: Brunswick Stew is one of those delectable things that benefit from long, slow cooking. It is a rule in some tidewater homes never to eat Brunswick Stew the same day it is made, because its flavor improves if it is left to stand overnight and is reheated the next day.

The Williamsburg Cookbook

Minestrone

Do not substitute other sausage. The Italian sausage gives the soup a delicious flavor. Soup is just as tasty leftover as fresh!

1 pound Italian sweet sausage
   (mild—in casing)
1 tablespoon vegetable oil
1 cup diced onion
1 cup sliced carrots
3 beef bouillon cubes dissolved
   in 1½ cups hot water
2 small raw zucchini,
   sliced, or 1 (16-ounce) can
   sliced zucchini
2 cups canned tomatoes,
   chopped
2 cups finely shredded cabbage

1 teaspoon crushed basil
   leaves
¼ teaspoon oregano
¼ teaspoon garlic powder
2 cups cooked Great Northern
   beans, or 1 (16-ounce) can,
   undrained
1 tablespoon sugar
1 teaspoon salt
¼ teaspoon black pepper
¼ teaspoon MSG (optional)
Chopped parsley

Slice sausage in ½-inch rings and brown in oil. Add onion and carrots and cook 5 minutes more. Add next 7 ingredients and heat to boiling. Cover and simmer 1 hour. Add beans, sugar, and seasonings, and cook 20 minutes more. Garnish with parsley to serve. Yields 3 quarts.

Mennonite Country-Style Recipes

Salads

Belmont, a Rappahannock River Manor near Fredericksburg, became the home and studio of Geri Melcher, famous painter of portraits and murals.

Red Raspberry Mold

A lovely and colorful addition to a luncheon. Goes especially well with poultry.

1 (10-ounce) package frozen
  red raspberries, thawed
2 (3-ounce) packages raspberry
  gelatin

2 cups boiling water
1 pint vanilla ice cream
1 (6-ounce) can frozen pink
  lemonade concentrate, thawed

Drain raspberries and reserve syrup. Dissolve gelatin in boiling water, add ice cream and stir until melted. Stir in lemonade and reserve syrup. Chill until thickened. Add raspberries; turn into a 6- to 8-cup mold and chill until firm. Serves 12.

A Heritage of Good Tastes

Cranberry Sour Cream Swirl Salad

A festive salad for holiday meals, but good the year round. A real crowd pleaser.

2 (3-ounce) packages cherry
  or red raspberry gelatin
1½ cups boiling water
1 (15-ounce) can crushed
  pineapple

1 (16-ounce) can whole
  cranberry sauce (break apart
  with fork)
1 cup (½ pint) dairy sour cream

Dissolve gelatin in boiling water. Stir in undrained crushed pineapple and cranberry sauce. Chill until partially set. Spoon into 8-inch square dish. Spoon sour cream on top and stir to swirl. Chill until firm. Cut into squares to serve.

Holiday Treats

When hunting cranes, the colonists saw that they fed on red berries which they named "crane berries." Somewhere along the way the "e" was lost and they've been called cranberries ever since.

Tutti-Frutti Glazed Salad

An attractive, great-tasting salad—so easy.

1 (29-ounce) can peach slices
1 (20-ounce) can pineapple
   chunks
1 (17-ounce) can pear chunks
1 cup seedless white grapes
   or 1 (17-ounce) can fruit
   cocktail

3 bananas, sliced
2 unpared red apples, cut into
   chunks, optional
½ cup orange juice, optional
1 (3¾-ounce) package vanilla
   or lemon instant pudding

Drain canned fruits; reserve pineapple juice. Dip bananas and apples in orange or pineapple juice; drain. Mix pudding with 1 cup pineapple juice (I like half orange juice). Pour over fruits. Chill.

Variation: If you like the tang of orange, add 1 tablespoon Tang to pudding. May use any combination of fruits desired.

Tip: Serve this salad in a pretty glass bowl—makes a great buffet salad for autumn.

Granny's Kitchen

Congealed Ambrosia Salad

1 (15¼-ounce) can pineapple
   tidbits (undrained)
1 (6-ounce) package orange
   flavored gelatin
1 pint orange sherbet
1 cup flaked coconut

2 (11-ounce) cans mandarin
   oranges
1 cup miniature marshmallows
1 (8-ounce) carton sour cream
Leaf lettuce (optional)

Drain pineapple, reserving juice. Add enough water to juice to measure 2 cups. Place juice in a saucepan; bring to boil. Add gelatin and stir until gelatin dissolves. Remove from heat, add sherbet and stir until sherbet melts. Chill until the consistency of unbeaten egg whites. Add pineapple and half of oranges. Spoon mixture into lightly oiled 6-cup ring mold, cover and chill until firm. Combine coconut, remaining oranges, marshmallows and sour cream; chill. Unmold salad onto a lettuce-lined plate; spoon fruit mixture into center.

Smyth County Extension Homemakers Cookbook

Quick and Easy Tomato Aspic

1 small box lemon gelatin
2 cups V8 juice
½ teaspoon onion salt
½ teaspoon Worcestershire
  sauce

Celery, chopped (optional)
Green pepper, chopped
  (optional)

Bring 1 cup V8 juice to boil and pour over gelatin. Stir to dissolve.
Add 1 cup cold V8, onion salt, and Worcestershire sauce. Add celery
and pepper if desired. Pour into mold. Refrigerate until firm.

THE What in the World Are We Going
to Have for Dinner? COOKBOOK

Sunshine Salad

1 (3-ounce) package lemon Jell-O
1 cup hot water
1 cup cold water
1 tablespoon vinegar

1 cup grated carrots
1 cup crushed pineapple,
  drained
½ cup chopped nuts (if desired)

Dissolve Jell-O in bowl with hot water. Add cold water and vinegar.
Then add carrots, pineapple and nuts. Refrigerate until set. Serves 8.

Spotsylvania Favorites

Molded Spinach Salad

1 (3-ounce) package lemon
  gelatin
¾ cup boiling water
1½ tablespoons vinegar
½ cup mayonnaise
¼ teaspoon salt

⅓ cup chopped celery
1 tablespoon minced onion
1 cup chopped frozen spinach,
  thawed and drained
¾ cup cottage cheese

Dissolve gelatin in boiling water; add vinegar, mayonniaise and salt. Put in freezer tray and chill until firm 1 inch around sides of tray. Turn into bowl and beat until fluffy. Add remaining ingredients. Place in 1-quart mold and chill in refrigerator until firm. Serves 6.

The Stuffed Cougar

Spinach Swinger

2 envelopes unflavored gelatin
¼ cup water
½ teaspoon salt
2 tablespoons lemon juice
1 cup mayonnaise
1 (10-ounce) can beef consommé
¼ cup chopped green onion
1½ teaspoons hot horseradish

1 (10-ounce) package frozen,
  chopped spinach, thawed and
  well drained
¼ pound crisp-fried bacon,
  chopped
4 hard-boiled eggs, finely
  chopped

Dissolve gelatin in water. Add salt, lemon juice and mayonnaise to dissolved gelatin. Then add consommé, onion and horseradish; stir well to mix. Gradually add spinach, bacon and eggs. Pour into 1½-quart mold. Serve with "horseradished mayonnaise." Serves 8.

Note: This salad served with ham, curried fruit and rolls is an easy and simple luncheon.

A Heritage of Good Tastes

Red Hill, Patrick Henry's last home and burial place, is a restored plantation and museum at Brookneal.

Asparagus Salad

¾ cup sugar
½ cup vinegar
½ teaspoon salt
1 cup water
2 envelopes gelatin
½ cup water
1 cup chopped celery

½ cup chopped pecans
1 (14-ounce) can green
  asparagus (use juice also)
1 small jar chopped pimento
1 tablespoon lemon juice
Grated onion, if desired

Boil together for 5 minutes the sugar, vinegar, salt and 1 cup water. Dissolve 2 envelopes of gelatin in ½ cup water and add to the above. Set aside to cool. While this is cooling, mix the celery, pecans, asparagus, pimento, lemon juice, and grated onion. Combine the above ingredients and pour into a 1½-quart mold and let set. This excellent recipe serves 9.

From Ham to Jam

Mushroom and Asparagus Curried Salad

2 cups asparagus, cut into
  1½-inch pieces
¼ pound fresh mushroom
  caps, sliced
¾ cup Hellmann's mayonnaise
3 tablespoons sour cream
1½ teaspoons curry powder

1 teaspoon grated onion
½ teaspoon sugar
¾ teaspoon lemon juice
Salt and pepper
Lettuce
Fresh parsley

Cook and chill asparagus. Mix remaining ingredients and combine with mushrooms and asparagus. Add salt and pepper to taste. Put on bed of lettuce and top with fresh parsley. Preparation: 15 minutes. Serves 4.

Virginia Seasons

The Governor's Palace in Williamsburg was the home of seven royal governors and the first two Virginia governors.

Broccoli Salad

1 large head broccoli	½ cup chopped English walnuts
10 slices bacon, cooked and crumbled	1 cup mayonnaise
5 green onions, sliced (optional)	2 tablespoons vinegar
½ cup raisins	¼ cup sugar

Trim off large leaves of broccoli, remove the tough ends of lower stalks and wash broccoli thoroughly. Cut the flowerets and stems into bite-size pieces. Place in a large bowl. Add bacon, green onions, raisins, and nuts. Combine the remaining ingredients, stirring well. Add dressing to broccoli mixture and toss gently. Cover and refrigerate 2–3 hours. Yields 6 servings.

Cooking with Class

Harder's Seven Layer Salad

1 medium head lettuce,
shredded (about 6 cups)
1 cup coarsely chopped celery
1 cup coarsely chopped green
peppers
1½ cups coarsely chopped
Spanish onion
2 cups small green peas,
drained; or frozen peas,
cooked

1–1½ cups real mayonnaise
2 tablespoons sugar
2½ cups shredded mild
Cheddar cheese
8 strips bacon, cooked,
drained and crumbled

Arrange lettuce in bottom of deep bowl. In layers add celery, green pepper, onion, and peas; do not toss. Spread mayonnaise evenly over layer of peas. Sprinkle with sugar and cheese. Cover and refrigerate for at least 4 hours. Sprinkle bacon over salad before serving.

Variation: Add 6 hard-boiled eggs, sliced, and Swiss cheese rather than Cheddar.

Variation: Add 1 (2-ounce) bottle capers, drained; 2 (10-ounce) cans artichokes; 1 (4-ounce) can grated Parmesan instead of Cheddar; and lemon-pepper marinade to taste.

From Ham to Jam

Spring Salad

1 cup mayonnaise
½ cup sour cream
3 boiled potatoes, cubed
3 hard-cooked eggs, chopped
½ cucumber, diced
3 pickles, chopped
¼ pound lean ham, chopped

4–5 green onions, chopped
½ (10-ounce) package cooked
peas
Salt
¼ head lettuce, cut in
⅛-inch strips

Mix mayonnaise and sour cream together. Combine potatoes, eggs, cucumber, pickles, ham, onions, peas, and salt to taste. Add about three-fourths of mayonnaise mixture. Chill. When ready to serve, fold in lettuce and mound onto a large serving plate. Ice with remaining mayonnaise mixture and garnish with cherry tomatoes and green onions.

Culinary Contentment

Hot Cabbage Slaw
(Microwave)

1 slice bacon
¼ teaspoon garlic salt
1½ teaspoons sugar
1 teaspoon wine vinegar

¼ teaspoon Worcestershire
  sauce
1 cup shredded cabbage

Place bacon in a 22-ounce casserole dish. Cover. Microwave on HIGH (100%) 1–1¼ minutes or until bacon is crisp. Remove bacon to paper towel to drain. When cool enough to handle, crumble bacon into small pieces. Set aside.

To bacon grease, add salt, sugar, vinegar and Worcestershire. Mix well. Add cabbage and stir until well coated. Microwave on HIGH (100%) 30–45 seconds or until heated to serving temperature. Sprinkle bacon pieces on top. Serve immediately.

The Microwave Affair

Potato Salad

6 medium potatoes
4 boiled eggs, chopped
¼ teaspoon celery seed
¼ teaspoon onion salt
2 tablespoons chopped
    pimento

⅓ cup pickle relish
½ cup sour cream
¼ cup sandwich relish
2 tablespoons mustard
½ cup mayonnaise

Cook potatoes until done. Boil eggs and let cool slightly. Mix all other ingredients together and blend with potatoes and eggs.

Recipes from Jeffersonville Woman's Club

Sweet Potato Salad with Orange and Lime

2 teaspoons grated lime rind
¼ cup fresh lime juice
2 teaspoons grated orange rind
¼ cup fresh orange juice
2 teaspoons Dijon-style
    mustard

Salt and pepper to taste
3 pounds sweet potatoes, peeled
    and cut into ¾-inch cubes
½ cup olive oil
¼ cup snipped fresh chives

In a large bowl whisk together lime rind, lime juice, orange rind, orange juice, mustard, and salt and pepper to taste. In a steamer set over boiling water, steam the potatoes, covered, for 7 minutes, or until they are just tender. Transfer them to the bowl, and toss with the dressing. Let potatoes cool, add oil, chives, and salt and pepper to taste. Toss well. Serves 4–6.

The Boar's Head Cookbook

Corn Salad

1 can whole-kernel corn
1 can shoepeg white corn
1 small jar chopped pimento
1 large onion, chopped finely
½ cup finely chopped celery

½ cup finely chopped green
    pepper
½ cup sugar
½ cup vinegar
1 teaspoon garlic salt

Drain corn and pimento. Combine the corn, onion, celery, green pepper, and pimento and set aside. Combine sugar, vinegar, and garlic salt; stir until sugar dissolves. Pour over vegetables and toss lightly. Cover and chill 8 hours.

WYVE's Bicentennial Cookbook

Curried Rice Salad

7 tablespoons light olive
  oil, divided use
½ teaspoon coriander
½ teaspoon ground cumin
½ teaspoon ground ginger
½ teaspoon ground cinnamon
¼ teaspoon celery seed
¼ teaspoon ground turmeric
¼ teaspoon cayenne pepper,
  or to taste

1½ cups converted rice
3 cups chicken broth
¼ cup red wine vinegar
4 tablespoons mango chutney
½ cup currants presoaked
½ cup chopped roasted and
  salted peanuts
Salt to taste

Heat 6 tablespoons olive oil in a heavy 3-quart Dutch oven. Stir in the next 7 ingredients. Cook over moderate heat for 3–4 minutes until they release their aroma. Stir in the rice and cook for 2 minutes or until the grains are well coated with oil. Pour in the chicken broth, stir once with a fork and bring to a slow boil. Cover and adjust the heat so that the liquid simmers.

Cook for 18–20 minutes or until all of the liquid has been absorbed. Remove the Dutch oven from the heat and let stand, covered, for 5 minutes.

In a small bowl, whisk together the vinegar, chutney, and remaining olive oil. While the rice is still warm, spoon it into a large bowl and stir in the chutney dressing. Fold in the currants. When the rice has reached room temperature, add the peanuts and taste salad to see if it needs more salt. Transfer to a serving bowl and garnish with sprigs of herbs. Serve at room temperature. Yields 6 servings.

Cardinal Cuisine

Chicken Salad Fit for a Queen

¾ cup mayonnaise
2 teaspoons lemon juice
1 teaspoon curry powder
2 teaspoons soy sauce
2 cups cooked chicken, in
    large chunks
¼ cup sliced water chestnuts

½ pound seedless grapes,
    halved
½ cup chopped celery
½ cup toasted slivered almonds
1 (8-ounce) can pineapple
    chunks, drained

Mix mayonnaise with lemon juice and seasonings, toss with remaining ingredients and chill several hours. Serve on lettuce leaves. Serves 5.

Note: This is the luncheon dish served to Queen Elizabeth II when she visited the University of Virginia and Monticello.

The Belle Grove Plantation Cookbook

June's Favorite Chicken Salad

1 cup mayonnaise
1 tablespoon curry powder
¼ cup chopped mango
    chutney
2 tablespoons grated lime peel
1 teaspoon lime juice
1 large pear, unpeeled, cored,
    seeded and cut into ¾-inch
    cubes
4 cups cooked chicken, cut
    into ¾-inch cubes
1 cup coarsely chopped pecans

1 cup coarsely chopped celery
1 cup coarsely chopped green
    onions, including some
    green tops
2 tablespoons chopped
    crystalized ginger
Romaine lettuce
Thin wedges of cantaloupe,
    honeydew or watermelon and
    wedges of fresh pineapple

In a 2-cup measure, combine mayonnaise, curry powder, chutney, lime peel and lime juice, mixing well. In a large bowl, combine pear cubes, chicken, pecans, celery, green onions, and ginger. Add mayonnaise dressing, mixing well. Cover and thoroughly chill. Spoon into a mound on a chilled serving plate lined with romaine leaves. Arrange wedges of melon or fresh pineapple around chicken salad. Serves 6.

Apron Strings

Chinese Chicken Salad

2 cups Chinese rice noodles
6 chicken breasts, boned and
  skinned
Soy sauce to cover plus 2
  teaspoons
4 tablespoons butter
4 tablespoons cooking oil

2 heads iceberg lettuce, shredded
  as finely as possible and crisped
2 tablespoons peanut oil
2 tablespoons vinegar
Mayonnaise
Chopped parsley

Fry rice noodles for a few seconds in deep hot oil. Remove as soon as they puff and before they brown. Marinate breasts in soy sauce for 20 minutes, then sauté in butter and cooking oil 5 minutes a side. Keep warm. Cut chicken into thin strips and toss with shredded lettuce, soy sauce, peanut oil, vinegar, and fried noodles. Add just enough mayonnaise to blend and season to taste with salt. Garnish with chopped parsley and a few fried noodles. Surround with snow peas, steamed 1 minutes and dress with Sesame Dressing. If you cook chicken ahead, keep at room temperature or reheat. Do not serve cold.

SESAME DRESSING:

¼ cup sesame seeds,
  lightly browned in oven
⅔ cup salad oil
2 tablespoons lemon juice

2 tablespoons vinegar
2 tablespoons sugar
1 garlic clove, crushed
1½ teaspoons salt

Put all in blender except sesame seeds and mix well. Add seeds.

The Boar's Head Cookbook

Salmon Gêlé John Paul Jones

1½ envelopes gelatin
1 cup chicken stock
1 large can salmon, drained
   and flaked
½ cup homemade mayonnaise
Juice ½ lemon

½ teaspoon salt
2¼ tablespoons horseradish
2¼ teaspoons dill weed
1 teaspoon chopped dried or
   fresh parsley
1 cup heavy cream

Soften gelatin in a little cool stock, then dissolve in remaining hot stock. Mix all ingredients together, including cream that has been whipped. Place in mold and refrigerate until solidified. Unmold and serve with crackers.

More Delectable Cookery of Alexandria

Shrimp and Crab Salad

1 (3- to 4-ounce) can black
   olives, divided
½ pound cooked and peeled
   shrimp
¾ cup mayonnaise

1 pound white crabmeat
1 cup diced celery
1 teaspoon lemon herb seasoning
Dash of garlic powder
Salt and pepper to taste

Reserve half the olives for garnish, and quarter those remaining. Mix ingredients in order given. Toss and serve on bed of lettuce. Garnish with whole black olives and tomato wedges if desired. Yields 4–6 servings.

The Great Taste of Virginia Seafood Cookbook

Seafood Pasta Salad

½ cup salad dressing
¼ cup zesty Italian
  dressing
2 tablespoons Parmesan
  cheese
2 cups corkscrew noodles,
  cooked and drained

1½ cups chopped imitation
  crabmeat
1 cup broccoli flowerets,
  partially cooked
½ cup chopped green pepper
½ cup chopped tomato
¼ cup green onion slices

Combine dressings and cheese; mix well. Add remaining ingredients; mix lightly and chill.

Smyth County Extension Homemakers Cookbook

Wild Rice and Seafood Salad

A delicious combination of seafood and rice!

1 (6-ounce) box long-grain
  and wild rice
8 ounces crabmeat, regular
  or backfin
10–12 ounces cooked shrimp
½ cup thinly sliced green
  onions, including tops
¾ cup finely diced celery
1 (8-ounce) can sliced water
  chestnuts, drained and halved

¾ cup mayonnaise
1 teaspoon white vinegar
½ teaspoon minced fresh parsley
1 teaspoon lemon juice
1½ tablespoons Dijon mustard
¼ teaspoon freshly cracked
  black pepper
½–¾ teaspoon salt

GARNISH:
6–8 large lettuce leaves
6–8 hard-boiled eggs,
  quartered

3–4 tomatoes, quartered
6–8 sprigs of fresh parsley,
  for garnish

Cook rice by directions on package. If using a box of rice with seasoning packet, do not use packet. Spread rice on plate to cool. Pick through crab three times to remove all shell. Combine all remaining ingredients except garnish. Stir gently and chill until ready to serve. Serves 6–8.

Serving suggestion: Serve on lettuce leaves garnished with eggs, tomatoes, and parsley. Serve with crusty hot rolls and corn on the cob for a superb seafood feast!

Note: Can be prepared one day ahead. Do not add salt until ready to serve. Salt can cause a salad to "weep" if salad is stored overnight.

Words Worth Eating

The Homestead's Raspberry Poppy Seed Dressing

1½ cups sugar
⅔ cup raspberry vinegar
1 teaspoon English mustard
1 teaspoon salt

2 tablespoons onion juice
2 cups vegetable oil
3 tablespoons poppy seeds

Mix everything together in a blender except oil and poppy seeds. Blend well. Add oil slowly until dressing reaches thick consistency. Add poppy seeds and blend. Serve over salad. Yields 1 quart.

Virginia's Historic Restaurants and Their Recipes

Boiled Salad Dressing

Yolks of three eggs beaten, one teaspoonful mustard, two teaspoonfuls salt, one quarter saltspoon cayenne, two tablespoons melted butter or oil, one cup cream or milk, half cup hot vinegar, whites of three eggs, beaten stiff; cook in double boiler until it thickens like soft custard; stir well. This will keep in a cool place for two weeks.

The Old Virginia Cook Book

Vegetables

An American farmhouse kitchen at the Museum of American Frontier Culture. Stauton.

German Red Cabbage

4 slices bacon
1 small onion, sliced
1 medium (about 1½
  pounds) head red cabbage
½ cup water, divided
¼ cup packed brown sugar

2 tablespoons flour
¼ cup vinegar
1 bay leaf
1 teaspoon salt
⅛ teaspoon pepper

Fry bacon until crisp; sauté onion in bacon drippings. Add red cabbage and ¼ cup of water. After 5 minutes add the brown sugar, flour, vinegar, bay leaf, salt and pepper, and rest of the water. Simmer, stirring frequently for 20 minutes.

Taste of Goodness

Cabbage Oriental

1 pound cabbage, coarsely
  chopped
4 ribs celery, coarsely
  chopped
1 green pepper, coarsely
  chopped

1 large onion, cut in rings
2 tablespoons oil
3 tablespoons soy sauce
¼ teaspoon paprika

Sauté cabbage, celery, pepper, and onion in oil over low heat for 10 minutes. Add soy sauce and paprika. Stir and serve. Serves 4.

Virginia Hospitality

The Natural Bridge is 215 feet high (17 stories) and 90 feet long. Thomas Jefferson bought the bridge and 157 surrounding acres from King George of England in 1774. The price of the purchase was 20 schillings. George Washington's initials are carved in it. It is one of the Seven Natural Wonders of the World.

Egg Foo Young

8 eggs, beaten	2 celery stalks including
3 scallions, sliced	tops, minced
1½ cups bean sprouts	1 recipe of Chinese gravy

Add all the vegetables to beaten eggs and stir together. Cook the mixture in a lightly oiled preheated frying pan as you would pancakes, turning once. Place in a shallow casserole dish and cover with Chinese gravy. Serve over cooked rice with a little soy sauce, if desired.

CHINESE GRAVY:

3 cups water	2½ tablespoons arrowroot
¼ cup soy sauce	

Blend ingredients together and cook over double boiler until thickened, stirring every few minutes.

The New Life Cookbook

Sweet Sour Baked Beans

8 bacon slices (or hamburger)	2 (15-ounce) cans butter beans
4 large onions	1 (1-pound) can green lima
½–1 cup brown sugar	beans
1 teaspoon dry mustard	1 (1-pound) can dark red
½ teaspoon garlic powder	kidney beans
1 teaspoon salt	1 (1-pound, 11-ounce) can New
½ cup vinegar	England-style baked beans

Pan fry bacon until crisp; drain and crumble. Cut onions into rings. Put onions in skillet; add sugar, mustard, garlic powder, salt and vinegar. Cook 20 minutes, covered. Add onion mixture to drained beans. Add bacon. Pour into 3-quart casserole. Bake at 350° for 1 hour.

Happy Times with Home Cooking

Black-Eyed Peas and Rice or "Hoppin' John"

Served on New Year's Day, this dish is supposed to bring good luck.

1½ cups dried black-eyed peas (field peas)	1 clove garlic, minced
1 teaspoon salt	1 ham hock
1½ cups diced onions	½ teaspoon pepper
1 bay leaf	Dash of cayenne

Pick over and wash peas. Soak overnight in about 3–5 cups of water. Next day, drain, saving the water. Remove any peas that float.

Heat water; add soaked peas and all above ingredients. Cover, bring to boiling point and simmer for about 1¼ hours, or until peas are tender and only a small amount of liquid is left. Pick meat from ham hock. Discard ham bone and add meat to the peas.

RICE:

Use amount of rice that will give each person a small serving. Cook according to package directions. Add 1 tablespoon butter and mix lightly with the peas. Cook for 2 or 3 minutes for flavors to blend. Yields 12 servings as a side dish or less if served as a main dish.

Keeping the Feast

Green Beans Caesar

3 tablespoons oil
¾ cup (½-inch) bread cubes
1 tablespoon vinegar
1 teaspoon minced onion
¼ teaspoon salt

1 (17-ounce) can green
  beans, or fresh
3 tablespoons grated
  Parmesan cheese

In 2 tablespoons oil, lightly fry the bread cubes until golden and crisp. Drain. Mix 1 tablespoon oil, vinegar, onion, and salt. Pour over drained green beans in skillet and stir until hot. Sprinkle with cheese and bread cubes. Serves 4.

The Best of the Bushel

Green Bean Casserole

2 (16-ounce) cans French-
  style green beans
1 (8-ounce) can sliced water
  chestnuts
1 can bean sprouts
1½ cans cream of mushroom
  soup

1 (8-ounce) can sliced
  mushrooms
1 medium onion, chopped
1 cup grated sharp cheese
1 can French fried onion rings

Drain beans, water chestnuts, bean sprouts, and mushrooms. In a 2-quart casserole layer half beans, chestnuts, sprouts, mushrooms, and onions.

Cover with half of soup. Sprinkle with salt and pepper and half of cheese. Repeat layering. Top with French fried onions. Bake at 400° for 20 minutes, covered. Remove cover and bake additional 10 minutes.

Command Performances

Belgian Endive

8 stalks endive
4 tablespoons melted butter
Juice of 1 lemon
¾ cup chicken stock

1 teaspoon salt
½ teaspoon sugar
½ teaspoon white pepper
1 teaspoon paprika

Wash and drain endive. Place in oven-proof baking dish. Pour over endive, butter, lemon juice, stock, salt, sugar, and pepper. Cover dish and bake in moderate oven 325°–350° for 40–45 minutes. Remove cover and place under broiler until golden. Sprinkle with paprika and serve.

This recipe was submitted by First Lady Jackie Kennedy when her husband was president.

The Hunt Country Cookbook

Asparagus Loaf

1 egg
1 cup milk
1 cup cracker crumbs
2 tablespoons butter, melted
1 tablespoon minced onion

1 (16-ounce) can asparagus
and liquid
¼ cup grated sharp cheese
Salt and pepper

Beat egg slightly. Heat milk and gradually add to egg. Add crumbs, butter, and onion and let stand until crumbs absorb milk. Cut asparagus into small pieces with scissors and fold asparagus and cheese into milk mixture, adding salt and pepper. Spoon into greased loaf pan. Bake at 350° for 25–30 minutes. Serves 6–8.

Virginia Seasons

Spinach Everyone Likes

2 (10-ounce) packages
spinach, chopped (1 package
whole leaf)
1 cup low-fat sour cream

½ package onion soup mix
½ cup bread crumbs or
herbed stuffing mix

Cook spinach according to package directions. Drain well. Add remaining ingredients except bread crumbs. Mix well. Pour into ungreased 2-quart casserole. Top with bread crumbs. Bake at 350° for 35 minutes. Serves 12.

Think Healthy

Spinach-Spinach Delectable

This dish can be prepared ahead of time and refrigerated before cooking.

½ pound sliced bacon
2 packages frozen chopped
  spinach
2 eggs
2 cups milk

1 teaspoon salt
⅔ cup soft bread crumbs
1½ cups shredded
  provolone cheese
Paprika

Dice bacon; parbroil until crisp. Drain well. Cook spinach according to package directions; drain well. Beat eggs slightly; add milk and salt. Stir in spinach, bread crumbs, bacon, half of the cheese. Pour mixture into 1½-quart baking dish, slightly greased. Sprinkle remaining cheese around edges; sprinkle paprika. Bake 375° for 30–45 minutes.

Taste of Goodness

Spinach-Artichoke Casserole
(Microwave)

½ cup chopped onion
½ cup butter or margarine
2 (10-ounce) packages frozen
  chopped spinach, thawed and
  drained
1 (14-ounce) can artichoke
  hearts (in water), cut up
  coarsely

½ cup grated Parmesan cheese
1 cup sour cream
1 (4-ounce) can chopped
  mushrooms
¼ teaspoon red pepper

Sauté onion in butter. Combine all other ingredients and add to onion. Bake in a deep casserole (2½- or 3-quart) covered at 350° for 25 minutes. Can be baked in microwave at 50% power for 25 minutes. Serves 4 when used as a main dish or 6 when used as a vegetable.

Historic Lexington Cooks

Students at Washington and Lee University in Lexington still benefit from stock donated to the school by George Washington. The nation's first president made a significant contribution to the school in 1796, saving it from financial collapse.

Lite Spaghetti Squash Primavera

1 medium spaghetti squash,
about 3½ pounds
1 cup fresh broccoli florets
1 cup sliced small zucchini
1 cup sliced mushrooms
1 cup sliced carrots
1 small garlic clove, crushed
¾ teaspoon reduced-calorie
margarine, melted
1 tablespoon skim milk

½ cup part-skim ricotta
cheese
1 tablespoon grated Parmesan
cheese
½ teaspoon imitation
butter flavoring
¼ teaspoon salt
½ teaspoon Italian seasoning
⅛ teaspoon coarsely ground
pepper

Wash squash, cut in half lengthwise and discard seeds. Place squash, cut-side-down, in a Dutch oven. Add 2 inches water and bring to boil. Cover and cook 20 minntes or until squash is tender. Drain squash and cool. Using a fork, remove spaghetti-like strands. Measure 3 cups of strands and set aside, reserving remaining strands for other uses. Steam vegetables 5–7 minutes or until crisp-tender; drain well. Combine squash and vegetables, tossing gently. Cover to keep warm; set aside.

Sauté garlic in margarine in a small saucepan; remove from heat. Add milk, cheeses, butter flavoring and seasonings to saucepan. Cook, stirring constantly, over low heat until mixture is hot. Do not boil. Spoon cheese mixture over vegetables, tossing gently. Serve immediately. Yields 6 servings.

Cardinal Cuisine

Champignons Au Gratin

1 clove garlic, minced
1 onion, grated
2 tablespoons chopped fresh
  parsley
1/8 teaspoon dried basil
1 teaspoon salt
1/4 teaspoon pepper
1/3 cup salad oil

2 tablespoons wine vinegar
1 1/2 pounds fresh mushrooms,
  trimmed and sliced
1/4 pound butter
1/2 cup fresh bread crumbs
1/4 cup freshly grated
  Parmesan cheese

Combine garlic, onion, parsley, basil, salt, pepper, oil, and vinegar in large mixing bowl. There will be very little liquid. Add mushrooms and marinate for 3 hours, stirring frequently.

Melt half the butter in heavy 10- to 12-inch skillet. Remove mushrooms from marinade with slotted spoon and cook over high heat for 1 minute, stirring.

Butter shallow 1-quart baking dish and place mushrooms in it. Sprinkle with bread crumbs and cheese. Dot with remaining butter. (Recipe can be prepared ahead to this point and held in refrigerator for at least 6 hours.) Place under preheated broiler 6–8 inches from heat, for 3–5 minutes, to brown before serving. Watch carefully to prevent burning.

Command Performances

Mushroom Pie

1 pound peeled and chopped
  fresh mushrooms
2 tablespoons melted butter
2 tablespoons flour
Salt and pepper to taste

2/3 cup cream
2 tablespoons grated
  Parmesan cheese
Baked puff pastry

Cook slowly 1 pound peeled and chopped fresh mushrooms in 2 tablespoons melted butter. Add 2 tablespoons flour, salt, and pepper to taste. Stir until smooth; add 2/3 cup cream and cook a few minutes; then sprinkle on 2 tablespoons of grated Parmesan cheese and cook until melted. Put into a warm crust of puff pastry and serve.

The Hunt Country Cookbook

Microwave Squash and Pepper Toss
(Microwave)

¼ teaspoon dried whole
  basil
¼ teaspoon dried oregano
¼ teaspoon thyme
½ teaspoon salt
¼ teaspoon pepper
1 tablespoon red wine
  vinegar

2 tablespoons water
2 pounds yellow squash, cut
  into slices
1 large omon, chopped
1 clove garlic, minced
1 sweet red pepper, cut
  into strips
2 tablespoons olive oil

Combine first 7 ingredients in a shallow 2½-quart casserole. Add squash. Cover with heavy plastic wrap. Microwave on HIGH for 3–4 minutes. Let stand covered, 3–4 minutes. Add onion and garlic, sweet pepper and olive oil; toss gently. Cover and microwave on HIGH for 3 minutes. Yields 6–8 servings.

Think Healthy

Carrots Grand Marnier

2 pounds carrots, cleaned
  and cut into ½-inch thick
  slices
½ teaspoon salt
¼ cup plus 2 tablespoons
  butter
1 cup sugar

1 (12-ounce) jar orange
  marmalade
¾ cup Grand Marnier, divided
4 medium oranges, halved
  with pulp and pith removed
Nutmeg

Combine carrots, water to cover, and salt in a small Dutch oven. Cover and cook over medium heat 25 minutes. Drain and set aside.

Melt butter in a large skillet over medium heat. Add sugar and marmalade; simmer about 10 minutes or until sugar is melted. Stir in carrots and ½ cup Grand Marnier. Simmer, uncovered, about 30 minutes, or until carrots are shiny and candied. Add remaining Grand Marnier. Sprinkle with nutmeg and serve in hollowed orange shells. Yields 8 servings.

The Enlightened Titan

Marinated Carrots

1 can tomato soup
¾ cup sugar
¼ teaspoon prepared
  mustard
¼ cup vinegar
½ cup salad oil
1 teaspoon Worcestershire
  sauce

1 teaspoon salt
Dash of pepper
1 green pepper, chopped
3 small onions, thinly sliced
2 pounds carrots, peeled, sliced,
  cooked with salt

Pour marinade over carrots. Refrigerate, covered, overnight. Serve cold or at room temperature. Keeps a week or longer in refrigerator.

More Than a Cookbook

Harvard Carrots

The tangy sauce gives sunshine carrots a flavor lift.

½ cup sugar
1½ tablespoons cornstarch
¼ cup vinegar
¼ cup water

4 cups cooked, sliced carrots
  (lengthwise)
¼ cup butter

Mix sugar and cornstarch. Add vinegar and water, cook until thick, stirring constantly. Add carrots and let stand over low heat 5–10 minutes. Add butter. Serves 6.

WYVE's Bicentennial Cookbook

Stewed Tomato Casserole

10 slices bread
1 large onion, sliced thin
3 (1-pound) cans stewed
   tomatoes

Salt and pepper
1 cup brown sugar

Toast bread and cut in cubes. Grease a shallow 9x13-inch pan. Spread half the bread cubes and half the onion in pan. Pour tomatoes over this, add salt and pepper, and cover with rest of the onion and bread cubes. Sprinkle brown sugar over all. Bake at 350° for 1 hour. Serves 10.

The Stuffed Cougar

Shields Tavern Sampler
Indian Meal Pudding

½ cup white cornmeal
1½ cups water
¼ pound butter
1 egg
3 egg yolks

½ cup sugar
¼ cup white wine
1 teaspoon nutmeg
½ teaspoon mace

Preheat the oven to 400°. Grease an 8-inch square baking dish.

Make a cornmeal mush. Combine the cornmeal with the water. Bring the mixture to a boil, stirring continuously. Reduce to low heat and cook the mixture for 20–30 minutes, stirring continuously until the mixture thickens. Mix the butter into the warm mush to melt the butter.

Combine and beat the egg and the egg yolks until they are light and fluffy. Add the sugar to the eggs and beat until thickened. Mix the egg mixture into the mush. Add the wine, nutmeg, and mace. Mix well. Pour into the prepared baking dish. Lower the oven temperature to 350°. Bake for 30–40 minutes. Serve hot or warm. Serves 8.

Note: This adaptation is quite sweet. You may wish to decrease the sugar to ⅓ cup.

The Williamsburg Cookbook

Corn Fritters

1 cup fresh corn
1 egg, divided and beaten
  separately

2 tablespoons flour
Salt and pepper, to taste

Combine all ingredients, except egg white. Fold in stiffly beaten egg white. Fry on hot griddle.

The Smithfield Cookbook

Both the Revolutionary War and the American Civil War ended official-ly in Virginia. Washington's stunning victory at Yorktown, Virginia, forced Cornwallis' troops to surrender; the South's Civil War surrender took place at Appomatox.

Scalloped Corn

2 eggs
1 cup milk
⅔ cup cracker or bread
  crumbs
2 cups cooked or canned corn

1 teaspoon minced onion
½ teaspoon salt
⅛ teaspoon pepper
1 tablespoon sugar
3 tablespoons melted butter

Beat the eggs and add milk and crumbs. Add the corn, onion, season-ing and melted butter. Mix together well and pour in a greased casse-role. Bake at 350° for 40 minutes. Serves 6.

Mennonite Community Cookbook

Mexican Corn-Zucchini Dish

1 pound small zucchini,
  thinly sliced
4 or 5 medium-size ears corn
¾ cup finely chopped onion
⅓ cup chopped green pepper
3 medium-size tomatoes,
  peeled and coarsely chopped

2 tablespoons vegetable oil
¼ teaspoon sugar
1 teaspoon salt
¼ teaspoon freshly ground
  black pepper
1½ cups diced stale bread
⅓ cup diced sharp cheese

Slice zucchini; cut kernels from corn cobs. You should have 2½–3 cups corn.

In flameproof casserole, combine zucchini, corn, onion, green pep-per, tomatoes, oil, sugar, salt and pepper. Cook, stirring gently over medium heat for about 10–12 minutes or until zucchini and corn are just cooked. Sprinkle vegetables with bread and cheese cubes and bake in preheated 350° oven until cheese melts and bread is crisp. Serve hot. Makes 6 servings.

Dan River Family Cookbook

Secretariat was the first Virginia-bred and Virginia-owned thoroughbred to win horseracing's coveted Triple Crown.

Broccoli and Water Chestnuts in Brie Sauce

1 bunch broccoli	1 tablespoon dry white wine
2 teaspoons butter	2 ounces brie, rind removed
2 tablespoons flour	1 can sliced water chestnuts
1 cup cold milk	

Shave broccoli stems and cut into serving pieces. Steam until tender crisp. Meanwhile, make white sauce. Heat butter in heavy pan over high heat. Add flour and whisk constantly until the roux becomes golden. Remove from heat, cool slightly and add all the milk and wine. Return to medium heat, add the brie and stir until the cheese melts and the sauce thickens. Season to taste with salt and pepper if desired. Arrange broccoli on plates; add drained water chestnuts to sauce to heat through. Pour sauce over broccoli. Serves 6–8.

The VIP Cookbook: A Potpourri of Virginia Cooking

Broccoli and Celery Casserole

10 ounces frozen chopped broccoli	¼ cup flour
	2 cups milk
2 cups celery, chopped in ½-inch pieces	½ teaspoon salt
	¼ teaspoon pepper
¼ cup butter	1 cup shredded Cheddar cheese

Preheat oven to 350°. Cook broccoli and drain. Cook celery in boiling, salted water until crisply tender, about 5–6 minutes. Combine the two vegetables in a buttered 1½- to 2-quart shallow baking dish. Melt butter in saucepan, add flour and blend. Add milk, stirring constantly and cook until smooth and thickened. Add salt and pepper, pour over vegetables. Cover with cheese. Bake for 15–20 minutes or until heated through. Serves 6.

Note: Can be prepared ahead.

Virginia Hospitality

Creamed Onions with Ham

This is a vegetable dish to accompany the main course. It is delicious served with roast beef.

16 small white onions
2 tablespoons butter
2 tablespoons flour
2 scant cups milk
½ cup minced cooked ham
½ cup buttered bread crumbs

Preheat oven to 375°. Grease a 1-quart casserole dish. Cook onions in slightly salted water until tender. Drain. Melt butter over medium heat. Stir in flour. Add milk, stirring constantly until smooth and slightly thickened. Place onions in prepared casserole and pour cream sauce over them. Top with ham and bread crumbs. Bake for about 20 minutes or until lightly browned and bubbly. Serves 8.

The Ham Book

Green Peppers and Eggplant

4 slices bacon, cooked crisp
1 cup chopped green pepper
½ cup chopped celery
½ cup chopped onion
1 clove garlic, finely chopped
1 medium eggplant, pared and
   cubed
2 small tomatoes, chopped
1 teaspoon lemon juice
3 tablespoons soy sauce
Dashes of basil, black pepper and
   oregano
Salt to taste

Cook bacon crisp; drain on paper towels. Sauté green pepper, celery, onion and garlic in bacon drippings until soft. Add eggplant and cook 10 minutes. Add tomatoes, lemon juice, soy sauce, basil, black pepper and oregano. Let simmer for 10 minutes or until tomatoes are soft. Add salt. Crumble bacon over top.

Kitchen Keys

Stuffed Eggplant

In need of a second dish for dinner? Or another plate to adorn your buffet table? Here is your answer—a delicious and delightful stuffed eggplant, Neapolitan style.

3 medium eggplants
Salt and pepper to taste
¼ pound sweet Italian
** sausage**
¼ pound ground beef
2 tablespoons olive oil
½ cup unflavored bread
** crumbs**

2 tablespoons fresh chopped
** parsley (or 1 tablespoon dried)**
1 cup Italian-style plum
** tomatoes**
1 cup water
2 ounces grated Parmesan
** cheese**

Preheat oven to 350°. Cut eggplants in half lengthwise. Scoop out pulp, leaving a ¼-inch thick shell. Chop pulp and set aside. Salt water. Place shells in a steamer for 5 minutes. Remove casing from sausage. Chop and add to chopped ground meat. Sauté in oil until brown. Add chopped pulp of eggplant to browned sausage and ground meat. Continue to sauté for 5 minutes. Remove mixture from heat. Add bread crumbs, parsley, salt, and pepper and mix well. Fill steamed eggplant shells. Squeeze moisture out of tomatoes. Chop and spread lightly over shells. Place shells in a 9x13-inch baking pan. Add water to pan and bake for 30 minutes. Remove shells from oven. Sprinkle grated Parmesan cheese and chopped parsley over stuffed shells. Serve hot or cold.

A Neopolitan Peasant's Cookbook

Eggplant Casserole

3 tablespoons olive oil
2 eggs
1 onion, chopped fine
1 pound fresh mushrooms,
  sliced
¼ teaspoon sage

¼ teaspoon poultry seasoning
2 eggplants, sliced
2 cups grated Monterey Jack
  cheese
¼ cup rye bread crumbs

Grease casserole dish with half of olive oil. Mix eggs, onions, mushrooms, and seasoning together. Alternate layers of eggplant, mixture, cheese, continuing in this manner, ending with cheese on top. Sprinkle with bread crumbs and bake at 350° for 40 minutes.

The New Life Cookbook

Escalloped Eggplant à la Parmesan

Absolutely fantastic!

1 medium eggplant, unpared
  and sliced in ½-inch slices
2 large homegrown tomatoes,
  peeled and sliced
1 large onion, sliced
¾ cup margarine, melted
  and divided

½ teaspoon dried basil
¾ teaspoon garlic salt
½ pound mozzarella cheese,
  sliced
2–3 slices whole-wheat bread,
  toasted and made into crumbs
2 tablespoons Parmesan cheese

Preheat oven to 450°. Arrange eggplant in the bottom of a 9x13-inch aluminum baking pan; top with tomatoes and onion. Drizzle ½ cup margarine over the entire casserole; sprinkle with basil and garlic salt.

Cover and bake for 20 minutes. Remove from oven and top with mozzarella cheese which has been cut into triangular pieces. Toss crumbs with ¼ cup melted margarine and spread over casserole; top with Parmesan cheese and bake uncovered for 10 minutes. Serves 6–8.

Note: The 450° temperature may sound high, but it's correct. Lower to 425° for a glass dish. This recipe can easily be halved.

Words Worth Eating

Ratatouille

½ pound eggplant, unpeeled
½ pound zucchini, unpeeled
1 teaspoon salt
3 cloves garlic, chopped fine
2 large onions, sliced thin
⅓ cup olive oil
2 green peppers, sliced and
  seeded
6–8 ripe tomatoes, or
  1 (28-ounce) can tomatoes,
  drained

3 tablespoons minced fresh
  parsley
1 teaspoon dry basil, or more
Salt and pepper to taste
Parmesan cheese and minced
  parsley

Cube eggplant and slice zucchini. Toss in a porcelain or stainless steel bowl with salt and let stand 30 minutes; drain. Meanwhile, sauté garlic and onions in oil until soft; add peppers and cook 5 minutes, stirring and tossing. Stir in eggplant and zucchini and cook 5 minutes. Peel tomatoes, cut in wedges, and remove seeds; add to eggplant mixture with herbs. Correct seasoning with salt and pepper. Simmer, covered, 30 minutes, stirring gently every now and then. Serve garnished with Parmesan cheese and more minced parsley. Serves 6–8.

Note: An electric skillet is ideal for this dish. An enameled or stainless steel skillet may be used, but avoid cast iron here. Ratatouille may be served cold as well as hot.

The Belle Grove Plantation Cookbook

Zucchini Sauce with Macaroni

5 quarts boiling water
2 tablespoons oil

8 ounces macaroni elbows
(small elbows)

In a large kettle, bring 5 quarts of water to a boil. Add oil and macaroni. Bring back to boil and cook 9 minutes. Drain; keep hot in colander over steaming water.

ZUCCHINI SAUCE:

4 cups diced zucchini (use
small, tender zucchini)
¾ cup chopped onion
¼ cup peanut oil
1 (16-ounce) can Italian-
style tomatoes
3 tablespoons (medium or
hot) piquant sauce

2 cloves garlic, squeezed
(use juice and pulp)
3 tablespoons chopped fresh
mint
3 tablespoons chopped fresh dill
1½ cups plain yogurt
1½ cups crumbled feta cheese

In large skillet sauté zucchini and onion in peanut oil (part at a time if size of skillet dictates) until tender, about 5 minutes each skilletful. Add tomatoes, piquant sauce, garlic, mint and dill. Cover and simmer for 15 minutes. This sauce is for 6 servings of macaroni. To serve, divide macaroni into 6 servings. Atop each serving spread 3–4 tablespoons of yogurt. Pour a sixth of the sauce over each serving and sprinkle each with feta cheese.

Historic Lexington Cooks

Stonewall Jackson's House in Lexington is the only home ever owned by the Civil War general. Before serving in the war, Jackson had been a teacher of natural philosophy and an artillery tactics instructor at Virginia Military Institute.

Zucchini Omelet

1 pound zucchini	Salt and pepper to taste
1 large onion	2 tablespoons grated
⅓ cup olive oil	Parmesan cheese
4 eggs	

Wash the zucchini under cold running water to remove grit and sand. Do not remove skin of zucchini. Cut zucchini crosswise into ¼-inch slices and set aside. Peel onion and slice thinly.

Place oil in a skillet. Add zucchini slices and onion and fry until slightly brown.

Beat eggs with salt, pepper and Parmesan cheese. Pour the eggs over zucchini and onions. Cook until slightly set on bottom. As the zucchini and onions continue to cook, lift the bottom of the frittata lightly from the sides with a spatula and let the uncooked egg run beneath the frittata. While the omelet is still moist on top, place a dish over the top of skillet and invert the omelet, then slide back into skillet. Cook until slightly brown on the bottom. Do not overcook eggs. Slide frittata onto a dish and serve. Yields 4 servings.

A Neopolitan Peasant's Cookbook

Zucchini Crab Cakes

2 cups grated zucchini	Onion salt
1 cup Italian bread crumbs	1 egg
2 tablespoons Old Bay	1 tablespoon Worcestershire
seasoning	sauce

Grate zucchini. In medium bowl, add all ingredients and mix. Shape into small croquettes and chill. Fry in ½ inch of oil. Can be served as an appetizer or as main dish. Tastes like crab.

The VIP Cookbook: A Potpourri of Virginia Cooking

Zucchini Pie

3 small zucchini, cubed
   (about 1–1¼ pounds)
1 small onion, chopped
1 cup Bisquick
½ cup oil

½ cup grated sharp cheese
4 eggs
Pinch of salt, pepper, parsley
   and basil

Mix together all ingredients. Pour into a lightly greased 10-inch pie plate. Bake at 350° for 30–40 minutes, until golden. Serves 4.

Think Healthy

Francie's Vegetable Pie

PIE SHELL:

1 egg, beaten

2 onions, chopped and
lightly sautéed

2 cups cooked rice

Butter

Preheat oven to 350°. Mix beaten egg with sautéed onion and 2 cups of cooked rice. Press into a buttered 9-inch pie plate.

VEGETABLE FILLING:

4 cups combined raw, sliced
vegetables, using what you
might have in the
refrigerator—carrots,
celery, mushrooms, zucchini,
summer squash, green beans,
broccoli, cauliflower, etc.

2 tablespoons olive oil

2 tablespoons butter

Salt, pepper and curry powder
to taste

Sauté the sliced vegetable combination in the olive oil and butter. Add salt, pepper and curry powder to taste. Place sautéed vegetables into rice shell.

CHEESE TOPPING:

¼ cup butter

¼ cup flour

1 cup milk

1 cup shredded Cheddar cheese

1 teaspoon dry mustard powder

Dash of cayenne pepper or
paprika

Parsley

Melt butter in pan and add flour. Mix well. Slowly stir in milk. Add cheese and stir. Add mustard and paprika or cayenne pepper. Salt and pepper to taste. Top vegetable pie with this mixture. Sprinkle with parsley. Bake in oven 30 minutes. Serves 6–8.

The Mount Vernon Cookbook

Mount Vernon, the home and burial place of George and Martha Washington, is America's most visited historic estate (pictured on cover).

Orange Sweet Potatoes

6 medium-sized sweet potatoes
⅓ cup white sugar
⅓ cup brown sugar
1 teaspoon salt

3 tablespoons melted butter
1 cup orange juice
2 teaspoons grated orange rind
1 tablespoon cornstarch

Cook potatoes in jackets until almost soft. Remove skins and cut in quarters lengthwise. Combine sugars, salt, butter, orange juice, rind, and cornstarch and cook until thickened. Arrange sweet potatoes in a greased baking dish and pour sauce over them. Bake at 350° for 35 minutes. Serves 6.

Mennonite Community Cookbook

Sweet Potato-Apple Soufflé

2 tablespoons sugar
1 teaspoon cinnamon
2 cups applesauce
1 tablespoon grated orange
 rind

3 cups cooked, mashed sweet
 potatoes
¾ teaspoon salt
⅓ cup butter, melted
4 eggs, separated

Combine sugar and cinnamon. Add to applesauce with orange rind. Mix well. Combine sweet potatoes, salt, applesauce mixture and butter. Add beaten egg yolks. Beat egg whites stiff and fold into applesauce-sweet potato mixture. Pile lightly into greased 3-quart casserole. Bake in 400° oven for 45 minutes. Serve immediately. Serves 6–8.

The Mount Vernon Cookbook

Honey and Cinnamon-Candied Yams

6 large yams	1½ teaspoons lemon rind,
1½ tablespoons cornstarch	grated
2 tablespoons cold water	2 teaspoons lemon juice
1½ cups honey	¼ cup orange juice
½ teaspoon cinnamon	1 teaspoon salt
⅛ teaspoon nutmeg	6 tablespoons butter

Preheat the oven to 375°. Butter a large ovenproof casserole.

Scrub the yams. Cook the yams in boiling salted water until tender. Drain. Rinse with cold water. Peel the yams and cut them in half lengthwise. Place the yams in the prepared casserole.

Dissolve the cornstarch in the cold water. Combine the honey, cinnamon, nutmeg, lemon rind, lemon juice, orange juice, and salt in a saucepan. Bring to a boil. Add the cornstarch mixture. Cook over medium heat, stirring constantly, until the mixture is thick and clear. Remove from the heat. Add the butter. Pour the mixture over the yams. Bake at 375° for 15 minutes. Serves 12.

Favorite Meals from Williamsburg

Candied Yams

Easy, economical and good!

2 large sweet potatoes	1 teaspoon ginger
1 cup sugar	½ cup water
1 teaspoon cinnamon	1 teaspoon lemon juice
1 teaspoon nutmeg	¼ cup butter, sliced

Boil sweet potatoes until tender and remove skins. Mix sugar, cinnamon, nutmeg and ginger; add water. Quarter the potatoes and put them in a heavy skillet. Pour sugar mixture plus lemon juice over potatoes and top with butter. Cook over low heat, turning several times. Cook 20–30 minutes. May freeze. Serves 3–4.

Virginia Hospitality

Sweet Potato and Orange Casserole

2 (1-pound) cans vacuum-
　packed sweet potatoes
⅓ cup firmly packed brown
　sugar
¼ cup butter, melted

½ teaspoon salt
2 tablespoons rum
1 (11-ounce) can mandarin
　oranges, drained
¼ cup chopped pecans

Mash sweet potatoes, and beat in ¼ cup of the brown sugar, half of the butter, the salt, and rum. Fold in oranges and turn into buttered 2-quart casserole. Mix together pecans and remaining brown sugar and butter, sprinkle over top. Bake at 375° for 30 minutes. Serves 8–9.

The Stuffed Cougar

Sweet Potato Bonbons (or Puffs)

Scrumptious with ham or turkey for the holidays or any time.

3 cups cooked, mashed sweet
　potatoes
¼ cup butter or margarine,
　melted
½ cup brown sugar
¼ teaspoon salt

2 tablespoons cream
8 large marshmallows
1 cup cornflake crumbs (or
　flaked coconut)
8 pecan halves, optional

Combine sweet potatoes, butter, sugar, salt, and cream. Cover marshmallows with potato mixture (if smaller balls are desired, cut marshmallow in half). Roll in cornflake crumbs (or coconut). Top with pecan half, if desired. Place into buttered baking dish and bake at 375° until lightly browned and marshmallows begin to ooze, about 10–15 minutes. Serves 8.

Sweet Potato Puffs: Place sweet potato mixture in a mound (I use ice cream dipper) on coconut in a buttered baking dish. Place a large marshmallow in center of each mound. Sprinkle with coconut. Bake at 350° until marshmallows and coconut are delicately browned, about 10 minutes. Easier than making Bonbons (or balls).

Festive Sweet Potatoes: Pile sweet potato mixture on pineapple slice. Top with marshmallows. Bake until marshmallows are browned.

Holiday Treats

Mashed Potatoes, Italian-Style

Your guests will exclaim, "I have never been served or have eaten potatoes as tasty and delicious as these." Your standard reply should be, "That's Italian, dear, strictly Italian!"

6 large potatoes	Salt and pepper to taste
4 tablespoons butter	6 ounces mozzarella, sliced
¼ cup of milk	Italian-style bread crumbs
Grated Romano or	as desired
Parmesan cheese as needed	

Peel potatoes, cut into cubes, and boil for about 20 minutes or until easily pierced with a fork. Drain potatoes and mash, adding butter, milk, salt, and pepper. Spoon a layer of potatoes into an oven-proof baking dish. Sprinkle grated cheese over potatoes and cover with mozzarella cheese, reserving a few slices of mozzarella. Add remaining potatoes and grated cheese. Cover with mozzarella slices. Sprinkle bread crumbs over potatoes and bake about 5 minutes or until mozzarella has melted or place in microwave oven for 2 minutes until cheese melts. Yields 4 servings.

A Neapolitan Peasant's Cookbook

Potato Princess

4 large baking potatoes	White pepper
3 onions, chopped	Caraway seeds
¼ pound butter	¼ pound Swiss cheese
Salt	Paprika

Parboil potatoes in unsalted water and remove skin. Sauté onions in butter; add salt and pepper to taste. Grease 1½-quart baking dish. Slice potatoes and place in baking dish, alternating layers of potatoes and onions, sprinkling with caraway seeds. Dot each layer with cheese; sprinkle completed casserole with paprika. Bake at 350° until cheese melts. Serve hot. Serves 6.

Note: This may be frozen before cooking. Provides a German accent to your meal.

A Heritage of Good Tastes

John's Favorite Potatoes

¼ cup peanut oil, divided
4 garlic cloves (minced)
½ teaspoon dry mustard
2 teaspoons thyme (fresh),
  or 1 teaspoon oregano (dry)
½ teaspoon cayenne pepper
1 teaspoon black pepper
  (fresh ground)

2 teaspoons salt
4 potatoes (peeled)
4 shallots (sliced)
4 tablespoons unsalted sweet
  butter

Preheat the oven to 400°. Use 2 tablespoons of peanut oil to grease the baking sheet. To the remaining peanut oil, add the garlic, the mustard, the fresh thyme, the cayenne, the black pepper, and the salt. Cut the potatoes in half lengthwise. Slice the potatoes across as thinly as possible and press down to fan out. Lifting the potatoes on the side of the knife, place them on a baking sheet side by side in two rows. Mold the potatoes slightly to allow room between them. Pour the peanut oil mixture to coat the tops. Place the sliced shallots in the valleys between the potatoes. Cut the butter into small chunks and distribute the chunks on top of the shallots. Bake the potatoes until brown and crispy, approximately 45–50 minutes. Serves 4.

The Great Chefs of Virginia Cookbook

Pommes Dauphinoise

6 large baking potatoes
1 large clove garlic, minced
Freshly ground black pepper
1 pint heavy cream
Milk
½ cup shredded Gruyère or
    Switzerland Swiss cheese

Peel potatoes and drop into a bowl of cold water. Preheat oven to 300°. Place a buttered shallow baking dish over direct low heat. Dry and thinly slice 1 potato at a time and spread the slices in the dish. When half the potatoes are in the dish, sprinkle with the garlic, salt to taste and use plenty of freshly ground pepper. Add enough of the cream to barely cover the potatoes and let cream come very slowly to a boil as the remaining potatoes are sliced and spread in the dish. When all potatoes are in the dish, add remaining cream and a little milk, if necessary, to just cover potatoes. Sprinkle with salt and pepper. Bring cream to a gentle boil, then transfer baking dish to preheated oven. Bake potatoes for 1½ hours. Sprinkle with cheese and continue to bake for 30 minutes longer. If you are not ready to serve, turn oven to low and potatoes will remain hot and creamy for quite a long time. Serves 6.

Spotsylvania Favorites

Cheesy Fries

3 medium potatoes
3 tablespoons butter or
    margarine
¼ cup Parmesan cheese
½ teaspoon garlic powder
½ teaspoon seasoned salt
½ teaspoon paprika

Scrub potatoes, leaving skins on. Cut each potato into 8 wedges. Melt butter or margarine in a large pie plate. Dip wedges in melted butter and arrange in a donut pattern on plate. Combine cheese and spices. Sprinkle evenly over potatoes. Bake at 375° until potatoes are just about tender.

Smyth County Extension Homemakers Cookbook

Browned Rice with Peas

1 cup rice
2½ cups boiling water
½ cup butter
¼ cup chopped onion
¼ cup sliced mushrooms, drained

10 ounces frozen peas, thawed
8 ounces canned water chestnuts, drained and diced
3 tablespoons soy sauce

Preheat oven to 350°. In dry skillet, brown rice, stirring often. Turn into a 1½-quart casserole; add water and stir with fork to separate grains. Cover and bake for 30 minutes or until rice is tender. Meanwhile in skillet, over low heat, melt butter, add onion and mushrooms and sauté. Remove from heat; add peas, chestnuts and soy sauce. Add to rice and blend gently. Bake uncovered for 15 minutes. Serves 8.

Hint: Add 1 tablespoon oil, butter or margarine to rice before boiling to make grains separate, and rice will never stick to pan.

Virginia Hospitality

Baked Rice

½ cup raw rice
⅛ cup chopped green pepper
⅛ cup chopped onion
1 (4-ounce) can mushrooms

½ cup butter, melted
1 (10¾-ounce) can beef consommé

Add all ingredients in order into a greased 1½-quart casserole. Stir and bake uncovered at 350° for 1 hour. Serves 4.

A Heritage of Good Tastes

The name "Shenandoah" comes from an Indian word meaning "daughter of the stars."

Wild Rice Stuffed Tomatoes with Basil

4 large ripe tomatoes
1½ cups cooked and cooled
  wild rice
3 tablespoons chopped fresh
  basil

3 scallions, finely chopped
  with some of the green tops
2 teaspoons olive oil
¾ teaspoon garlic salt

Cut a 1-inch slice off the top of each tomato. Scoop out the inside pulp, being careful not to bruise the tomato shell. Chop the tomato pulp and drain excess liquid. Combine pulp with the wild rice, basil, scallions, olive oil and garlic salt. Toss lightly. Fill tomato cases with the rice mixture. Serve on a bed of lettuce leaves. May also be served as a hot vegetable. One-third cup of uncooked wild rice will equal about 1½ cups of cooked rice. Serves 4.

The Mount Vernon Cookbook

Italian Macaroni

Boil it well in water, put alternate layers of grated cheese and macaroni, add a little pepper; let the last layer be cheese; pour over melted butter and bake.

The Old Virginia Cook Book

Pasta Fantasy

Pasta fit for a king—a marvelous flavor—even those who don't like pasta will ask for seconds!

1 pound mushrooms, thinly
  sliced
6 tablespoons butter, melted
2 cups heavy cream, at room
  temperature
1 cup freshly grated Parmesan
  or Romano cheese
12 ounces fully cooked,
  smoked ham, diced

8 ounces spinach, washed,
  stems removed and torn into
  bite-size pieces
Salt and pepper
Pinch of nutmeg
8 ounces spinach linguine
8 ounces egg linguine
Additional Parmesan cheese

In a large heavy skillet, sauté mushrooms in 4 tablespoons butter over moderate heat until tender but not browned. In a large heavy saucepan, combine remaining 2 tablespoons butter and cream. With a whisk, blend in cheese; simmer, whisking occasionally, until mixture is slightly thickened. Add ham and spinach, mixing well; continue to cook over low heat for 4–5 minutes, until spinach is tender but firm. *Do not overcook* spinach. Add seasonings. Cook spinach and egg linguine in boiling salted water until tender but firm (al dente); drain well. Fold linguine into sauce, mixing well. Adjust seasoning, if desired. Serve immediately and garnish each serving with additional grated Parmesan cheese, if desired. Makes 8–10 servings.

Apron Strings

Stuffed Cannelloni Shells

One of the most famous Italian dishes is stuffed cannelloni smothered with tomato sauce. The fillings are varied with ground beef, pork, Italian sausage, or prosciutto. Most home cooks use store-bought, dry macaroni shells. My family has always used handmade crêpes and stuffed them with a simple filling that is pure Neapolitan: eggs, ricotta cheese, diced mozzarella, grated Parmesan cheese, and fresh parsley; this is covered with a marinara tomato sauce or pasta meat sauce and baked. Put this delightful dish before your guests and then hear them sing hallelujah!

CONTINUED

CRÊPES:

4 eggs	1 teaspoon salt
1½ cups cold water	1½ cups flour

RICOTTA FILLING:

3 pounds ricotta cheese	2 tablespoons chopped fresh
3 eggs	parsley (or 1 tablespoon dried)
1 cup grated Parmesan cheese	Salt and pepper to taste
1 cup diced mozzarella	

Using an electric mixer or hand-held electric mixer, beat eggs and water together. Add salt. Add flour gradually and beat mixture to the consistency of a thin pancake batter. Lightly grease a six-inch skillet with butter or margarine. Do not grease again.

Put enough batter in hot skillet to coat bottom of skillet (usually one tablespoon). Cook one side of crêpes only. Remove crêpes and stack between sheets of waxed paper. Let crêpes cool and proceed to fill with Ricotta Filling.

Preheat oven to 350°. Mix all the ingredients together. Place one full tablespoon of filling at the edge of each crêpe. Fold over and roll. Coat the bottom of a 9x13-inch baking pan with marinara sauce and place stuffed crêpes, seam-side-down, in pan. Cover each cannelloni with marinara sauce. Cover pan with aluminum foil and bake for 20 minutes. Do not stack one upon the other in pan. Serve hot.

BASIC MARINARA SAUCE:

It is almost incredible that a simple marinara pasta sauce can vary in taste by merely adding individual assorted seafood such as shrimp, mussels, crabs, or clams to the sauce.

¼ cup olive oil	1 (6-ounce) can tomato paste
1 small onion, cut into four	½ teaspoon sugar
quarters	Salt and pepper to taste
1 garlic clove, chopped	
1 (28-ounce) can Italian-style	
tomatoes, seeded and blended	

Place oil in sauté pan; add onion. Cook onion to limp stage. Remove onion. Add garlic and brown. Remove garlic. Pour tomatoes into pan and simmer for 15 minutes. Add tomato paste and stir until dissolved. Add sugar, salt, and pepper. Continue to simmer sauce for 35 more minutes with cover of pan slightly ajar. Yields 4 servings.

A Neapolitan Peasant's Cookbook

Linguine Pesto

1½ pounds linguine
2 eggs, beaten
3 tablespoons butter
¾ cup heavy cream

2 cups grated Parmesan
1 tablespoon salt
2 cups sliced mushrooms

Cook linguine according to package. Rinse in very hot water and drain well. Combine linguine with eggs, butter, cream, cheese, salt, and mushrooms.

PESTO SAUCE:
½ cup butter
½ cup chopped fresh parsley
4 tablespoons basil
¼ teaspoon pepper

¾ cup olive oil
¾ cup sliced water chestnuts
2½ cloves garlic, crushed
½ teaspoon salt

Combine all ingredients and heat thoroughly. Toss with linguine and serve at once. Serves 8.

The Best of the Bushel

Brandied Cranberries

4 cups cranberries
2 cups sugar

1 cup brandy

Combine cranberries and sugar in a 12x8x2-inch pan, mixing well. Bake, uncovered, in a moderate oven (350°) for 1 hour. Stir brandy into cranberry mixture, blending well. Serve hot or cold. Makes 6–8 servings.

Apron Strings

Sandra's Cranberry Casserole

3 cups chopped apples
2 cups fresh cranberries
½ cup oats
2 cups sugar
½ cup brown sugar

½ cup chopped pecans
1 teaspoon cinnamon
½ teaspoon nutmeg
6 pats butter

Place fruit in 3-quart buttered casserole. Combine dry ingredients and pat on top. Dot with butter. Decorate with pecan halves. Cook, covered, for 45 minutes at 325°. Serves 6–8.

A Heritage of Good Tastes

Grandma Seller's Green Tomato Relish

2½ pounds green tomatoes
6 large onions
6 sweet peppers
1 pint vinegar
1½-inch stick cinnamon

1 teaspoon whole cloves
1 whole allspice
1 tablespoon salt
1 teaspoon mustard seed
2 cups sugar

Grind or chop tomatoes, onions and peppers fine; cover with boiling water and boil 15 minutes. Drain well. Put vinegar, cinnamon, cloves, and allspice together; bring to a boil. Strain out the spices. Add salt, mustard seed, and sugar to vinegar mixture. Add to vegetables; boil 20 minutes. Put in hot sterilized jars and seal. Makes 4½ pints.

Happy Times with Home Cooking

Country Corn Relish

1 tablespoon cornstarch
1 teaspoon turmeric
1 cup plus 1 tablespoon vinegar
2 green peppers, seeded and
   diced
2 sweet red peppers, seeded
   and diced
2 large tomatoes, peeled and
   diced

1 large cucumber, pealed and
   diced
½ pound white onions, diced
2 ears fresh corn, cut from cob
4 stalks celery, diced
1¼ cups sugar
¼ teaspoon mustard seed

In large kettle or pot, blend cornstarch and turmeric with small amount of vinegar. Add remaining vinegar and mix in all the other ingredients. Bring to a boil, then reduce heat and simmer, uncovered, for 50–60 minutes, or until thick. Pour into hot sterilized jars and seal. (Relish may also be cooled and poured into refrigerator or freezer containers. Refrigerate for immediate use or freeze for future serving.) Makes 1½ quarts.

Apron Strings

Candied Tomatoes

1 onion, chopped
1 tablespoon butter
1 quart tomatoes, quartered

½ cup chopped green pepper
½ teaspoon salt
1 cup sugar

Brown onion in butter in iron skillet. Add tomatoes, green pepper, salt, and sugar. Simmer over low heat 1½ hours; stir occasionally. Serves 4.

The Hunt Country Cookbook

Apple Butter
(Oven Method)

7 pounds apples (16 cups
  sauce)
3 pounds brown sugar
1 cup vinegar or cider

2 tablespoons powdered
  cinnamon or 1 cup of crushed
  pineapple

Cook apples until soft and press through a sieve. Add remaining ingredients and put in the oven. Bake 3 hours at 350°. Stir occasionally. Pour into jars and seal. Makes 5 quarts.

Mennonite Community Cookbook

Curry Powder

One ounce turmeric, one do. coriander seed, one do. cummin seed, one do. white ginger, one of nutmeg, one of mace, and one of cayenne pepper; pound all together, and pass them through a fine sieve; bottle and cork it well; one teaspoonful is sufficient to season any made dish.

The Virginia House-wife

Meats

Virginia's hunt country features some of the most scenic landscape in America, including magnificent rolling fields and handsome estates and plantation lands.

Leg o' Lamb with Marinade

2 tablespoons chili sauce
1½ tablespoons Worcestershire
  sauce
1½ tablespoons cider vinegar
3 tablespoons (or less)
  vegetable oil
Dash of salt, pepper, thyme,
  crushed bay leaf
1 can beef broth
2 tablespoons minced onion
1 clove garlic
1 leg o' lamb

Combine all ingredients except lamb in saucepan, heating through. Pour over lamb before cooking and baste during cooking.

Make a foil tent over lamb and roast 30–35 minutes to the pound at 300°. Thirty minutes before it's done, pour the juices into a saucepan, put into freezer to let the fat come to the top, skim off the fat, and make gravy or just use the juice.

Keeping the Feast

Lamb Chops en Papillote

4 shoulder lamb chops, ½ inch
  thick, trimmed of fat
1 teaspoon celery salt
Few twists of fresh pepper
¼ teaspoon crumbled chervil
  (1 teaspoon fresh)
2 onions, peeled and sliced
3–4 zucchini, quartered
  lengthwise
3–4 carrots, peeled, quartered,
  2 inches long
4 new potatoes, peeled and sliced
Salt

Preheat oven to 350°. Cut 4 (16-inch) squares of heavy-duty foil. Place a chop on each; sprinkle each side with celery salt, pepper, and chervil. Top with vegetables and sprinkle lightly with salt. Wrap tightly and place on jellyroll pan. Bake for 1 hour. Can be served in packet. Serves 4.

Virginia Seasons

Spicy Lamb in Foil

2 tablespoons flour
1 teaspoon salt
1 teaspoon curry powder
½ teaspoon garlic powder
⅛ teaspoon pepper
1 (5- to 6-pound) leg of lamb

½ cup chutney, chopped
¼ cup bottled steak sauce
2 tablespoons ketchup
1 tablespoon red wine vinegar
1 tablespoon Worcestershire
   sauce

Arrange 2 large sheets of aluminum foil in opposite directions in the bottoms of a shallow roasting pan. Combine flour, salt, curry powder, garlic powder, and pepper, mixing well; rub mixture thoroughly into surface of lamb. Arrange lamb in the center of foil.

In a small bowl, combine chutney, steak sauce, ketchup, wine vinegar, and Worcestershire sauce, mixing well; spoon over roast. Close foil, sealing edges securely. Bake in a moderate oven (350°) for 30 minutes per pound, about 2½–3 hours. Uncover during the last half hour of roasting and increase oven temperature to hot (400°.) To serve, carve roast into thin slices and spoon spiced lamb drippings over each serving.

Richmond Receipts

Medallions of Beef and Sautéed Shiitake Mushrooms with Red Wine Sauce

6 tablespoons butter or margarine, divided	¼ pound mushrooms (fresh, sliced shiitake, if possible)
4 small shallots (minced)	1½ pounds beef tenderloin (medallions)
1 garlic clove (minced)	
½ cup Worcestershire sauce	Cognac as needed
½ cup red wine (Bordeaux)	1 teaspoon flour

To make the sauce: In a sauté pan, melt 2 tablespoons of the butter. Sauté the shallots; then add the garlic. After 2 minutes, add the Worcestershire and the wine. Simmer until the sauce is reduced by one third. Add the mushrooms.

To prepare the beef: In a separate pan, melt the remaining butter and, when hot, sauté the beef to the desired degree of doneness. Flame the beef with cognac. Remove the beef. Add the flour to the pan and stir. Mix the beef drippings into the sauce. Set the medallions on a bed of rice and pour the sauce over. Serves 4.

The Great Chefs of Virginia Cookbook

Beef Bourguignon

This recipe can be multiplied several times. Bob and Phoebe Harper have prepared it for 65 people for a ski weekend. They made several batches and froze them. If after freezing, the sauce seems too thick, add a little more red wine. Serve over medium-size flat noodles. Serve with Claret or Cabernet Sauvignon.

1½ cups lean salt pork, diced
3 tablespoons lard
12 small white onions, peeled
2 cups sliced fresh mushrooms
2 pounds beef shank, cut
   into small cubes with fat
   removed
Salt and pepper to taste
2–4 tablespoons flour

½ teaspoon thyme
1 bay leaf, crumbled
4 sprigs parsley
½ teaspoon salt
¼ teaspoon pepper
1½ cups dry red wine
2½ cups beef broth
Chopped parsley for garnish

Place salt pork in a small saucepan and cover with cold water. Bring to a slow boil and simmer for 10 minutes. Drain, rinse in cold water and pat pieces of pork dry.

Place half of the lard in a heavy frying pan over medium heat and add onions and salt pork. Sauté until pork is yellow. Remove onion and salt pork and drain on paper towels. In the same lard, adding more if necessary, sauté mushrooms until tender. Remove mushrooms, drain and set aside for later use.

Sprinkle meat with salt and pepper and coat with flour. Sauté in same lard until meat is brown on all sides. Put meat into an oven-proof casserole. Add spices, salt and pepper, wine and beef stock. Cover and cook in a preheated 350° oven for 2 hours. Add onions, mushrooms and salt pork. Check seasonings and adjust if necessary. Return covered casserole to oven and cook for another ½ hour. The sauce will have reduced by half. Thicken gravy if desired. Serve hot, over noodles, garnished with parsley. Serves 4.

Virginia Wine Country

Veal of Hanover

Located in historic Hanover County, Thyme and Sage of Hanover exhibits a casual atmosphere, featuring antique church pews and chairs as part of the decor. Veal of Hanover, an entrée specialty, is frequently requested by patrons.

2 pounds very thinly sliced boneless veal (scallopine)

About ½ cup flour

1 tablespoon clarified butter, melted

1 tablespoon hot cooking oil

1 cup thinly sliced mushrooms

1 tablespoon minced peeled shallots

¼ cup dry white (chablis) wine

½ cup heavy cream, at room temperature

3 tablespoons browning and seasoning sauce

Salt and pepper to taste

Between sheets of waxed paper, flatten veal pieces, as desired, with a meat mallet. On a sheet of waxed paper, dredge veal pieces in flour, coating each well. In a large heavy skillet, sauté veal in butter and oil over moderate heat, about 30 seconds per side. Remove veal, draining well, and set aside. Add mushrooms and shallots to skillet; sauté vegetables in hot pan drippings, stirring frequently, until vegetables are tender. Add wine and continue cooking until liquid is almost gone. Add cream, and browning and seasoning sauce, blending well. Season with salt and pepper to taste; continue cooking for 30 seconds. Return veal to pan, spooning sauce over veal. Serve immediately.

Note: If sauce becomes too thick, a few drops of water may be added.

Variation: Two pounds of boneless turkey breast cutlets may be substituted for veal. Proceed with recipe as previously directed.

More Richmond Receqts

Elegant Filet Mignon

Topped with a superb butter sauce!

4 filets mignons (approximately
  1½–2 inches thick)
2–3 teaspoons freshly
  cracked black pepper
2 teaspoons extra virgin
  olive oil
4–7 tablespoons butter, divided

3–6 shallots, sliced in half
½ cup beef bouillon
2–3 tablespoons red wine vinegar
1–2 tablespoons Worcestershire
  sauce
Sliced green onions, for garnish

Dry filets and sprinkle each side generously with ½ teaspoon pepper; press pepper into beef. Place on plate and cover; refrigerate 2–3 hours. In a skillet, heat olive oil and add 1 tablespoon butter; cook filets quickly on each side (approximately 4–6 minutes per side). Place meat on a warm platter; keep warm.

Pour excess pan drippings from skillet; add 2–3 tablespoons butter to pan. Sauté shallots for one minute over medium heat; add beef bouillon. Increase heat and boil to reduce pan juices to 2 tablespoons. Be sure to scrape bottom of pan well while sauce is cooking; add red wine vinegar and Worcestershire sauce; boil one minute. Add remaining 2–3 tablespoons butter and mix with pan juices; pour over filets. Garnish with sliced green onions. Serve immediately. Serves 4. Do not overcook this elegant beef dish!

Note: Sliced mushrooms can be substituted for shallots. Use only extra virgin olive oil for this recipe.

Words Worth Eating

In 1755, the Virginia colony exported over 42 million pounds of tobacco. The crop was introduced by John Rolfe (who married Pocahontas), and its cultivation was taught to the area's farmers in 1612. Philip Morris is the largest cigarette producer in the nation.

Gin Stew

¼ cup olive oil
3–4 pounds chuck, carefully
  trimmed and cut into cubes
½ cup flour
1 tablespoon salt
1 teaspoon pepper for
  dredging
3 cups onions, cut in chunks
3 cups mushrooms, cut in
  large chunks

3 cups carrots, cut in chunks
1 large can tomatoes, undrained
  or 3 cups fresh tomatoes in
  chunks
3 cloves garlic
1 tablespoon Italian seasoning
Salt, pepper, chopped parsley
½ cup gin
2 cups full-bodied red wine

Put olive oil in bottom of large pot. Add a layer of beef (dredged in flour, salt and pepper; browning is not necessary) and vegetables in casserole. Add 2 cloves minced garlic, Italian seasoning, gin and wine. Simmer until beef is tender, about 3 hours. The stew is better if not eaten the day it is made. At time of reheating, add 1 clove minced garlic, parsley and any additional salt and pepper.

Lovely served with buttered noodles. Stew may be frozen. I usually make a large quantity and freeze in several small serving containers. Makes 5 quarts.

The Foxcroft Cook Book

Foxcroft Mulligan Stew, Adapted

4 pounds veal, cut up
1 duck, cut up
4 tablespoons salt
3 (1-pound, 12-ounce) cans
  Italian tomatoes
1 can tomato paste with 1
  can of water
4 packages frozen lima beans

4 packages frozen cut corn
1 stalk celery, cut in
  ½-inch pieces
1 pound onions, chunked
1 pound rice
½ pound butter
2 pints cream
2 teaspoons pepper

Cook veal and duck in water, to cover, 2 hours, with 2 tablespoons salt. (I suggest dividing in half and using two very large pots). Let cool overnight, then remove and discard the cake of grease on top. Pull meat off skin and bones and put back in stock in which it was cooked. Cut duck pieces up so they don't make long strings. Add tomatoes, tomato paste, lima beans, corn, celery, onions and rice (half to each pot) and cook 4 hours or until all meats have disappeared. Stir frequently as the rice sticks easily. If it scorches on the bottom a little, it will taste more like the old school product than if it doesn't. Finally add the butter and cream and the rest of the seasonings. This freezes very well and is well worth making. Easier than it sounds and everybody loves it. (This is really a very thick soup).

To serve Mulligan Stew as a stew for a crowd: for every six people, cook 1 pound of veal, cut up until tender—maybe an hour. Save the stock and add the veal to the defrosted Mulligan Stew. Serve over barley, on plates instead of in bowls.

Barley: Cook the barley in boiling stock for about 2 hours with a stalk of celery. One pound should serve 10 people. Or you can add the barley directly to the stew with or instead of the rice. Season to taste with salt, pepper and butter. Makes 11 quarts for 40–50.

The Foxcroft Cook Book

Gourmet Goulash

2 tablespoons butter
2½ pounds round steak,
  cubed
3 cups chopped onion
1 (8-ounce) can tomato sauce
1 teaspoon Worcestershire
  sauce
1 clove garlic, minced

2 tablespoons brown sugar
1 tablespoon paprika
1½ teaspoons salt
1 teaspoon caraway seed
1 teaspoon dill seed
¼ teaspoon pepper
1 cup sour cream (optional)

Melt butter in large skillet; add meat and brown well. Add onion. Combine tomato sauce, Worcestershire sauce, garlic, brown sugar, paprika, salt, caraway seed, dill seed and pepper. Add to meat and onion and cook covered until meat is tender—about 1½ hours. If desired, add sour cream. Serve on parsley-buttered noodles. Serves 6–8.

A Heritage of Good Tastes

Hurry-Up Meat Loaf

¾ pound ground beef
1 (8-ounce) can tomato sauce
  (divided)
½ cup soft bread crumbs
1 egg, slightly beaten
1 tablespoon dried onion flakes

½ teaspoon salt
⅛ teaspoon pepper
1 tablespoon brown sugar
2 teaspoons dried parsley flakes
1 tablespoon Worcestershire
  sauce

Combine ground beef, ½ cup tomato sauce, bread crumbs, egg and onion flakes, salt, and pepper; mix well. Shape meat mixture into 4 individual loaves. Place on slightly greased baking pan (11x7x1½). Bake at 450° for 30 minutes. Combine remaining tomato sauce, brown sugar, parsley flakes, and Worcestershire sauce. Mix well and pour over loaves and bake an additional 5 minutes. Yields 2 servings.

WYVE's Bicentennial Cookbook

Chili

1¼ pounds ground beef
2 cups diced onion
1 (6-ounce) can tomato paste
1 (14½-ounce) can whole
  tomatoes (with juice)
2½ tablespoons chili powder
2½ teaspoons cumin
1½ teaspoons salt
1¼ cups water or beef stock
⅓ teaspoon garlic powder
  or 3 garlic cloves (minced)

1 small bay leaf
1 teaspoon oregano
¼ teaspoon cayenne pepper
1 (15-ounce) can kidney beans
1½ cups grated Cheddar
  cheese
¾ cup coarsely chopped onion
6 tablespoons sour cream

To prepare the chili: Sauté the meat and the onions over medium heat until the meat loses its pink color. Add all of the remaining ingredients, except the beans and toppings. Simmer, stirring occasionally for 1 hour. Add the beans and simmer the mixture for 15 minutes longer. (The chili will hold, refrigerated for 4 days at this point; the flavors will mellow and improve with time).

For service: Heat the chili slowly to a simmer. Continue to simmer for 20 minutes, until thoroughly heated, stirring occasionally. Serve the chili in heated crocks or bowls. Top each serving with grated Cheddar cheese, chopped onion and sour cream. Serves 6.

The Great Chefs of Virginia Cookbook

Crazy Beans

1½ pound ground beef
½ pound bacon
1 can each: kidney, pinto,
  navy and pork and beans

¼ cup ketchup
½ cup brown sugar
2 tablespoons Worcestershire
  sauce

Brown ground beef; drain. Cook the bacon and crumble. Mix all the ingredients; put in crockpot and cook on high for 4–5 hours.

Smyth County Extension Homemakers Cookbook

Lasagna Pie

½ cup container small-curd
  cottage cheese or ricotta
¼ cup grated Parmesan cheese
1 pound extra lean ground
  beef
1 medium onion, chopped
1 green pepper, chopped
1 teaspoon dried oregano
½ teaspoon dried basil
1 (6-ounce) can tomato paste
1–1½ cups shredded mozzarella
  cheese, divided
Salt and pepper to taste
1 cup milk
⅔ cup packaged biscuit mix
2 eggs

Preheat oven to 400°. Lightly grease 10-inch pie pan. Place the cottage cheese in a layer on the bottom, then top with the Parmesan cheese. Brown beef over low medium heat; and add onion and green pepper, cooking until the onion is translucent. Add oregano, basil, tomato paste, ¾ cup of mozzarella, salt and pepper to taste. Spoon over the cheese layers in pie pan.

Beat milk, biscuit mix, and eggs for 1 minute until smooth (1 minute or so with hand beater). Pour into pie pan. Bake for about 30 minutes, or until golden brown. Knife inserted halfway between center and edge will come out clean. Sprinkle with remaining mozzarella. Let stand for 5–10 minutes before serving.

The Other Side of the House

Lasagna Rollups

1 pound sweet Italian sausage
½ cup chopped onion
2 (6-ounce) cans tomato paste
1⅔ cups water
1 teaspoon oregano leaves
½ teaspoon basil leaves
1 (10-ounce) package frozen
  chopped spinach, cooked
  thoroughly, drained

2 cups ricotta cheese
1 cup grated Parmesan cheese
1½ cups shredded mozzarella
  cheese
1 egg, slightly beaten
½ teaspoon salt
¼ teaspoon pepper
8 lasagna noodles, cooked
  and drained

Remove casings from sausage; crumble. Brown sausage with onion in saucepan. Pour off drippings. Add tomato paste, water, oregano and basil. Cover; boil gently 20 minutes.

Combine spinach, ricotta cheese, Parmesan cheese, 1 cup of mozzarella cheese, egg, salt, and pepper; mix thoroughly. Spread about ½ cup of mixture on each noodle. Roll up. Place seam-side-down in 12x7½x2-inch baking dish. Pour sauce over rolls. Top with remaining mozzarella cheese. Bake at 350° for 30–40 minutes or until heated through.

Culinary Contentment

Hot Wheel Burgers

1½ pounds lean ground beef
1 (10¾-ounce) can tomato
  soup
1½ teaspoons dried minced
  onion
1 tablespoon Worcestershire
  sauce

1 tablespoon prepared mustard
1 teaspoon horseradish
1 teaspoon salt
Hamburger buns
Sliced tomatoes
Cheese slices

Combine first seven ingredients. Spread thinly on hamburger bun halves. Broil about 4 inches from heat for 12 minutes. Top with tomato slices and cheese. Broil until cheese melts. Makes 6.

Children's Party Book

Moose

1½ pounds hamburger	3 (8-ounce) cans tomato sauce
3 tablespoons butter	1 (12-ounce) package noodles
⅛ teaspoon garlic powder	1 (3-ounce) package cream cheese
1 teaspoon salt	2 cups sour cream
1 teaspoon pepper	6–8 scallions
1 tablespoon sugar	½ cup grated cheese

Brown hamburger in butter. Add garlic powder, salt, pepper, sugar and tomato sauce. Cover with lid and simmer for 20 minutes. Cook noodles in boiling salted water according to package directions. Drain. Mix softened cream cheese with sour cream and add chopped scallions. In buttered casserole, layer noodles, cream cheese mixture and hamburger sauce. Repeat. Sprinkle top with grated cheese. Bake at 350° until hot and bubbly in center. Freezes beautifully. Serves 6.

Of Pots and Pipkins

Sunday Supper Snack

1 pound ground chuck	¼ teaspoon thyme
1 medium onion, chopped	¼ teaspoon oregano
1 clove garlic, crushed	1 can biscuits (12 to a can)
½ cup barbecue sauce	Several slices sharp processed
½ teaspoon salt	cheese

Brown hamburger, onion and garlic together. Add barbecue sauce and seasonings and simmer until hamburger is cooked. Meanwhile, press biscuits into muffin tins, forming cups. Fill cups with hamburger mixture and top with a piece of cheese. Bake about 10 minutes in 375° oven, until crust is done. Serves 6.

Of Pots and Pipkins

Super Supper Stacks

1 (10-ounce) package frozen
  broccoli spears or 1 (16-ounce)
  can asparagus spears
6 eggs
3 English muffins, split,
  buttered and toasted
½ can condensed cream of
  mushroom soup
2 tablespoons milk
2 tablespoons creamy Italian
  salad dressing or
  ranch-style dressing

6 slices of almost any cold meat
  (sliced roast beef, pork, country
  ham, turkey, cold cuts, corned
  beef, etc.)
6 slices cheese (Cheddar,
  American, Swiss, Muenster,
  etc.)
Parsley for garnish

Cook broccoli according to package directions and drain; or heat asparagus and drain. Poach eggs. Set aside. Prepare English muffins. Prepare special sauce: Heat mushroom soup, milk, and salad dressing together, stirring, until it begins to bubble. Remove from heat. On platter, stack up ingredients as follows: English muffin half, slice of meat, slice of cheese, couple of broccoli or asparagus spears, poached egg. Top with special sauce and a sprig of parsley for garnish. Makes 6 servings.

From Ham to Jam

149

Lady Pick's Scotch Loaf

This very old and most unusual receipt has been handed down from one generation to another for nearly 200 years. It was given to Lady Pick by her old Scotch nurse.

1 pound ground steak (no fat)
½ pound lean bacon (have
 bacon ground with steak)
2 unbeaten eggs

1 pint bread crumbs (Italian
 flavored)
2 fresh nutmegs (grated)

Knead last 3 items with ground meat. Roll mixture in ¼ yard unbleached floured cloth folded over twice, tied tight with string at each end and pinned in center. Put in boiling water to cover in deep pot with lid for 3 hours. Remove and roll in extra bread crumbs. Put in refrigerator to chill. Slice and serve cold.

Delectable Cookery of Alexandria

Haystacks

1¼ cups rice
2 tablespoons margarine
3 cups hot water
1 teaspoon salt
1 pound hamburger

1 small onion, chopped
2 tablespoons chopped green
pepper
1 (1¾-ounce) envelope taco
seasoning mix

TOPPINGS:

Chopped lettuce
Chopped mushrooms
Sliced tomatoes
Bean sprouts
Chopped green peppers

Crushed corn chips
1 (10-ounce) can Cheddar cheese
soup, or 2 cups your own
cheese sauce

Fry dry rice in margarine in pan until lightly browned. Add hot water and salt and heat to boiling. Cover tightly and simmer 20 minutes. Sauté hamburger, onion, and pepper in skillet until lightly browned. Drain. Add seasoning mix. May add a little water to make mixture slightly juicy. Spoon over rice to serve. Yields 6 servings.

Use any or all toppings as desired. Heat cheese soups or cheese sauce and spoon over top.

Mennonite Country-Style Recipes

Bring Home the Bacon

1 cup grated cheese
1 cup cottage cheese
3 cups rice (cooked according
to package directions)
12 strips of bacon, fried crisp
and crumbled
1 cup sliced fresh mushrooms
or 1 (8-ounce) can, drained

1 pound fresh asparagus spears,
or 1 (16-ounce) can, drained
½ teaspoon salt
Dash of pepper
½ cup butter or margarine
1 cup milk

In small bowl, blend cheeses and set aside. Mix together rice and bacon; place in 9x13x2-inch greased casserole dish. Spread mushrooms over rice. Arrange asparagus spears on top of mushrooms. Sprinkle on salt and pepper. Top with cheese mixture and dot with butter and pour cup of milk over top. Bake 45 minutes at 350°. Serves 6–8.

The VIP Cookbook: A Potpourri of Virginia Cooking

Baked Virginia Ham

Visitors to Wiliiamsburg who plan to carry home a Virginia ham as a souvenir are advised to heed these preliminary directions or they may be sadly disappointed:

Scrub the ham to remove the coating of seasonings, cover it with water, and soak it for 24 hours. Place the ham, skin side down, in a pan with enough fresh water to cover, bring to a boil, reduce the heat, and simmer, covered, for 20–25 minutes per pound. When done, skin the ham and trim off excess fat.

Note: *These directions apply to a Virginia ham that has been cured for at least 12 months. If the ham has been cured less than 12 months, follow the instructions on the wrapper or hang the ham and allow it to age.*

1 (10- to 12-pound) Virginia ham
2 tablespoons light brown sugar
1 tablespoon bread crumbs

1 teaspoon cloves
3 teaspoons honey, dry sherry, or sweet pickle vinegar

Preheat the oven to 375°. Combine the brown sugar, bread crumbs, and cloves. Press the mixture into the ham. Place the ham in a roasting pan. Bake at 375° for 15 minutes or until the sugar melts.

Drizzle honey, sherry, or sweet pickle vinegar over the ham. Bake at 375° for 15 minutes.

Favorite Meals from Williamsburg

Jelly Glaze

¼ cup ham juices (pan
   drippings or ham stock)
1 teaspoon dry mustard
Dash of cinnamon
Dash of ground cloves

1 cup currant jelly, orange
   marmalade, cranberry jelly,
   apricot preserves or pineapple
   preserves

Combine and beat until smooth. Spread on ham last 30 minutes of baking.

The Ham Book

Spicy Raisin Sauce for Ham

1 cup sugar
½ cup water
1 cup raisins
2 tablespoons butter or
   margarine
3 tablespoons vinegar

½ tablespoon Worcestershire
½ teaspoon salt
¼ teaspoon ground cloves
Ground mace (few grains)
Black pepper (few dashes)
1 small jar apple currant jelly

Cook sugar and water together 5 minutes, stirring. Add remaining ingredients. Serve in sauce boat with your holiday ham.

The Enlightened Titan

Mustard Sauce for Ham

½ cup brown sugar
½ cup vinegar
¼ cup dry mustard

½ cup butter
3 egg yolks

Put all ingredients in double boiler and cook, stirring constantly, until mixture is consistency of custard. Chill and serve with ham. Can be reheated in double boiler, stirring to prevent curdling. Yields 1½ cups.

The Mount Vernon Cookbook

The world famous Smithfield hams are cut from peanut-fed hogs, then dry salt smoked, a technique they learned from the Indians. In 1902, P. O. Gwaltney, Jr. cured one and it is still edible, though it has never been refrigerated. It sports a brass collar that says, "Mr. Gwaltney's Pet Ham."

Ham Mousse

3 envelopes gelatin
2 cans consommé, heated
6 cups ground ham
1 tablespoon Worcestershire
  sauce

Dash of Kitchen Bouquet
1 cup chopped parsley
1 quart whipped cream

Soak the gelatin in a little cold water; add it to the hot consommé. Cool, but do not let it jell. Add the ground ham and the seasonings, and a cup of chopped parsley. When beginning to set, fold in the whipped cream. Pour into an oiled mold and let it set. Serve with raw tomatoes and a green salad. It is rich. This makes a large mold—about three quarts.

The Hunt Country Cookbook

Champagne Ham

This was a nineteenth century innovation first described in Key to the Pantry *in 1898. It is delicious. Virginia Gearhart Gray, historian and lecturer on cookbooks, marked this recipe as of special interest and significance in her family collection. Her daughter, Miss Sally Gray, cookbook author and librarian at the College of William and Mary, shared this recipe.*

Brown sugar
1 tablespoon allspice
1 teaspoon ground cloves
1 cup vinegar

1 cup Champagne
½ cup sugar
1 cup Champagne

Rub a whole cooked ham with brown sugar. Combine allspice, cloves, vinegar, 1 cup Champagne and sugar. Pour over top of ham and bake slowly, 300°, for 1 hour. Add 1 cup Champagne. Serve pan juices as gravy for ham.

The Ham Book

William and Mary is the second oldest college in the United States. It and Virginia Polytechnic Institute were the first to admit women (1918).

Ham Skillet Casserole

This top-of-the-stove casserole is quick and absolutely delicious. Even if your taste does not fancy squash, you will love this dish.

1 onion, chopped
1 (10-ounce) package squash
or 4 medium-size yellow
squash, cut into pieces
1 (10-ounce) package frozen
cauliflower or 1 small head
cauliflower, broken into buds

1 cup water
2 tablespoons butter
1 cup cubed ham
1 (8-ounce) package grated
mozzarella cheese
1 tomato, cut into wedges
1 pepper, cut into strips

Place first 5 ingredients in skillet. Steam until tender. Add ham. Steam for a few minutes. Cover casserole with mozzarella cheese. After cheese melts, arrange around skillet the tomato wedges and pepper strips. Steam for a few more minutes, then serve at once.

The Ham Book

Sweet Ham Roll Up
(Microwave)

1 (8-ounce) can whole cranberry
sauce
½ cup instant rice
⅛ cup chopped green pepper
⅛ cup celery, sliced thin
2 tablespoons water
1 teaspoon butter or margarine

½ teaspoon molasses
¼ teaspoon cornstarch
¼ teaspoon dried minced onion
⅛ teaspoon salt
1 dash black pepper
1 (3-ounce) ham slice

Combine all ingredients, except ham, in a small bowl. Mix well. Cover. Microwave on HIGH (100%) 1½–2 minutes or until rice is tender. Place ham slice on serving plate. Place mixture in the middle of ham slice, reserving ⅛ of a cup. Roll up ham slice and secure with a toothpick. Spoon remaining mixture over top of ham. Cover loosely with waxed paper. Microwave HIGH (100%) 1¼–1½ minutes or until heated.

The Microwave Affair

Marinated Pork Roast with Apricot Sauce

Really delicious.

2 garlic cloves, peeled and
  minced
½ cup plus 2 tablespoons
  dry sherry
½ cup plus 1 tablespoon
  soy sauce

2 tablespoons dry mustard
2 teaspoons thyme
1 teaspoon ginger
1 (5- to 6-pound) boneless pork
  loin, rolled and tied
1 (10-ounce) jar apricot preserves

In a 2-cup measure, combine garlic, ½ cup sherry, ½ cup soy sauce, mustard, thyme and ginger, blending well. Arrange pork loin in a deep bowl or dish; pour marinade over meat. Cover and refrigerate for 2–3 days, turning meat frequently. Remove meat from marinade. Insert meat thermometer into center of roast, away from fat. Arrange roast on a rack in a shallow roasting pan and bake in slow oven (325°) for 2½–3 hours or until thermometer registers 170°. In a saucepan, combine preserves, 2 tablespoons sherry and 1 tablespoon soy sauce; heat until bubbly hot; serve sauce with the roast. Makes 8–10 servings.

Apron Strings

Rice and Pork Casserole

1 cup uncooked rice
1½ quarts water
2 teaspoons salt
6 pork chops

1 tablespoon fat
2 red or green peppers
1 (10½-ounce) can tomato soup
¼ teaspoon pepper

Boil rice in salt water and drain. Brown pork chops slightly in fat. Place browned chops in the bottom of a casserole. Add a layer of sliced pepper rings. Add the rice and top with another layer of sliced peppers. Pour the tomato soup, which has been diluted with ½ cup water, over the mixture. Bake at 375° for 40 minutes. Serves 6.

Mennonite Community Cookbook

Bavarian Chef's Mandelschnitzel

2 eggs
2 cups fine bread crumbs
2 ounces blanched almonds,
  sliced

4 (6-ounce) pork tenderloins
Flour for dredging
3 tablespoons butter

Beat eggs. In separate bowl, combine bread crumbs and almonds. Lightly dredge pork in flour. Dip in egg batter, and roll in bread crumb mixture to cover. Melt 3 tablespoons butter in large skillet and sauté pork until golden brown on both sides. Remove from pan, place on platter and keep warm. Serves 4.

SAUCE:

2 tablespoons butter
1 small onion, chopped
1 cup chicken stock or broth
5 ounces strawberry
  preserves
2 tablespoons sugar

1 ounce gin
1 ounce kirschwasser (or kirsch)
¼ cup cornstarch
¾ cup water
Cayenne to taste
1 lemon, sliced

Melt 2 tablespoons butter in skillet and sauté onions until soft. Add chicken stock, strawberry preserves, sugar, gin and kirschwasser. Mix cornstarch and ¾ cup water in cup and stir until cornstarch is dissolved. Add to sauce and stir until thickened. Sprinkle with cayenne to taste. Place sauce on warmed plates and lay pork on top. Garnish with lemon slices. Serves 4.

Virginia's Historic Restaurants and Their Recipes

Raspberry Pork Chops

6 thick pork chops, trimmed
Salt and pepper to taste
Flour for dredging
3 tablespoons safflower oil
5 tablespoons unsalted butter,
  divided use

3 medium onions, thinly sliced
2 cups chicken stock, or
  more if necessary
1 tablespoon raspberry vinegar
½ pint raspberries

Preheat oven to 350°. Season chops with salt and pepper; dredge in flour. In oven-proof skillet, heat oil and 3 tablespoons butter. Brown chops on both sides. Remove chops; discard fat. Line skillet with layer of onions. Top with chops; add 2 cups chicken stock. Cover and bake for 1 hour and 15 minutes, adding more stock if necessary.

Remove chops to platter; keep them warm. Skim off fat in skillet. Add vinegar and remaining 2 tablespoons of butter. Add raspberries (reserve a few for garnish) and mash gently. Boil until slightly thickened. Spoon over chops; garnish with raspberries. Yields 6 servings.

Cardinal Cuisine

Sausage Casserole Ramsay

Outstanding for brunch or Sunday supper.

1½ pounds sausage
2 cups chopped celery
1½ cups chopped green
  onions
1½ cups chopped green
  pepper

2 cans cream of chicken soup
1 can chicken stock or broth
3 cans water
3 cups rice
Salt, pepper, and parsley flakes
  to taste

Brown sausage, then remove all fat but 2 tablespoons. Add celery, onions, and green pepper. Sauté until all are tender. Place uncooked rice in large casserole and add other ingredients. Stir. Bake covered for about 1 hour (until rice is tender) in 350° oven. Serves 8.

More Delectable Cookery of Alexandria

Pork Chops and Cheesy Potatoes

A simple meat and potato dish, but oh so good.

8 potatoes, sliced	1 soup can milk
1 onion, chopped	Salt and pepper to taste
6 slices Cheddar cheese	6 pork chops, browned
2 cans cream of mushroom soup	

In a 1½-quart buttered dish, place alternate layers of potatoes, onions, and cheese. Combine soup, milk, and seasonings; pour over all (do not stir). Top with browned pork chops; cover and bake at 350° for 1½ hours. Serves 6.

Holiday Treats

Caper Sauce

¼ cup minced onion	1 cup beef broth
1 garlic clove, minced	1 cup sour cream
Butter	¼ cup capers, drained
4 tablespoons flour	Salt and pepper to taste

Sauté onions and garlic briefly in butter. Blend in flour, then add beef broth, sour cream, and capers. Cook over medium low heat, stirring constantly, until mixture thickens. Add salt and pepper as desired.

Note: This is good with beef, lamb, or pork. For lamb, you can substitute lamb broth, if available. For chicken, substitute chicken broth for the beef broth. Yields 8 servings.

The Other Side of the House

When standing in the middle of State Street in Bristol, you can have one foot in Tennessee and one foot in Virginia.

Boar Pie

1½ pounds diced boar (pork
   shoulder may be substituted
   by the less daring)
3 cups Monticello red wine
3 tablespoons butter
4 tablespoons flour
⅓ cup raisins
½ cup prunes

½ cup dates
⅓ cup diced apples
½ teaspoon ginger
½ teaspoon nutmeg
½ cup mincemeat
½ teaspoon cloves
Salt and pepper

Simmer the meat in a skillet with wine until browned. Melt the butter
in a saucepan and add flour, cooking gently for for 1 minute. Drain the
hot stock off the meat and stir into well-blended roux.

Put the meat and all other ingredients in the sauce and pour into a
deep 8x9-inch pie dish lined with pastry dough. Top with dough and
bake at 375° for 45 minutes or until well browned. Serves 4–6.

The Boar's Head Cookbook

Barbecue Shoat

Take a piece of shoat and make incisions at regular distances, and stuff
with a rich force meat; put in pan with a pint of water, cloves of garlic,
pepper, salt, and gill of red wine and two gills of mushroom or tomato
ketchup; bake it, and thicken the gravy with butter and browned flour.
It must be jointed and the ribs cut across before it is cooked; lay the
dish with the ribs up and garnish with force meat balls.

The Old Virginia Cook Book

Leu's Venison

Venison
Milk-egg batter
Parmesan cheese, grated

Cracker crumbs
Oregano
Garlic salt

Use any cut of venison. Cut in long pieces ¼ inch thick. Pound with
coke bottle. Cut pieces 2 inches long by 1 inch wide. Place in batter.
Mix equal amounts of cheese and cracker crumbs. Add spices; mix.
Remove meat from batter; roll in cheese and crumb mixture; fry in hot
oil 1–2 minutes each side. Eat hot.

More Than a Cookbook

Buttermilk Marinated Venison Roast

1 venison roast
Buttermilk to cover half of
  roast
3 strips bacon

1 large onion, sliced
½–1 teaspoon basil
1 teaspoon salt
¼ teaspoon pepper

Thaw roast, if frozen, and wash well to remove any remaining clotted blood. Place roast in glass or ceramic dish and marinate in buttermilk for 24 hours, turning often to coat well.

Remove roast from dish and place in oven cooking bag that has been dusted with flour. Place bacon strips on top of roast and season with onion, basil, salt and pepper. Place on rack in roasting pan and bake at 300° 20 minutes per pound or until meat thermometer registers 150°.

Kitchen Keys

Essie's Barbequed Rabbit

Essie made even older rabbit tender and succulent by this recipe.

Rabbit
Salt
Bacon strips or salt pork

Water
2 hot pepper pods
1 cup vinegar

Put whole rabbit in heavy roasting pan. Salt generously. Cover each rabbit with one or two bacon strips or salt pork. Add enough water to stand ¼ inch deep in bottom of roaster. Baste with a mixture of 2 hot pepper pods crumbled in 1 cup vinegar. Cover roaster tightly and bake at 450° for 15 minutes. Reduce heat to 325° and cook for 1 hour or until very tender, basting often. Add more pepper and vinegar as necessary. The cover may be removed the last few minutes of cooking to allow the rabbit to brown, if desired.

'Possums, raccoons and muskrats may be prepared in the same manner as rabbit and squirrel. To insure tenderness, they are usually parboiled first.

The Smithfield Cookbook

Cheesy Corn Pups

1 (8-ounce) can refrigerated
dinner rolls
8 hot dogs
8 strips Cheddar cheese
(3x½x¼-inch)

3 tablespoons barbecue sauce
½ cup cornmeal
Wooden skewers

Preheat oven to 400°. Lightly grease cookie sheet. Separate dough into 8 rolls. Insert cheese in a narrow strip in each hot dog. Shape one roll evenly around each hot dog and pinch together to seal. Brush with barbecue sauce and roll in cornmeal. Insert wooden skewer in end of each hot dog. Place on cookie sheet and bake for 15–20 minutes until brown. Serve with ketchup and mustard. Serves 8.

Children's Party Book

Tomata Catsup

Gather a peck of tomatoes, pick out the stems, and wash them; put them on the fire without water, sprinkle on a few spoonsful of salt, let them boil steadily an hour, stirring them frequently, strain them through a colander, and then through a sieve; put the liquid on the fire with half a pint of chopped onions, a quarter of an ounce of mace broke into small pieces, and if not sufficiently salt, add a little more, one tablespoonful of whole black pepper, boil all together until just enough to fill two bottles; cork it tight. Make it in August.

The Virginia House-wife

Poultry

A silversmith shows his wares in the streets of Williamsburg.

Belle Grove Inn Fried Chicken

1 chicken (2¾ to 3 pounds),
  cut up
Salt and pepper to taste
1¼ cups flour

¾ cup lard or vegetable
  shortening
¼ cup butter

Wipe chicken pieces lightly with a wet towel, sprinkle salt and pepper on both sides, and coat each piece carefully with flour. Place on a cookie sheet and set aside.

Heat a heavy cast-iron or aluminum frying pan to medium high, then add lard or vegetable shortening and butter. If butter begins to brown, lower heat to medium. Add pieces of chicken, without crowding. Fat should be halfway up on each piece; add more fat if necessary. Cook to an even golden brown, turning pieces 2 or 3 times for 25–30 minutes cooking time per piece. Keep fat sizzling hot. When all pieces are evenly browned, put a lid on the pan and cook 5 minutes more. Transfer chicken to drain on a cookie sheet lined with paper towels, and place in a 300° oven while making gravy.

GRAVY:

3 tablespoons fat
4 tablespoons flour

2 cups milk
Salt and pepper

Pour off all fat, leaving brown crumbs in frying pan. Measure 3 tablespoons of the fat back into the pan, stir in flour, and brown quickly. Add scalded milk, stirring vigorously to avoid lumps. When gravy thickens, season with salt and pepper. Serves 4–6.

Note: This is the way my mother fried chicken for guests when she and my father operated Belle Grove as an inn in the 1920s. The chickens were raised on the farm, the lard rendered at butchering time, and the butter churned in the kitchen. These ingredients, along with the iron skillet, wood range, careful attention and patience, were my mother's essentials.

The Belle Grove Plantation Cookbook

Southern-Fried Chicken, Virginia Style

Many Richmonders use only bacon drippings for frying chicken. It gives a very special flavor.

1 cup flour
1 tablespoon salt
1 tablespoon paprika
1½ teaspoons poultry
   seasoning
¾ teaspoon pepper

3 (3-pound) frying chickens,
   cut into serving pieces
1½ cups shortening, cooking oil,
   or bacon drippings (or a
   combination)

Combine the first 5 ingredients in a paper or plastic Ziploc bag. Place 3–4 chicken pieces in bag at a time, close, and shake to coat well with seasoned flour. In a large skillet, melt fat, add chicken pieces, and cook over moderate heat (350°) until browned and crisp on both sides (do not crowd chicken pieces in skillet). Transfer chicken to 2 (9x13x2-inch) baking pans and cover securely with aluminum foil. Bake in a moderate oven (350°) for 40 minutes. Uncover and continue baking for 15–20 minutes longer, or until chicken is tender and outside is crisp. Yields 12 servings.

Richmond Receipts

Chicken Florentine

This is a simple, yet elegant dish!

2 (10-ounce) packages chopped frozen spinach, cooked and drained
2 tablespoons margarine
3 tablespoons flour
1 teaspoon Ac'cent
1 teaspoon salt
¼–½ teaspoon cayenne
2 cups milk
½ cup Parmesan cheese
2 cups cooked chicken, chunked
1–1½ cups soft bread, torn into pieces
1–2 tablespoons butter

Place the spinach in the bottom of a 1½-quart buttered casserole. Melt the margarine in a saucepan and stir in the flour; let bubble one minute, stirring constantly. Add spices and milk; stir constantly until mixture thickens. Add cheese and chicken. Pour chicken mixture over spinach; top with bread crumbs and dot with butter. Bake at 350° for 20–25 minutes or until casserole is heated completely. If bread crumbs need additional browning, place under broiler for a minute or two. Serves 4–6. The flavor is superb!

Note: This casserole can be prepared at least one day ahead. Do not add bread crumbs until ready to bake.

Words Worth Eating

Chicken Rockefeller

4 chicken breasts, skinned
  and boned
1 (10-ounce) package frozen
  chopped spinach, cooked and
  drained
8 fresh mushrooms, sliced
½ cup grated Parmesan
  cheese, divided

¼ cup plain yogurt
1 small onion, finely chopped
1 egg yolk, beaten
2 teaspoons lemon juice
⅛ teaspoon ground nutmeg

In wide steamer, place 1 inch of water. Heat to boiling over medium temperature. Place chicken in single layer, in steaming basket, lower into steamer. Cover and cook until fork can be inserted in chicken with ease, about 20 minutes. Remove chicken.

In bowl, mix together spinach, mushrooms, ¼ cup of Parmesan cheese, yogurt, onion, egg yolk, lemon juice, and nutmeg. Place chicken in medium shallow baking pan. Spread spinach mixture over chicken. Sprinkle with remaining ¼ cup Parmesan cheese. Place under broiler until cheese is golden brown, about 3 minutes. Yields 4 servings.

The Enlightened Titan

Chicken and Spinach Casserole

2 packages frozen chopped
  spinach, defrosted and
  drained
4 whole chicken breasts,
  halved, skinned, boned and
  cooked
1 cup mayonnaise

2 (10¾-ounce) cans cream
  of chicken soup
1 tablespoon lemon juice
1 cup shredded sharp Cheddar
  cheese
½ cup buttered bread crumbs

Place drained spinach in a 9x13-inch ungreased dish. Place chicken breasts on top. Combine and mix mayonnaise, soup and lemon juice. Spread over chicken. Sprinkle with cheese. Top with buttered crumbs. Bake at 350° for 30–40 minutes. Makes 8 servings.

Historic Lexington Cooks

Chicken Suzanne

Our absolutely number one favorite dish at the restaurant. We have had more requests for this recipe than any other.

6 (8-ounce) boneless chicken breast halves
1 cup flour
1 egg, beaten with 1 cup milk
3 cups good quality fresh bread crumbs
½–1 cup light cooking oil

Dip chicken breasts in flour, dip in egg/milk mixture, then thoroughly coat in bread crumbs.

Sauté in hot oil until well browned on each side. Cook until done (do not overcook). Serve with a dollop of herb butter. Serves 6.

HERB BUTTER:
½ cup chopped green onions
½ cup chopped fresh parsley
2 cloves garlic
1 teaspoon basil (2 tablespoons fresh)
½ teaspoon oregano (½ tablespoon fresh)
1 teaspoon marjoram (1 tablespoon fresh)
1 teaspoon tarragon (1 tablespoon fresh)
1 teaspoon dill weed (1 teaspoon fresh)
1 teaspoon black pepper
Dash of Tabasco
1 pound unsalted butter

Mix all above thoroughly in food processor.

The herb butter is delicious on toasted French bread, or toast triangles. Can also be used on steaks, hamburgers, veal scaloppini or steamed vegetables.

Cooking with Heart in Hand

 Busch Gardens in Williamsburg is the home of the world-renowned Anheuser-Busch Clydesdale horses.

Chicken Pillows

1 whole chicken breast, halved, skinned, and boned
1 clove garlic, halved
2 slices (1 ounce) prosciutto or boiled ham
2 slices (1 ounce) mozzarella cheese, thinly sliced
2 tablespoons seasoned bread crumbs
2 tablespoons medium dry sherry
2 tablespoons clarified butter
Salt and freshly ground pepper
1 tablespoon chopped parsley

Pound chicken breast pieces to a thickness of ¼ inch. Rub each chicken breast piece with cut clove of garlic. Place prosciutto and cheese over chicken. Sprinkle with bread crumbs. Roll up, starting at broader end, and secure with wooden picks. Place in lightly greased shallow baking dish.

Combine sherry and butter and heat briefly. Pour over chicken. Season with salt and pepper. Bake at 350° for 20–25 minutes or until chicken is done. Sprinkle with parsley.

Command Performances

Margaret's Chicken

4–6 chicken breasts, boned and skinned
4–6 slices Swiss cheese
1 can cream chicken soup
½ can dry white wine
½ cup slivered almonds

Place chicken breasts in greased baking dish. Cover each breast with a slice of Swiss cheese. Mix soup and wine. Spoon over chicken. Top with slivered almonds. Bake at 350° for 1 hour.

THE What in the World Are We Going to Have for Dinner COOKBOOK?

Simply Marvelous Cordon Bleu
(Microwave)

2 tablespoons flour
½ teaspoon seasoned salt
¼ teaspoon ground thyme
  leaves
1 (6- to 8-ounce) chicken
  breast, skinned, deboned
1 tablespoon butter or
  margarine

1 (½-ounce) slice ham
1 (½-ounce) slice Swiss cheese
¼ teaspoon dry minced onion
1 tablespoon dry Hollandaise
  sauce mix
2 tablespoons white wine or
  water

Using a small plastic bag, combine flour, salt and thyme together. Mix. Add chicken and coat well.

Using a 6-inch browning skillet, microwave 1 tablespoon butter or margarine for 20–30 seconds. Add chicken. Cover. Microwave on HIGH (100%) 1 minute. Turn chicken over. Cover. Microwave on HIGH (100%) 1¼ minutes or until done.

Using a paring knife, cut a slit in the side of the breast forming a "pocket." Lay ham and ½ slice of Swiss cheese inside the chicken piece. Top with other ½ of cheese. Set aside.

In browning skillet, add onion, Hollandaise sauce mix and wine or water. Microwave on HIGH (100%) 20–30 seconds or until thickens. Stir until smooth.

Place chicken on serving plate. Spoon sauce over top. Cover. Microwave on HIGH (100%) 30–45 seconds or until cheese melts.

The Microwave Affair

Lazy Day Chicken

2–3 pounds chicken breasts
⅓ cup flour
1 package dry onion soup mix
2–3 sliced carrots
2–3 stalks sliced celery

1 can mushrooms, drained
  (optional)
½ cup sherry
1 can cream of chicken soup
Paprika

Oil large baking dish. Dredge chicken in flour and place in dish. Sprinkle onion soup over top. Place sliced vegetables on soup. Combine sherry and cream soup. Spread over chicken and vegetables. Dot with paprika. Cover with foil and bake at 350° for.at least 1 hour 15 minutes.

A Southern Lady's Spirit

Chicken Croquettes

SAUCE:

4 tablespoons butter	½ cup heavy cream
4 tablespoons flour	Curry powder to taste
1½ cups chicken stock	Salt and pepper to taste

Melt the butter in a small heavy saucepan. Stir in the flour. Blend well, cooking slowly over low heat. Slowly stir in the chicken stock and the cream. Stirring constantly, bring the mixture slowly to a boil and cook for about 2 minutes or until the sauce has thickened. Season the sauce to taste with the curry powder and the salt and pepper. Cool one cup of the sauce and hold the remaining one cup warm (covered).

2 cups chicken (cooked, chopped)	¼ teaspoon onion juice
½ teaspoon salt	1 teaspoon parsley (fresh chopped)
¼ teaspoon celery salt	2 eggs (beaten)
Cayenne pepper to taste	½ cup bread crumbs
1 teaspoon lemon juice	

Mix together the chicken, the salt, the celery salt, the pepper, the lemon juice, the onion juice, the parsley, and enough of the cooled sauce to keep the mixture soft but stiff enough to hold its shape. Chill the mixture; then shape into 8 croquettes. Heat vegetable oil to 375° to 385°. Dip the croquettes into the beaten eggs, roll them in bread crumbs, and then fry them for 2–4 minutes. Serve the croquettes with the hot cream sauce. Serves 4.

The Great Chefs of Virginia Cookbook

Raspberry Chicken

This is an elegant, different luncheon dish. The ladies groups love it. (Men do, too!)

6 whole chicken breasts,
  divided to make 12 servings
Flour
½ cup clarified butter or oil
4 tablespoons butter
1 medium onion, minced
½ cup canned diced tomatoes

¼ cup raspberry vinegar
  (or tarragon vinegar)
2 tablespoons crème de cassis
1½ cups heavy cream
2 (10-ounce) boxes frozen
  red raspberries, thawed
Salt and pepper to taste

In a large frying pan, sauté chicken breasts which have been lightly dredged in flour, in butter or oil, until light brown. Cover and cook 12–15 minutes until chicken breasts are cooked through; check to make sure when pricked with a fork that the juices run clear. Do not overcook.

Sauté the onion in 4 tablespoons butter until melted. Add rest of ingredients. Boil down until desired consistency and flavors have mingled. Adjust seasonings (a little lemon juice can be added just before serving). The taste should be a sweet-tart flavor.

Cooking with Heart in Hand

Zesty Deviled Chicken

3 tablespoons butter or
  margarine
1 cup dry bread crumbs
1 teaspoon sugar
1 teaspoon paprika

¼ teaspoon onion powder
1 egg, beaten
¼ cup prepared mustard
1 (2½- to 3-pound) broiler-fryer,
  cut up and skinned

Melt butter in a 12x8x2-inch baking dish. Set aside. Combine bread crumbs, sugar, paprika, and onion powder in a shallow dish. Combine egg and mustard; brush evenly on chicken. Coat chicken with bread crumb mixture and place in prepared dish. Bake at 400° for 25 minutes; turn chicken in baking dish. Bake an additional 20 minutes. Yields 4 servings.

WYVE's Cookbook/Photo Album

Chicken, Sausage and Wild Rice

1 pound pork sausage
1 pound sliced mushrooms
2 medium large onions, sliced
1 (2½- to 3-pound) chicken,
  cooked, boned and cut in
  bite-size chunks
2 cups wild rice*
¼ cup flour

½ cup heavy cream
2½ cups chicken broth
1 teaspoon monosodium
  glutamate
Pinch each of oregano, thyme
  and marjoram
1 tablespoon salt
⅛ teaspoon pepper

Sauté sausage and set meat aside. In fat, sauté mushrooms and onions; add sausage and chicken. Cook wild rice according to package directions. Mix flour with heavy cream until smooth; add chicken broth and cook until thickened. Add seasonings and combine with rice, sausage, chicken, and vegetables. Put in baking dish and bake 25–30 minutes in 350° oven. Serves 10–12.

*You may substitute 1 box Uncle Ben's Wild Rice and eliminate monosodium glutamate and herbs.

The Stuffed Cougar

Favorite Chicken Casserole

A real favorite of everyone and so easy to prepare.

2 cups diced, cooked chicken
  [1 (3-pound) chicken]
1 can cream of chicken soup
½ cup milk
1–1¼ cups chicken broth
½ cup chopped celery
¼ cup chopped onion

1 egg, beaten
½ bag (2 cups) Pepperidge
  Farm herb stuffing
1 tablespoon parsley flakes,
  optional
Paprika

Spread chicken in bottom of a 2-quart flat casserole dish. Dilute soup with milk. Pour over top of chicken. Cook celery and onion in broth until tender (if you don't have broth, substitute 1 cup water with ½ stick butter and 1 chicken bouillon cube). Make dressing by combining broth, celery, onion, egg, stuffing, and parsley flakes. Spread dressing on top of soup. Sprinkle with paprika. Bake at 350° for 35–40 minutes or until bubbly and brown.

Granny's Kitchen

Martha Washington's To Make A Frykecy
Original receipt by Martha Washington

Take 2 Chicken, or a hare, kill & flaw [skin] them hot. take out theyr intrills & wipe them within, cut them in pieces & break theyr bones with A pestle. Y(n) put halfe a pound of butter into y(e) frying pan, & fry it till it be browne, y(n) put in y(e) Chiken & give it a walme [boil] or two. Y(n) put in halfe a pinte of faire water well seasoned with pepper, & salt, & a little after put in a handfull of parsley, & time, & an ounion shread all smal. fry all these together till they be enough, & when it is ready to be dished up, put into y(e) pan y(e) youlks of 5 or 6 eggs, well beaten & mixed w(th) A little wine vinegar or juice of leamons. stir thes well together least it Curdle, y(n) dish it up without any more frying.

Though Martha Washington's receipt is used here as an early example of chicken fricassee, the one given below has been adapted for modern use from a combination of Colonial recipes. Serves 6–8.

½ cup unsalted butter	¼ teaspoon pepper
1–2 tablespoons lard	1 teaspoon thyme
8 large chicken breast halves,	1 teaspoon marjoram
or a combination of breasts	1 teaspoon rosemary
and thighs	¼ teaspoon ground cloves
4–5 cups chicken stock, or	3 egg yolks, slightly beaten
as needed	¼ cup minced fresh parsley
1 large onion, chopped	1 tablespoon lemon juice
1 teaspoon salt	

HEARTH:

1. In a large spider or Dutch oven over hot coals, melt butter and lard. Add chicken and sauté until golden brown. Barely cover with stock; add onion and seasonings.
2. Cover pan and bring stock to simmer. Maintain heat by replenishing coals until chicken is tender, about 45 minutes. Remove chicken to heated platter and place near edge of fire to keep warm.
3. Measure stock; there should be 3–3½ cups (see note at end of recipe). Gradually add ½ cup hot stock to egg yolks, stirring constantly to prevent eggs from curdling. Return mixture to rest of stock and toss in parsley. Correct seasoning and allow sauce to simmer briefly, stirring all the while. Blend in lemon juice. Pour sauce over chicken and serve.

CONTINUED

MODERN:
1. One tablespoon cooking oil may replace lard if desired.
2. Brown chicken over medium high heat and, after adding stock, bring it to a boil, reduce heat, cover pan, and allow to simmer until chicken is fork-tender, about 30–40 minutes.
3. Recipe can be prepared ahead of time up to this point. When ready to serve, reheat slowly, until sauce bubbles and chicken is heated through. Proceed, following hearth direction 3.

Note: If you end up with only 2 cups broth, use only 2 yolks. The rule of thumb here is 1 yolk per 1 cup liquid. The liaison of egg yolks, seasoned broth, and lemon juice results in a delicious, elegant sauce.

Hearthside Cooking

Mushrooms and Chicken Livers in Wine

1½ pounds fresh mushrooms, sliced
½ cup butter or margarine
¾ cup chopped green onions
3 (8-ounce) packages frozen chicken livers, thawed
½ cup dry red wine
1 tablespoon soy sauce
2 teaspoons cornstarch
Dash of pepper

Cook mushrooms in ¼ cup butter in a 12-inch skillet, stirring frequently, until tender. Remove from skillet with juices and reserve. In same skillet, cook onion in remaining ¼ cup butter until almost tender. Cut chicken livers in half and add to onion. Cook, stirring carefully, until livers are tender. Return mushrooms to skillet.

Blend wine and soy sauce into cornstarch and pepper. Stir into livers and mushrooms. Cook and stir until mixture thickens and bubbles. Serve in chafing dish. Garnish with thinly sliced green onion tops. Serves 12.

Kitchen Keys

Southern Cornbread Chicken Sandwich

1 baked hen or 8 baked
 boneless chicken breasts, sliced

BREAD:

2 cups cornmeal
½ teaspoon baking soda
1 cup buttermilk
1 teaspoon salt

2 eggs, beaten
1 teaspoon baking powder
6 tablespoons melted shortening

Combine bread ingredients; thin with sweet milk, if necessary. Bake in greased iron skillet at 400° for 20 minutes. Cut into squares.

SAUCE:

2 tablespoons minced onion
2 tablespoons minced celery
½ cup butter
4 tablespoons flour

3 cups strong chicken broth
¾ cup cream
Salt and pepper to taste

Brown onion and celery in butter to a light golden color. Add remaining ingredients and cook until sauce thickens.

To assemble, put slices of chicken between 2 slices of cornbread and cover with sauce. Preparation: 1 hour. Serves 8. This recipe can easily be doubled. It is very rich. A salad is all you need to accompany this dish. Any recipe for good cornbread can be used.

Virginia Seasons

Hot Peanutty Chicken Salad

¾ cup peanuts, chopped
2½ cups cooked and chopped
  chicken
¼ cup chopped green pepper
¼ cup chopped onion
1½ cups cooked rice

¾ cup mayonnaise
1 (3-ounce) can mushrooms,
  drained
2 cans cream of mushroom soup
1 cup shredded Cheddar cheese
Salt and pepper

Reserve ¼ cup peanuts. Mix remaining ingredients thoroughly. Turn into a 2-quart casserole. Sprinkle with reserved peanuts. Bake at 400° for 30–40 minutes or until hot and bubbly. Serves 6–8.

Gourmet by the Bay

Chicken Oriental and Bean Sprouts

1 tablespoon oil
1 pound chicken, white meat
  (cut into one-inch cubes)
1 can bean sprouts
1 can water chestnuts, drained
1 stalk celery, diced

1 small can mushrooms, not
  drained
¼ cup soy sauce
¼ cup water
1 tablespoon cornstarch
3 small onions

In skillet place oil and heat; put chicken in, stirring constantly (approximately 4–5 minutes), until chicken is white and completely cooked. Add bean sprouts, water chestnuts, diced celery, and mushrooms. Mix soy sauce, water, cornstarch in separate container, then pour in frying pan, stirring throughout chicken mixture, then simmer for approximately 15 minutes. Dice onions into ½-inch cubes and put in frying pan with other ingredients, then cover and simmer for another 10 minutes. Serve over hot cooked rice.

WYVE's Bicentennial Cookbook

Pheasant Smithfield

1 young pheasant
½ cup cooked wild rice
1 slice Smithfield ham

Cointreau
2 ounces Perigoudine Sauce

Bone pheasant breast and stuff with wild rice. Shape breast and hold with piece of foil around the bottom. Secure legs with toothpick. Roast in 350° oven for 1 hour. Serve on slice of ham. Sprinkle Cointreau over pheasant, and mask with Perigoudine Sauce (a basic Madeira sauce with chopped truffles). Serves 1. (Courtesy of The Williamsburg Inn.)

Virginia Hospitality

Quail, Stuffed and Baked

Clean and wash birds thoroughly; be sure all shot and hidden feathers are removed; make a stuffing of bread crumbs, chopped celery, boiled chestnuts, butter, pepper, and salt; moisten all with a little hot water and stuff the birds; lay a thin slice of bacon on the top of each one; baste them while cooking with a little melted butter; serve hot with tossed salad.

Chesapeake Bay Country

Seafood

The Waterside festival marketplace and one of the "tall ships" that sails in the Norfolk Harbor.

Sautéed Mountain Trout Homestead

A traditional Homestead favorite, this is a simple and delicious way to prepare any delicate fish and protect its flavor. Use only fresh trout—ours come from nearby Allegheny streams. If you have a rushing mountain stream nearby and can catch your own, your reward will be doubled.

6 fresh trout, weighing 10–12 ounces each before boning	½ cup half-and-half
	Salt
1 tablespoon chopped fresh parsley	Freshly ground white pepper
	1 cup flour
Juice of 3 lemons	¼–½ cup peanut oil
½ cup canned or peeled fresh grapes (4–5 per serving)	6 tablespoons butter
	6 lemon wedges
⅓ cup sliced blanched almonds	Sprigs of fresh parsley or dill

Recommended equipment: A boning knife, small mixing bowl, waxed paper (or plate), small chefs knife, 12-inch sauté pan, turning spatula, paper towels, serving platter (or plates).

One by one, rinse the trout thoroughly under cold running water and then, using the boning knife, butterfly them: split the trout open along the belly, leaving the halves attached along the back, and carefully remove the entrails, all bones (including the backbone), the head, and gills. Do not remove the skin. Then trim away about ¼ inch along the belly flaps.

Rinse the parsley, spin or pat dry, chop, and reserve. Juice the lemons. Prepare the grapes and, if you wish, toast the almonds. (Preheat oven to 250° and toast the almonds on a pan until they are golden brown. When they are done, remove them from the oven and reserve.)

Mix the half-and-half in the small bowl with some salt and pepper, spread the flour on the waxed paper (or plate), and holding the butter-fly fillets carefully, dip them one by one into the cream, being sure to coat both sides. Let any excess cream drip off and then place fillets on the flour; pat lightly into flour, turn over and repeat with the other side; remove, and shake gently to dislodge the excess flour. (Do this just before you are ready to sauté the fillets; otherwise they will be pasty.)

Set the sauté pan over high heat, pour in oil to a depth of ⅛ inch, and when the oil is hot, put the trout into it skin side up. It is impor-tant not to crowd the pan. Cook fillets in separate batches as necessary, changing the oil after the first two. When the trout starts to sizzle,

CONTINUED

reduce heat to medium high and sauté for 3 minutes. Turn fillet over and, after sizzling starts, sauté for 2 minutes. Remove to paper towels to drain and then place on warm serving platter (or plates).

When all fillets are cooked, pour oil from pan and wipe out. Add butter and set over medium heat. Shake pan gently to swirl butter around as it melts until it begins to turn light golden brown. When this happens, add the lemon juice immediately to prevent the butter from browning any further. (The butter at this stage is "beurre noisette" and has a nutlike flavor.) Stir in the parsley, almonds, and grapes, remove from heat, and pour sauce over the fish. Garnish with sprigs of parsley (or dill) and lemon wedges and serve at once. Yields 6 servings.

Dining at the Homestead

Baked Haddock à la Grecque

2 tablespoons olive oil
1 large onion, chopped
2 garlic cloves, chopped
1 (16-oumce) can tomatoes
4 tablespoons chopped fresh
    parsley
1 teaspoon salt or ⅓ cup
    white wine
Pepper to taste

1 cup water
3 stalks celery, chopped
3 carrots, sliced thinly
1 box frozen spinach, thawed
    and drained well
2 pounds haddock, fresh or
    frozen (thawed)*
1 lemon, sliced

Heat oil in a pot. Sauté onion and garlic until soft. Squeeze tomatoes into a bowl; cut into small pieces. Add to pot with spices, salt or wine, pepper, water, celery and carrots. Cook uncovered 15–20 minutes, or until vegetables are tender.

Remove from heat, add drained spinach and mix well. Pour vegetable mixture into baking dish that will accommodate the fish. Place fish on top. Arrange lemon slices around fish. Bake 35 minutes in 400° oven or until fish is tender and flaky. Serve over cooked rice.

*Any fish may be substituted for haddock. If using shrimp, reduce baking time to 15–20 minutes.

Command Performance

Atlantic Stuffed Flounder Supreme

24 Ritz Crackers
4 tablespoons butter
Tabasco sauce to taste
Garlic powder to taste
3 onions
1 bell pepper
6 mushrooms

½ cup water
2 tablespoons vegetable oil
1 (8-ounce) package cream cheese
8 slices toast
2 pounds flounder fillets
1 lemon

Topping:
Crumble the Ritz Crackers by hand or with a food processor. Melt the butter and stir into the crackers. Season well with Tabasco sauce and garlic powder, and stir.

Stuffing:
Slice the onions, bell pepper, and mushrooms and place in a skillet. Add water and boil until most of the water is gone and the vegetables begin to stick to the surface of the pan. Reduce heat, add vegetable oil, and stir-fry until the vegetables have browned. Turn off the heat, add the cream cheese, and stir until well mixed. Slice or tear the toast into pieces, add to the pan, and stir until well mixed. Preheat oven to 425°. Grease an 8x12-inch pan and spread the stuffing evenly upon it. Layer the flounder fillets over the stuffing. Sprinkle the topping evenly over the fillets. Bake for 20 minutes or until the topping begins to brown. Putting the pan under the broiler very briefly will result in a nicely browned top. Serve with lemon wedges as an entrée or as a meal-in-itself. Other fish may be substituted for the flounder. Do not over-cook! Yields 4 servings.

The Great Taste of Virginia Seafood

Red Snapper with Artichoke Lemon Sauce

¼ cup marinated artichoke
  hearts, drained
1 tablespoon capers, drained
1 tablespoon minced fresh
  mint leaves
¼ teaspoon minced garlic
1 tablespoon chicken broth
1 large egg yolk, room
  temperature

1 tablespoon fresh lemon juice
¼ cup olive oil, plus additional
  for coating fish
6 (6 to 7 ounces each) red snapper
  fillets with skin
Salt and pepper to taste
6 thin lemon slices, quartered
6 mint sprigs, garnish

In a blender, purée the first 7 ingredients, scraping down the sides with a rubber spatula. With the motor running, add ¼ cup oil in a stream, blending the sauce until it is smooth; add salt and pepper. Sauce will improve if made a day ahead. Keep covered and chilled in refrigerator.

Rub fillets with additional oil; salt and pepper to taste. Wrap each fillet, skin-side-up, in a sheet of foil; grill the fillets on a rack set 2 inches over glowing coals for 7 minutes, or until they just flake. Unwrap the foil and place each fillet, skin-side-up, on a platter. Spoon the sauce around the fillets and garnish with the lemon quarters and mint. Yields 6 servings.

Variation: The fillets may be baked in the same manner. Place on a baking sheet in a preheated 450° oven for 8 minutes.

Cardinal Cuisine

The Chesapeake Bay-Bridge Tunnel connects the mainland to the Eastern shore, a slender finger of land separating the Atlantic Ocean from the Chesapeake Bay. Requiring 3½ years and the construction of four man-made islands, the tunnel (17.6 miles) is the world's largest bridge-tunnel complex.

Crispy Potato Cakes with Irish Smoked Salmon, Leeks, and Cream

1 large leek, white part only,
  cleaned and cut into thin
  strips 1¼ inches long
3 cups heavy cream
Salt and pepper to season

6 (5-ounce) Crispy Potato
  Cakes (see below)
1 cup clarified butter
¼ pound smoked salmon, cut
  into ¼-inch cubes

Equipment: 5-quart saucepan, tongs or slotted spoon, two stainless-steel bowls, cutting board, French knife, two 2½-quart saucepans, medium-gauge strainer, paring knife, mandolin, whisk, two baking sheets with sides, film wrap, stainless-steel ladle, two nonstick sauté pans (one large), rubber spatula, metal spatula.

Blanch the leek strips in boiling salted water until tender but still slightly crunchy, 45 seconds to 1 minute. Pour the leeks into a strainer and place the strainer in ice water. When the leeks are cold, drain thoroughly, cover with film wrap, and refrigerate until needed.

Heat the cream in a 2½-quart saucepan over medium heat. Season lightly with salt and pepper. When the cream begins to simmer, lower the heat so the cream will continue to simmer slowly, but not boil. Place a stainless-steel ladle in the saucepan with the cream and occasionally stir the cream to keep it from foaming out of the saucepan. Simmer until it has reduced by half, about 45–50 minutes.

Preheat the oven to 350°. When the cream is almost ready, begin to fry the potato cakes.

Strain the reduced cream into a separate nonstick sauté pan. Add the leeks and smoked salmon and bring to a simmer. When the potato cakes are hot, ladle equal portions of the cream mixture onto each of 6 warm plates. Place a hot cake in the center of each and serve immediately.

CRISPY POTATO CAKES:

3 pounds Idaho baking
  potatoes
Salt and pepper to season

1 egg, lightly beaten
1 cup clarified butter

Cook the unpeeled potatoes in boiling salted water for 35 minutes. Drain the potatoes and transfer to a stainless-steel bowl. Cool under slowly under running water for 10 minutes. When potatoes are cool, drain and refrigerate for 25–30 minutes.

Peel the cooled potatoes and cut into strips ⅛ inch by ⅜ inch using

CONTINUED

a mandolin or a French knife. Place the strips in a stainless-steel bowl and season with salt and pepper. Add the beaten egg to the potatoes and gently combine by hand. Divide into the desired number of portions. Form the portions into ¾-inch-high cakes. Transfer the cakes to a baking sheet.

Preheat the oven to 350°. When the cream is almost ready, begin to fry the potato cakes. Heat ½ cup clarified butter in a large nonstick sauté pan over medium-high heat. When hot, fry 3 or 4 potato cakes until evenly golden brown, 3½–4 minutes on each side. Transfer to a baking sheet and hold at room temperature. Discard any remaining butter from the pan, wipe the pan dry, and repeat the cooking procedure with the remaining 3 or 4 cakes. When all the cakes have been fried, place the baking sheet in the preheated oven for 10 minutes. Serve hot and crispy. Yields 6 (5-ounce) cakes or 8 (4-ounce) cakes.

The Chef's Touch: These cakes are terrific as a side dish, appetizer, or as the centerpiece for a main course. Serve them hot and crispy on the outside and warm and moist on the inside!

After 35 minutes of boiling, the potatoes will be properly cooked. They should still be slightly firm; otherwise, they will not cut well and will lose the textural quality needed to form attractive potato cakes.

Uncooked potato cakes may be kept refrigerated, covered, for up to twenty-four hours before cooking.

The Trellis Cookbook

Suprêmes de Saumon Amoureuse
Fillets of Salmon with Pernod and Tarragon Sauce

Invented by a Dr. Ordinaire, a Frenchman living in Couvet, Switzerland, the formula for absinthe liqueur was sold to a M. Pernod in 1791. French soldiers returning from Algeria in the 1850s contributed to its popularity, and by the turn of the century "la Verte" was virtually the apéritif national. *However, by this time, it was clear that wormwood, its main ingredient, was responsible for much more than the amorous and euphoric moods attributed to it. In 1915 it was outlawed and replaced by* pastis *and the Pernod called for here. A handsome entrée, this dish is particularly stunning when each serving is garnished with fresh tarragon sprigs, two or three lightly blanched fresh Snow Peas, and a cooked, peeled shrimp. Boiled Ponimes de Terre Parisienne are the perfect companion for this salmon. Small portions of the fish alone make a superb first course for a special dinner.*

1 tablespoon finely chopped shallots	3 cups whipped cream
2–2¼ pounds boned and skinned fresh salmon fillets (5–6 ounces per serving)	1½ tablespoons lobster base (for live lobster see Note)
	1 tablespoon Pernod
Salt	Dash of cayenne pepper
Freshly ground white pepper	1 tablespoon chopped fresh parsley
½ cup dry white wine	Butter for the baking dish
2 sprigs fresh tarragon	and waxed paper

Recommended equipment: A large chefs knife, enameled cast-iron baking dish or lined copper plat à sautér, waxed paper or aluminum foil, 4-quart saucepan, wire whisk, fine-mesh sieve, double boiler.

Preheat oven to 325°. Butter the baking dish or plat à sauter. Using the chefs knife, mince the shallots and strew them in the baking dish. Rinse the salmon fillets gently under cold water, drain, and pat dry. Season them lightly with salt and pepper and lay them in the dish. Pour the wine around the fillets, cover loosely with buttered waxed paper (or buttered foil), bring to a low simmer over medium heat, then place on middle rack in preheated oven. Bake for 8–10 minutes (thin fillets cook quickly) or until fish just comes apart when pulled with a fork.

While the fish is baking, rinse and dry the fresh tarragon; remove the leaves, chop, and reserve them. Put the stems and pieces into the saucepan with the cream, lobster base, and Pernod. When the fish is done, remove from oven and reserve, covered loosely with the waxed paper so the steam may escape. Set the saucepan over medium heat,

CONTINUED

bring to a boil, stirring occasionally with the whisk, reduce heat to a low simmer, add cooking liquid from the baking dish, and reduce by one-half (or until the sauce coats a wooden spoon, about 10 minutes).

Next, strain sauce through the sieve into a clean saucepan. Add the chopped tarragon leaves (or dried tarragon), simmer 1 minute, and adjust seasoning with salt, pepper, and a dash or two of cayenne. Chop the parsley and stir it into the sauce. (If you are not quite ready to serve, pour sauce into a double boiler to keep warm and coat the surface with dots of butter to prevent the formation of a skin layer.)

When ready to serve, heat the salmon for 1 minute in the oven, put on warm serving plates, spoon the sauce over the fillets, and garnish as you wish. Serve immediately. Yields 6 servings.

Note: Lobster base is available in specialty food shops, but to give the eye and palate a real treat, try fresh lobster. If using fresh lobster, get one that weighs 1 to 1¼ pounds. Separate the tail from the body. Cut the tail crosswise into three pieces and bake in the same pan with the salmon. Crush the body and claws and cook in 1 tablespoon of olive oil in a hot sauté pan, stirring occasionally, until the shells turn red. Then add ¼ cup dry white wine and simmer over medium heat for 3 minutes. When you are ready to reduce the cream sauce, add contents of the sauté pan to the saucepan.

The rich flavor created by using fresh lobster is enhanced by the luxurious garnish it provides. Slice the tail meat into medallions (after removing the shell) and decorate the fillets with this delightful delicacy.

Dining at the Homestead

Virginia is one of four states designated as a commonwealth. Three other states, Kentucky, Massachusetts, and Pennsylvania, chose to be called commonwealths after independence from Great Britain.

Salmon Steaks in Lemon/Dill Sauce
(Microwave)

1 pound salmon steaks, cut
  1 inch thick
1 tablespoon butter

1 tablespoon fresh lemon juice
¼ teaspoon dill
1 lemon, sliced thin

Place salmon steaks in a microwave-safe dish that has been lined with paper towels. Cover with a paper towel and microwave on HIGH 3½–4½ minutes (rotate dish once) or until salmon flakes apart with ease. Remove steaks from oven and set aside. In a 1-cup glass measuring cup, microwave butter on HIGH setting 30–45 seconds or until butter is melted. Stir in lemon juice and dill. Place steaks on serving platter and spoon sauce over all. Garnish with lemon slices. Serves 4.

Historic Lexington Cooks

Bluefish, Onions and Parmesan

3 small onions, sliced thinly
  into rings
2 tablespoons butter, unsalted
4 (½-pound) bluefish fillets
½ cup mayonnaise, divided
  (homemade would be nice)

½ cup freshly grated
  Parmesan cheese
½ cup fine bread crumbs
Salt
Pepper, freshly grated

Sauté onions in butter until brown and tender. Oil broiler pan rack (or spread heavy-duty foil on rack and oil it). Arrange fillets skin-side-down and season with salt and pepper. Spread each fillet with 1 tablespoon of mayonnaise and broil 4 inches under preheated broiler for 3 minutes. Divide onions among fillets; spread remaining ¼ cup mayonnaise over them. Sprinkle with mixture of Parmesan cheese and bread crumbs. Broil 2–3 minutes, or until they flake when tested with fork and top is golden brown. Remove with large spatula. Serves 4.

Virginia Seasons

Poached Cod Steaks with Hot Mayonnaise

COD:

4 cod steaks, about 1½
   inches thick and about ¾
   pound each
Approximately 6 cups water
¼ cup milk

1 bay leaf
4 sprigs parsley
Salt, if desfred
20 peppercorns

Place steaks in pan large enough to hold in single layer. Add water, milk, bay leaf, parsley, salt, and peppercorns. If liquid doesn't cover fish, add water until it does. Bring to simmer and cover. Let simmer 3 or 4 minutes or until fish flakes easily when tested with fork. Take care not to overcook or fish will toughen and become dry. Drain, remove bay leaf and serve with Hot Mayonnaise.

HOT MAYONNAISE:

1 egg, separated
1 tablespoon Dijon mustard
1 tablespoon white wine vinegar
Salt, if desired

Freshly ground pepper to taste
1 cup corn oil or other
   polyunsaturated vegetable oil
1 teaspoon finely minced garlic

Put 1 inch of water in skillet large enough to hold mixing bowl. Bring to boil and remove from heat. With mixing bowl in water, add yolk, mustard, vinegar, salt, and pepper. Gradually add oil, beating briskly with whisk. Continue beating until all oil is used and mixture is thickened and smooth. As you beat, the mixture should become slightly hotter than lukewarm. Beat egg white until stiff and fold in. Let stand in hot water, stirring until thoroughly hot without cooking. Stir in garlic. Serve this meal with carrots and potatoes with caraway. Serves 4.

Think Healthy

Assateague Island is famous for its miniature ponies that have roamed the barrier island for hundreds of years. In July the ponies make their annual swim across the channel to Chincoteague.

Sea Scallops Virginia

Sea Scallops Virginia was created in 1980 while Paul was a member of the 1980 American Culinary Team competing at the Culinary Olympics in Frankfurt, Germany. The recipe won a gold medal and many accolades for its wonderful flavor and incorporation of native Virginia products.

2 pounds large sea scallops	2 tablespoons butter or
4 tablespoons hot olive oil	margarine, melted and
2 firm ripe tomatoes,	divided
peeled, cored, seeded, and	4 ounces fully cooked smoked
chopped	Smithfield-style or other
2 sprigs of parsley, minced	cured ham, cut into a
1 tablespoon minced peeled	julienne (see Note)
shallots	2 medium leeks, cut into a
1 teaspoon minced peeled	julienne
garlic	

In a large heavy skillet, sauté scallops in olive oil, stirring frequently, until tender, opaque in color, and lightly browned, about 2–3 minutes. Do not overcook, as scallops become tough. Transfer scallops in skillet to a very, very slow oven (200°) to keep warm. In a small heavy skillet, sauté tomatoes, parsley, shallots, and garlic in 1 tablespoon butter over moderate heat until leeks are tender. Spoon ham mixture onto 4 dinner plates, dividing evenly. Arrange sautéed scallops over julienne ham and leeks, dividing evenly. Spoon a small amount of hot tomato sauce over each portion. Serve immediately. Yields 4–6 servings.

Note: To prepare a julienne, cut ham and leeks with a very sharp knife into very thin match-like strips.

More Richmond Receipts

Virginia is among the top ten wine-producing states in the country. From the Hunt Country to the Shenandoah Valley, there are forty licensed wineries.

Fresh Sea Scallops in White Wine Sauce

The Doniers own a cottage on the seashore and enjoy pairing seafood with wine. The delicate sauce and the flavor of the fresh sea scallops are enhanced by the rich flavor of Johannisberg Riesling. Served with a fresh spinach salad, this is a perfect summertime meal. Serve with Johannisberg Riesling.

1 large clove garlic, crushed	⅛ teaspoon white pepper
12 tablespoons butter	⅛ teaspoon paprika
1 pound fresh sea scallops	Salt to taste
3 teaspoons flour	½ pound thin vermicelli,
½ cup Johannisberg Riesling	cooked al dente
2 teaspoons minced parsley	

In a large skillet heat 6 tablespoons of butter and sauté garlic for a few minutes. Add scallops and stir; cook 3–4 minutes until tender. Remove scallops from pan and save butter and juices in a separate container. Melt the other 6 tablespoons butter in the same pan. Whisk in 3 teaspoons flour, stir and cook for 2–3 minutes. Add wine, parsley, seasonings, and juices from scallop cooking. Cook until thickened. Add more wine if too thick. Return scallops to sauce and heat. Serve over cooked vermicelli. Serves 4.

Virginia Wine Country

Simply Scrumptious Virginia Bay Scallops in Wine Sauce

¾ cup bread crumbs
¼ cup grated Parmesan cheese
4 tablespoons butter
2 tablespoons margarine
2 stalks celery, leaves removed, sliced
1½ medium onions, chopped
6 tablespoons flour
1 cup milk
½ cup white wine
4 ounces medium sharp Cheddar, sliced
1 pound Virginia bay scallops

Preheat oven to 350°. Prepare topping by combining bread crumbs and Parmesan cheese in a small bowl. Melt butter and margarine in a medium (2-quart) saucepan. Sauté celery and onions in melted butter and margarine. Blend in flour to make a paste; cook one full minute over medium heat. Gradually add milk, stirring after each addition. Stir wine into sauce. Add cheese and let it melt into sauce, stirring frequently. Fold in scallops. Pour into a greased 2-quart casserole dish. Sprinkle on topping. Bake for 20–30 minutes until bubbly. Serve over noodles or rice. Yields 5 servings.

The Great Taste of Virginia Seafood Cookbook

Shrimp Casserole Harpin

A buffet supper classic, this recipe brings back lots of memories.

2½ pounds large raw
  shrimp, shelled and deveined
1 tablespoon fresh, frozen
  or canned lemon juice
3 tablespoons salad oil
½ cup long-grain white rice
2 tablespoons butter
¼ cup minced green pepper
¼ cup minced onion
1 teaspoon salt

⅛ teaspoon pepper
Dash of cayenne pepper
⅛ teaspoon mace
1 (10¾-ounce) can condensed
  tomato soup, undiluted
1 cup heavy cream
½ cup sherry
¾ cup slivered blanched almonds

Early in the day, cook shrimp in salted boiling water for 5 minutes. Drain. Place in 2-quart casserole; sprinkle with lemon juice and salad oil. Meanwhile, cook rice as label directs. Drain. Refrigerate all.

About 1¼ hours before serving, start heating oven to 350°. Set aside about 8 shapely shrimp for garnish. In the butter in the skillet sauté green pepper and onion for 5 minutes. Add sautéed pepper and onion, with the rice, salt, pepper, cayenne pepper, mace, soup, cream, sherry and ½ cup almonds to shrimp in casserole. (This can be refrigerated.) Bake uncovered 35 minutes. Then top with ¼ cup almonds and 8 shrimp. Bake 20 minutes longer or until mixture is bubbly and shrimp are slightly browned. Makes 6–8 servings.

Historic Lexington Cooks

Blandford Church in historic Petersburg is one of only five buildings in the world where every window was designed by Louis Comfort Tiffany.

Seafood Brochettes

Chef David Jordan of the Virginia Museum in Richmond, Virginia, stated that when using Virginia's fine seafood, he prefers to keep the preparation simple, thereby enhancing the freshness, quality, and nutrients. This recipe, served at the 1983 Governor's Tasting, is simple to prepare, and will serve as an hors d'oeuvre or entrée, depending on the portions.

2 pounds flounder fillets   **Dry sherry as needed**
2 pounds bay or ocean scailops   **Juice of fresh lemon**
1 pound bacon   **Salt and pepper to taste**

Cut the flounder fillets into 1- to 2-inch pieces. Wash and drain scallops. Begin threading skewer: bacon, scallop, bacon, flounder, etc. Proceed to desired size, making sure the bacon intertwines each seafood piece. Marinate in sherry. Chill for several hours. Before cooking add juice of fresh lemon and a dash of salt and pepper. Broil under medium heat until bacon is well done. Do not overcook. Yields 10–12 servings.

The Great Taste of Virginia Seafood Cookbook

Deviled Eggs and Shrimp in Mornay Sauce

12 hard-boiled eggs
¼ teaspoon dry mustard
⅓ cup chopped parsley
½ cup mayonnaise

1½ cups small cooked shrimp
¾ cup freshly grated
  Parmesan cheese

Preheat oven to 350°. Cut eggs in half lengthwise and put yolks in a bowl. Thoroughly mash yolks and mix in mustard, parsley, and about ½ cup of mayonnaise or enough to make a smooth paste. Fill each egg white half with the yolk mixture. Place in buttered oven-proof serving dish and distribute shrimp evenly around eggs. Prepare sauce.

MORNAY SAUCE:

6 tablespoons butter
6 tablespoons flour
1 cup chicken broth

1 cup light or heavy cream
4 ounces Gruyère cheese, grated
1 tablespoon dry sherry to taste

Melt butter and stir in flour until well blended. Gradually add chicken broth and cream, stirring constantly. Cook over low heat, stirring until sauce is thickened and smooth. Add the Gruyère, and heat, stirring until cheese melts. Add sherry.

Spoon sauce over eggs and shrimp. Sprinkle with Parmesan cheese and heat for 15 minutes to warm thoroughly. Remove from oven and place under broiler for 3–4 minutes or until top is golden brown. Serves 6.

The Boar's Head Cookbook

Steeplechase racing in Virginia began when gentlemen in "pinks," after the fox hunt was over, had a friendly chase "to yon steeple." They cleared shrubbery and downed fences on their "natural course." Today steeplechasing is a spring family picnic affair surrounded by other outdoor activities.

Curry of Shrimp

⅓ cup butter or margarine
½ cup chopped onion
½ cup chopped green pepper
2 cloves garlic, minced
2 cups dairy sour cream
2 teaspoons lemon juice
4 teaspoons curry powder

¾ teaspoon salt
½ teaspoon ginger
Dash of chili powder
Dash of pepper
3 cups cleaned, cooked shrimp,
   split lengthwise (about 2 pounds
   in shell)

Melt butter; add onion, green pepper, and garlic. Cook until tender but not brown. Stir in sour cream, lemon juice, and seasonings. Add shrimp. Cook over low heat, stirring constantly, just until hot through. (Sauce is traditionally thin.) Serve over hot rice or yellow rice (recipe below.) Offer condiments such as coconut, chopped peanuts, raisins, chutney. Makes 6 servings.

YELLOW RICE:
2 cups boiling water
1 teaspoon salt

15 grains saffron
1 cup uncooked rice

To boiling water add salt and saffron. Stir in rice. Return to boil, reduce heat to low, cover and cook until tender, about 25 minutes. Makes 3 cups.

A Southern Lady's Spirit

Ice House's Shrimp Scampi

4 teaspoons butter
2 ounces oil (olive or peanut)
2–3 garlic cloves, sliced
1 pound medium shrimp,
   shelled
½ teaspoon lemon juice
½ medium onion, chopped

1 tomato, chopped
½ green pepper, chopped
1 teaspoon black pepper
1 teaspoon salt
1 tablespoon fresh parsley
¼ cup white wine

In skillet, melt butter, add oil and sauté garlic lightly. Add shrimp, cooking until it turns pink and begins to curl. Add lemon juice, onion, tomato, green pepper, black pepper, salt, parsley and wine. Cook only a minute or so until tender. Remove shrimp and pour sauce from skillet over top. Serves 4.

Virginia's Historic Restaurants and Their Recipes

Shrimp Tetrazzini

4 tablespoons butter
2 medium onions, chopped (or about 3 tablespoons instant minced onion)
1 pound shelled deveined shrimp, fresh or frozen
1 pound fresh mushrooms, sliced
½ cup flour
½ cup mayonnaise
2 teaspoons salt

1 quart milk
½ cup sherry
1 (16-ounce) package thin spaghetti, cooked a minute or two less than the directions on the package call for, then drained
Grated Parmesan cheese
Shredded mozzarella cheese (optional)

Preheat oven to 350°. Melt butter in Dutch oven. Sauté onion until just tender. Add shrimp and mushrooms and cook, stirring frequently, until shrimp are just done. Remove from pan (along with liquid) and drain in colander. Blend flour and mayonnaise in pan; add salt, milk, and sherry. Cook until thickened, stirring as you would any cream sauce. Toss with shrimp and spaghetti and turn into 3-quart casserole. Top generously with cheeses. Bake for 30 minutes. Yields 8 servings.

Note: This can be fancied up further if you wish by adding a can or two of artichoke hearts, halved, or hearts of palm, sliced about ½-inch thick.

The Other Side of the House

Crab Quiche Surprise

Crust for a 9-inch quiche pan
½ cup grated Swiss cheese
½ cup grated Cheddar
  cheese
1 tiny zucchini, peeled and
  sliced
1 tiny yellow squash, peeled
  and sliced
1 small onion, diced
1 tablespoon olive oil
3 ounces crabmeat
2 eggs
½ cup sour cream
Salt and pepper to taste
1 teaspoon parsley

Preheat oven to 350°. Mix cheese together and sprinkle ¾ cup in bottom of crust. Sauté zucchini, yellow squash, and onion in olive oil for 3 minutes (just to get them started). Spread crabmeat, zucchini, squash, and onion on top of cheese. Mix together eggs, sour cream, remaining cheese, salt, and pepper to taste and spread on top of quiche. Sprinkle the parsley on top. Bake for 35–40 minutes until set. Yields 9-inch pie.

The Great Taste of Virginia Seafood Cookbook

Crabmeat Casserole

2 tablespoons butter
3 tablespoons flour
1 cup milk
1 cup backfln crabmeat
2 hard-boiled eggs, chopped
1 tablespoon soft bread
   crumbs
¼ cup diced green peppers

1 teaspoon parsley
1 teaspoon dry mustard
1 teaspoon Worcestershire
   sauce
1 teaspoon salt
Dash of black pepper
Dash of cayenne pepper

Make cream sauce with butter, flour and milk. Add remaining ingredients, except bread crumbs, to slightly cool cream sauce. Put in buttered 1½-quart casserole dish. Cover with bread crumbs and dot with butter. Bake at 375° for 30–40 minutes. Serves 4.

Of Pots and Pipkins

Crab and Spinach Casserole

1 package frozen spinach,
   chopped
1 cup grated sharp cheese
¼ cup butter plus 2
   tablespoons butter, melted
2 tablespoons minced onion
2 tablespoons flour

1 cup milk
⅛ teaspoon curry powder
½ teaspoon salt
1 tablespoon lemon juice
1 pound crabmeat
½ cup bread crumbs

Cook spinach and drain well. Put in the bottom of a greased casserole dish. Sprinkle cheese over spinach. Melt ¼ cup butter and sauté onions until transparent. Melt the remaining 2 tablespoons of butter and stir in flour. Add milk, stirring constantly, until thickened. Add curry powder and salt. Stir lemon juice and crabmeat into sauce. Pour over spinach and cheese. Add bread crumbs on top. Bake at 350° for 30 minutes.

Gourmet by the Bay

Sherwood Forest Crabmeat Casserole

1 cup crabmeat (white)
2 cups bread crumbs
  (slightly toasted)
1 cup mayonnaise

½ cup milk
4 hard-boiled eggs, mashed
1 teaspoon onion, chopped
Tabasco, lemon juice and salt

Mix all ingredients. Put in greased casserole. Bake at 350° until bubbly.

The Virginia Presidential Homes Cookbook

Virginia's Crabmeat

1 pound backfin crabmeat
1 tablespoon horseradish
1 teaspoon grated lemon rind
½ teaspoon Ac'cent
Dash of hot sauce

1 tablespoon grated onion
1½ cups mayonnaise
¾ cup grated sharp Cheddar
   cheese

Mix the first 7 ingredients in baking dish. Sprinkle grated sharp Cheddar cheese on top and bake in 350° oven for 25 minutes. Serves 4.

The Boar's Head Cookbook

Crab Cakes

1 tablespoon butter
¼ cup minced green pepper
¼ cup minced onion
1 pound crabmeat
1 tablespoon Worcestershire
   sauce
2 tablespoons chopped
   pimiento

1 teaspoon hot pepper sauce
½ cup mayonnaise
1 teaspoon salt
2 tablespoons chopped parsley
1 egg, well beaten
Bread crumbs
Cracker meal

Sauté onion and pepper in butter until transparent. Add to crabmeat with all other ingredients except cracker meal. Add enough bread crumbs to make mixture stiff enough to shape into cakes. Coat each cake with cracker meal and fry over moderate heat in a heavy, well oiled skillet until browned. Makes 6 generous crab cakes.

Variation: For Crab Casserole, omit bread crumbs and turn mixture into greased casserole dish. Top with buttered bread crumbs. Bake at 350° for 30–45 minutes or until browned and bubbly.

The Smithfield Cookbook

Deviled Crab Morattico

2 tablespoons mayonnaise
  (Hellmann's preferred)
2 tablespoons prepared mustard
2 tablespoons vinegar

Dash of Worcestershire
Dash of Tabasco
Salt and pepper to taste
1 pound crabmeat

Mix all ingredients together, adding crabmeat last. Toss gently. Place in shells. Do not pack. Top with bread crumbs, paprika and a large pat of butter on each. Bake at 350° for 30 minutes. Makes 8 servings or 4 large servings for dinner.

The Rappahannock Seafood Cookbook

Oysters and Wild Rice

1 (6-ounce) box long-grain and
  wild rice, cooked
¼ pound butter, melted
4 dozen oysters, well drained
Salt and pepper to taste
Dash of Tabasco sauce
Sprinkle of celery seed
1 cup heavy cream

2 chicken bouillon cubes,
  dissolved in ¼ cup hot water
1 cup light cream
1 medium onion, finely chopped
¾ teaspoon thyme
1 tablespoon curry powder
  (optional)
Fresh chopped parsley

Preheat oven to 300°. Toss rice and butter until thoroughly mixed. Place half of rice in bottom of 13x9-inch baking dish. Layer oysters on top of rice and season with salt and pepper and Tabasco sauce. Top with remaining rice.

In heavy pan, add celery seed to heavy cream and heat; pour in chicken bouillon. Stir, then add light cream. Remove pan from heat and add remaining ingredients. Pour over casserole. Bake at 300° for 45 minutes. Garnish with chopped parsley.

Recipes from Jeffersonville Woman's Club

Baked Oysters with Crumbs & Garlic

2 tablespoons butter
1 cup fresh white bread crumbs
  (French or Pepperidge Farm
  bread, put in blender)
1 teaspoon finely chopped
  garlic

2 tablespoons finely chopped
  fresh parsley
2 dozen fresh oysters
3 tablespoons Parmesan cheese
2 tablespoons butter, cut in
  tiny pieces

Preheat oven to 450°. Butter oven-proof platter. Melt butter in small pan and add crumbs and garlic. Sauté until golden brown (2–3 minutes). Stir in parsley. Spread two-third crumbs in platter. Arrange oysters in one layer. Mix rest of crumbs with cheese, and spread over oysters. Dot with butter. Bake 12–15 minutes until bubbly.

A Southern Lady's Spirit

Clams Posillip

48 little neck or cherry stone clams	3 cups canned tomatoes
½ cup olive oil	1 (6-ounce) can tomato paste
2 cloves garlic, minced	Freshly ground pepper
2 dried, hot peppers	1 tablespoon dried oregano
½ cup dry white wine	¼ cup finely chopped parsley

Wash clams well and drain. Heat oil in large heavy skillet or casserole and add garlic and hot pepper. Cook briefly and add wine. Cook to reduce liquid by half. Add tomatoes and tomato paste. Add pepper to taste and oregano. Cover and bring to a boil. Cook for 15 minutes. Add clams and cover tightly. Cook until clams open (about 5–10 minutes). Sprinkle with chopped parsley. Serves 4. A hot pasta dish of your choice should accompany this dish.

The Rappahannock Seafood Cookbook

Although Chincoteague calls itself the "Clam Capital of the World," it first became known for its production of salt oysters. Chincoteague's history is highlighted in the Oyster Museum. Chincoteague's National Wildlife Refuge covers 9,460 acres and is a well-known retreat for hikers, bicyclists and nature lovers.

Cakes

The beautiful Rotunda of the University of Virginia at Charlottesville.

Almond Cake with Raspberry Sauce

A favorite recipe.

¾ cup sugar
½ cup unsalted butter, softened
8 ounces almond paste
3 eggs
1 tablespoon kirsch or

¼ teaspoon almond extract
¼ cup all-purpose flour
⅓ teaspoon baking powder
Powdered sugar
Sauce

Butter and flour 8-inch round pan. Combine sugar, butter, and almond paste in medium mixing bowl and blend well. Beat in eggs, liqueur, and almond extract. Add flour and baking powder, beating until just mixed through; do not overbeat. Bake at 350° until tester comes out clean, about 40–50 minutes. Let cool. Invert onto serving dish and dust lightly with powdered sugar.

SAUCE:

1 pint fresh raspberries or
  1 (12-ounce) package frozen,
  thawed

2 tablespoons sugar or to taste

Combine raspberries with sugar in processor or blender and purée. Gently press sauce through fine sieve to remove seeds. Serve cake on bed of sauce on individual dessert plates.

Note: Sugar can be omitted when using frozen raspberries.

Gourmet by the Bay

Almond Cold-Oven Cake

½ cup sliced almonds
1 cup butter
½ cup margarine
3 cups sugar
5 eggs

3 cups all-purpose flour
½ teaspoon baking powder
1 cup milk
1½ teaspoons almond extract

Grease and flour a 10-inch tube pan. Sprinkle sliced almonds on bottom of pan. Cream butter, margarine and sugar. Add eggs, one at a time, beating well after each addition.

Sift together flour and baking powder. Alternately add flour and milk to mixture. Beat well. Add extracts. Blend well. Pour into prepared tube pan. Place in a cold oven and bake at 350° for 1 hour and 30 minutes. Cool cake. Remove from pan. Yields one 10-inch tube cake.

Cardinal Cuisine

Virginia Cherry Filbert Cake

1½ cups butter, softened
2 cups sugar
6 eggs, separated
¾ cup milk
¼ cup cognac
3½ cups sifted flour

½ teaspoon cream of tartar
¼ teaspoon salt
3 cups toasted filberts, chopped
1 cup red candied cherries,
 halved
Confectioners' sugar

Preheat oven to 275°. Cream butter and gradually beat in sugar. Add egg yolks, one at a time, beating until light and fluffy. Combine milk and cognac, and add with flour to creamed mixture. Beat egg whites with cream of tartar and salt until stiff. Fold in the filberts and cherries, then fold egg whites into batter. Spoon into greased and waxed paper-lined tube pan and bake for 2 hours and 15 minutes. Peel off paper and sprinkle with confectioners' sugar. Cake keeps well; wrap well and store in a cool place.

Virginia Hospitality

Pecan Whiskey Cake

3 eggs (separated)
1 cup sugar
1 ounce butter (room
    temperature)
½ cup light brown sugar
1 pound cake flour

1 pound pecans
12 ounces golden raisins
½ teaspoon baking powder
½ teaspoon nutmeg
½ cup bourbon whiskey

Preheat oven to 250°. Beat the egg whites to soft peaks and set aside. Beat half of the sugar (½ cup) with the egg yolks and set aside. Cream the butter. Gradually beat the brown sugar and ¼ cup of the granulated sugar into the butter. Add the egg yolk mixture to the butter mixture and beat well. Mix half of the flour (1 cup) with the pecans and the raisins. Sift the rest of the flour together with the baking powder and the nutmeg. Add the sifted mixture to the butter mixture. Add the bourbon whiskey. Stir in the flour, nut, and raisin mixture. Gently fold in the reserved egg whites. Fill a buttered loaf pan with the mixture. Bake the cake for 2 hours or until done. Serves 6.

The Great Chefs of Virginia Cookbook

Riddick's Folly Tipsy Cake

This was always served for Christmas dinner at Riddick's Folly. There was a special Tipsy Cake platter and a cut glass pitcher for the sauce. Served by Mother from the table, this dessert was the glorious conclusion to a big family dinner!

2 quarts whole milk
6 eggs
Bourbon (for glow)
Sherry (for flavor)

1 large sponge cake
½ pound almonds (blanched)
1 pint cream (whipped)

Make custard (I make 1 quart with 3 eggs at at time). Cool, sweeten and flavor with bourbon and sherry to taste (about 1½ cups each). If the cake is round, slice through to make two layers. Place one layer on a large platter, pour a third sauce over, and sprinkle with half of the almonds. Repeat, saving a third of sauce for serving, and refrigerate.

At serving time, pile on the whipped cream and add additional sauce to each serving with wine jelly on the side if desired.

A Southern Lady's Spirit

Special Request Cake

1 yellow cake mix (Duncan
  Hines)
⅔ cup vegetable oil
4 eggs

½ cup brown sugar
1 cup sour cream
2 teaspoons maple flavoring

Put all ingredients into a large mixing bowl and beat until smooth and well blended. Divide batter into 3 (8-inch) cake pans that have been greased and floured. Bake in preheated oven at 350° for about 25–30 minutes. Remove from oven and cool on rack. Put fruit filling between layers and frost. Let sit for at least 24 hours before serving. Keep in refrigerator.

FILLING:

2 packages diced mixed dried
  fruit

½ cup brown sugar
½ cup orange or apple juice

Combine and cook slowly, until orange juice is absorbed and fruit is tender. May need to add a little more juice to cook fruit soft. Cool to lukewarm. Spread on cake layers.

FROSTING:

2 cans Pillsbury vanilla
  frosting

2 teaspoons maple flavoring

Add 1 teaspoon flavoring to each can of frosting; mix well. Frost sides and top of cake, and sprinkle frosting with chopped nuts, if desired. Cake may be frozen.

Taste of Goodness

Coconut Pound Cake

A grand holiday cake.

½ cup butter, softened
½ cup shortening
1 (8-ounce) package cream
  cheese, softened
3 cups sugar
6 large eggs, room temperature
3 cups all-purpose flour, sifted

¼ teaspoon baking soda
¼ teaspoon salt
1 (6-ounce) package frozen
  coconut, thawed
1 teaspoon vanilla extract
1 teaspoon coconut flavoring

Cream butter, shortening, and cream cheese. Gradually add sugar, beating at medium speed of electric mixer until light and fluffy. Add eggs one at a time. Beat 60 seconds after each addition.

Combine sifted flour, soda, and salt. Add to creamed mixture, stirring just until blended. Stir in coconut and flavorings. Spoon batter into greased and floured 10-inch tube pan. Bake at 350° in preheated oven. Bake 1 hour and 15 minutes. A wooden pick should come out clean when inserted. Cool in pan 10 minutes. Remove. Cool completely. Yields 1 (10-inch) cake. Can be frozen to be served later.

Keeping the Feast

Black Walnut Pound Cake

1 cup butter
½ cup shortening
3 cups sugar
5 eggs
2 teaspoons vanilla

1 teaspoon baking powder
3 cups flour
1 cup milk
1 cup black walnuts

Beat butter, shortening, and sugar together until fluffy. Add eggs, one at at time. Beat after each addition. Add vanilla. Add baking powder to flour. Start adding flour mixture alternating with milk. Add walnuts. Pour into greased and floured 10-inch tube pan. Bake at 325° for 1 hour and 10 minutes.

Cooking with Class

Million Dollar Pound Cake

6 eggs	¼ teaspoon salt
1 pound butter or margarine	1 teaspoon almond extract
1 cup sweet milk	4 cups flour
3 cups sugar	

Have eggs, butter, and milk at room temperature. Cream butter, sugar, and salt well. Add almond extract. Add eggs one at a time, beating really well. Add flour and milk a little at a time and beat well until batter is smooth. Grease a 10-inch tube pan well and dust with flour. Bake in a preheated 325° oven for 1 hour and 40 minutes. Test for doneness with a toothpick; when it comes out clean, the cake is done. (This is the best pound cake I've ever eaten, but it is a large cake and needs a large mixing bowl and a heavy-duty beater.)

CARAMEL ICING:

2 cups brown sugar	6 tablespoons butter
½ cup half-and-half cream	

Cook slowly in a heavy pan until it forms a soft ball when tested in water. Remove from heat and beat by hand until it starts creaming. This is a long, tiring process, but well worth the effort. If icing hardens before you are finished, you may add a little cream or milk to keep it spreadable. Serves 15–20.

The Best of the Bushel

Rum Pound Cake

This is the best recipe for pound cake that I have ever used.

3 cups sifted flour
½ teaspoon baking soda
1 cup butter, softened
3 cups sugar
5 large eggs

1 cup sour cream
3 tablespoons dark rum or
   rum flavoring
Sifted confectioners' sugar
   (optional)

Sift together the flour and baking soda. Cream butter until smooth. Add sugar gradually, beating well. Add eggs, one at a time, and continue beating until light and fluffy. Add dry ingredients to creamed mixture alternately with sour cream and rum, beginning and ending with dry ingredients, stirring until well blended after each addition. Spoon into a greased and floured 10-inch tube pan. Bake in a slow oven (300°) for 1 hour to 1 hour 15 minutes or until cake tester inserted in center comes out clean. Cool in pan for 10 minutes, then remove from pan and transfer to a wire rack, right side up, to finish cooling. Sprinkle with confectioners' sugar, if desired. One 10-inch tube cake.

Apron Strings

Sour Cream Pound Cake

½ pound butter
3 cups sugar
6 eggs
1 cup sour cream
3 cups all-purpose flour, sifted

¼ teaspoon baking soda
Pinch of salt
½ teaspoon almond extract
1 teaspoon vanilla

All ingredients should be at room temperature. Cream butter in large mixing bowl. Add sugar gradually, beating continually. Add 2 eggs, one at a time. Add sour cream. Add 4 eggs, one at a time. Scrape from sides and bottom of bowl; beat well. Sift together flour, soda, and salt and add to above mixture. Beat and beat, scraping often. Add almond and vanilla. Bake in greased and floured tube pan at 325° (preheated oven) for 1½ hours. This is a very moist cake, keeps well, and may be frozen.

Of Pots and Pipkins

Granny's Blueberry Pound Cake

A summer treat!

**2 sticks butter or
  margarine, softened**
2 cups sugar
4 eggs
1½ teaspoons vanilla

**1 pint blueberries, washed
  and drained well**
3 cups flour, divided
1 teaspoon baking powder
½ teaspoon salt

Preheat oven to 325°. Grease and flour a 10-inch tube pan. Use mixer to cream butter and sugar; add eggs one at a time. Beat well after each egg is added. Add vanilla and beat until fluffy.

Dredge berries with ¼ cup of flour and set aside. Sift remaining flour with baking powder and salt; fold into cake batter until well blended. Gently stir in berries. Pour into pan and bake for approximately 1 hour and 10 minutes or until cake tester, inserted near center, comes out clean. Place pan on rack and cool in pan for 10 minutes before removing from pan. Serves 12–16. This delicious cake is nice to take to picnics since it is easy to wrap and pack!

Note: Well-drained frozen or canned berries can be used.

Words Worth Eating

Dream Cheesecake

Allow one hour minimum preparation. This cheesecake tastes best when made at least one day before serving.

4 tablespoons butter or margarine, melted
1 cup fine graham cracker crumbs
1 teaspoon cream of tartar
6 eggs, separated
19 ounces cream cheese

1½ cups plus 3 tablespoons sugar
3 tablespoons flour
½ teaspoon salt
1 pint sour cream
1 teaspoon vanilla

Butter generously a 9-inch springform pan. Mix butter and crumbs well. Reserve ¼ cup of crumbs and press remainder firmly on bottom of pan. Add cream of tartar to egg whites and beat until stiff. Set aside. Beat cheese until soft in a separate bowl. Mix sugar, flour, and salt and gradually beat into cheese. Add egg yolks one at a time, beating thoroughly after each. Add sour cream and vanilla. Mix well. Fold in egg whites thoroughly. Pour mixture into prepared pan. Sprinkle with reserved crumbs. Bake in moderate oven at 325° for 1 hour and 15 minutes or until firm. Turn off heat and open oven door. Let cake stand in oven for 15 minutes. Remove and place on cake rack away from drafts. Refrigerate after cake comes to room temperature. Yields 8–10 servings.

Gourmet by the Bay

Raspberry Topped Cheesecake

1 package yellow cake mix
4 eggs
2 tablespoons oil
2 (8-ounce) packages cream
  cheese
½ cup sugar

1½ cups milk
3 tablespoons lemon juice
3 tablespoons vanilla
Fresh raspberries, frozen if
  necessary

Preheat oven to 300°. Reserve 1 cup dry cake mix. In large bowl, combine remaining cake mix, 1 egg, and oil. Blend thoroughly and press this crust into bottom and sides of a springform cake pan. Blend cream cheese and sugar. Add 3 eggs and 1 cup cake mix. Beat 1 minute at medium speed. At low speed, add milk and flavorings. Pour into crust. Bake 55–60 minutes. Chill before serving. Top with fresh raspberries. Serves 10–12.

The VIP Cookbook: A Potpourri of Virginia Cooking

Cheese Cake

1 (6-ounce) package zwieback
1⅔ cups sugar, divided
1 teaspoon cinnamon
½ cup margarine, melted
1 cup sour cream

½ pound cream cheese, softened
2 tablespoons lemon juice
1 teaspoon vanilla
¼ teaspoon salt
6 eggs, separated

Roll zwieback fine. Mix with 1 cup sugar, cinnamon and butter. Reserving ½ cup of mixture to sprinkle on top, spread the rest on sides and bottom of 9-inch springform pan. Mix together ½ cup sugar, sour cream, cream cheese, lemon juice, vanilla and salt. Add 6 well beaten egg yolks. Set aside.

Whip 6 egg whites with ⅙ cup sugar and add to the mixture. Pour into pan. Bake 50 minutes in a preheated 300° oven. Then turn to 275° for another 50 minutes. Cool before removing from pan.

Note: Zwieback can be found in the baby food department of the grocery store.

Recipes from Jeffersonville Woman's Club

Pinky's Cheddar Cheesecake

CRUST:

2 cups sifted flour
⅛ teaspoon salt
1 cup confectioners' sugar

1 cup butter or margarine,
   at room temperature
1 egg, slightly beaten

To prepare crust, combine flour, salt, and sugar in a bowl. Cut butter into dry ingredients and blend until a smooth ball is formed. With a fork, stir in egg. Lightly grease a 9-inch springform pan. Using a knife, spread crust mixture to a depth of ¼ inch over bottom of pan.

Bake in a moderate oven (350°) for 10 minutes, or until light golden in color. When pan has cooled, "frost" or spread sides of pan with ¼-inch layer of dough (do not bake). Place in refrigerator until ready to fill.

FILLING:

4 (8-ounce) packages cream
   cheese, at room temperature
1 cup finely grated mild
   Cheddar cheese, at room
   temperature
1¾ cups sugar
3 tablespoons flour

1 teaspoon lemon juice
1½ teaspoons grated
   orange peel (optional)
1 teaspoon vanilla extract
5 eggs plus 2 egg yolks
½ cup heavy cream

Increase oven temperature to very hot (450°). Prepare filling. In a large bowl, beat cheeses and sugar together until well blended and creamy. Add flour, lemon juice, orange peel, and vanilla. Beat at high speed just to blend. Add eggs and egg yolks, one at a time, beating just enough to blend thoroughly. Stir in cream and pour into prepared pan. Bake for 8 minutes. Reduce oven temperature to very slow (250°) and bake for 1 hour longer, or until set.

Note: Any remaining crust mixture may be spread into an 8-inch square pan. Spoon ¼–⅓ cup strawberry or raspberry preserves over crust. Bake in a moderate oven (350°) for 10 minutes. Cool for 5–7 minutes and cut into 1-inch squares.

Richmond Receipts

The Douglas MacArthur Memorial in Norfolk highlights the life and times of the famous general.

Chocolate Cheesecake

10 chocolate wafers,
  crumbled fine
1 tablespoon butter, melted
1 (15-ounce) container part
  skim-milk ricotta cheese
⅓ cup unsweetened cocoa
  powder
Pinch of salt

½ cup sugar, divided
1 envelope unflavored gelatin
½ cup low-fat (1%) milk
1 teaspoon vanilla extract
2 egg whites at room temperature
½ cup nondairy dessert topping

Preheat oven to 350°. In an 8-inch springform pan, combine chocolate wafer crumbs and butter; spread onto the bottom. Bake 5 minutes. Cool. In blender or food processor, purée ricotta with cocoa and salt until smooth; set aside. In small saucepan, combine ¼ cup sugar and gelatin; stir in milk and let stand 1 minute. Heat over medium-low heat, stirring constantly 5 minutes until gelatin is dissolved. Remove from heat. Add to ricotta mixture in blender and process until smooth. Blend in vanilla. Transfer to a bowl and refrigerate, stirring occasionally, until mixture mounds slightly when dropped from a spoon, 30–40 minutes.

In mixer bowl, beat egg whites until foamy. Gradually beat in remaining ¼ cup sugar until soft peaks form. Fold into ricotta mixture. Pour into prepared pan. Refrigerate until set, at least 4 hours or overnight. Remove sides of pan. Spoon topping into a pastry bag and decorate top of cake. Preparation time: 25 minutes plus chilling. Serves 12.

Think Healthy

Chocolate Mousse Cake

There is no flour in this cake because it is really a chocolate mousse that when baked turns into a rich, fudgy cake. If the cake is baked the day before and chilled thoroughly, it will be easier to unmold and slice. Serve with Riesling.

6 eggs	2 teaspoons vanilla extract
½ cup sugar	3 cups heavy cream
16 ounces semisweet chocolate	2 tablespoons sugar
¼ cup strong brewed coffee	1 tablespoon Grand Marnier
¼ cup Grand Marnier or	or dark rum
dark rum	Shaved chocolate

Put the eggs and sugar into a bowl and begin to beat on high speed. Continue beating for at least 5 minutes or until the mixture is thick and creamy.

Put the chocolate in the top of a double boiler. Add coffee and Grand Marnier or rum and melt until smooth. Remove from heat. Add vanilla and set aside.

Whip 1 cup of the cream until thick and stiff. Fold the chocolate into the beaten egg mixture and then gently fold in the whipped cream. Make sure the batter is well mixed and then pour it into a 9-inch spring-form pan.

Set the springform pan into a larger pan and fill the larger pan with about 2 inches of hot water. Bake the cake in a preheated 350° oven for 1 hour until the center of the cake seems firm to the touch.

When cake is done, remove it from the oven and carefully lift it out of the water bath. Set it on a rack to cool completely. Cover and chill at least 8 hours or overnight.

To serve the cake, whip the other 2 cups of cream with the 2 table-spoons of sugar and 1 tablespoon of Grand Marnier or rum. Whip until thick and stiff. Remove the cake from the refrigerator. Run a knife around the side, and gently release the sides of the springform pan. Invert the cake onto a serving platter and carefully lift off the bottom. Frost top and sides of cake with whipped cream. Decorate with shaved chocolate. Surround the cake with fresh fruit, if desired. Serves 8–10.

Virginia Wine Country

Chocolate Eclair Cake

4 (1-ounce) squares unsweetened
  chocolate, melted
½ cup boiling water
¼ cup sugar
2¼ cups cake flour, sifted
1½ cups sugar
3 teaspoons baking powder

1 teaspoon salt
½ cup vegetable oil
7 egg yolks
¾ cup cold water
1 teaspoon vanilla
7 egg whites
½ teaspoon cream of tartar

Combine and cool first 3 ingredients. Stir together dry ingredients. Make a well in center of dry ingredients and add in order the next 4 ingredients. Beat until smooth. Stir in chocolate mixture.

In a small bowl, beat egg whites with cream of tartar until very stiff peaks form. Fold into cake batter. Pour into ungreased 10-inch tube pan. Bake at 325° for 65 minutes. Invert pan to cool; remove from pan.

FILLING:

¼ cup sugar
¼ cup cornstarch
3 cups milk

2 eggs, beaten
2 teaspoons vanilla

In a saucepan, combine sugar and cornstarch. Add milk and stir in eggs. Cook and stir over medium heat until thickened and bubbly; add vanilla. Cover with waxed paper and cool. Split cake into 3 layers and spread filling between layers. Frost cake with Chocolate Icing. Immediately pipe Powdered Sugar Icing around top.

CHOCOLATE ICING:

1 (4-ounce) package sweet
  cooking chocolate
3 tablespoons butter

1½ cups powdered sugar
3–4 tablespoons hot water

In a saucepan, melt chocolate and butter over low heat. Remove from heat; stir in powdered sugar and enough hot water to make pouring consistency. Pour over cake.

POWDERED SUGAR ICING:

1 cup powdered sugar, sifted
¼ teaspoon vanilla

1¼ tablespoons milk
  (approximately)

Stir together all ingredients to make of drizzling consistency.

The Enlightened Titan

German Chocolate Upside-Down Cake

Easy and delicious—indulge and bulge!

1 cup flaked coconut
1 cup chopped pecans
1 package German chocolate
　cake mix
1 stick butter or margarine

1 (8-ounce) package cream
　cheese, softened
1 (1-pound) box confectioners'
　sugar

Combine coconut and pecans; spread evenly on bottom of a greased 9x13x2-inch pan. Mix cake mix according to directions on package; pour over coconut-pecan mixture. Put butter and cream cheese into a saucepan; heat until mixture is warm enough to stir in confectioners' sugar. Spoon mixture over top of cake batter. (As cake bakes, the cream cheese mixture will settle to bottom with coconut and pecans, making a delicious "Frosting.") Bake at 350° for 50–60 minutes, or until done. Serve from pan; do not cut until cake is cooled.

Holiday Treats

Smilin' Pineapple Upside Down Cake
(Microwave)

1½ tablespoons pineapple
　juice or water
½ cup yellow cake mix
1 teaspoon butter or margarine

2 tablespoons brown sugar
1 (8-ounce) can crushed
　pineapple, drained

In a small mixing bowl, combine water or juice with cake mix. Blend well. Set aside. Using a 6-inch browning skillet or a 4½x7-inch paper container, coat with vegetable cooking spray. To skillet or paper container add butter and brown sugar. Mix. Spread in the bottom of the container evenly. Add crushed pineapple and spread evenly over top of sugar. Add cake batter. Spread evenly over the pineapple.

Microwave on MEDIUM HIGH (80%) 5–6 minutes or until middle of cake springs back when lightly touched. Let cool at least 15 minutes. Invert onto serving plate.

The Microwave Affair

Do-Nothing-Cake
(Pineapple Goody Cake)

2 cups flour	½ teaspoon salt
2 cups sugar	1 teaspoon vanilla
2 eggs	1 (20-ounce) can crushed
1 teaspoon soda	pineapple, undrained

Put all ingredients in large bowl and mix with spoon (not mixer). Pour into 13x9x2-inch pan. Bake at 350° for 30–40 minutes or until center is done. Spoon topping on cake while hot. So easy.

TOPPING:

1 stick butter or margarine	1 cup chopped nuts
1 cup sugar	1 cup coconut
⅔ cup evaporated milk	

Combine butter, sugar, and milk in small saucepan. Cook 5 minutes. Add nuts and coconut. Spoon on cake while hot. Yummy!

Granny's Kitchen

Coconut Cake

1 box cake mix (yellow or white)	Cool Whip (large)
	Frozen coconut
1 small can cream of coconut	
1 can Eagle Brand condensed milk	

Mix cake mix as directed on box. Bake in 9x13–inch pan at 350° for 20–25 minutes. Pierce holes in cake with a large wooden spoon handle.

Mix cream of coconut and Eagle Brand condensed milk and pour over warm cake. When cool, ice with Cool Whip and sprinkle with coconut. Refrigerate.

Culinary Contentment

A seven-day calendar clock designed by Thomas Jefferson still marks the hours in the entrance hall of his home, Monticello.

Citrus Chiffon Cake

2½ cups sifted all-purpose
  flour
1 tablespoon baking powder
1 teaspoon salt
1⅓ cups sugar, divided
½ cup vegetable oil

3 egg yolks, beaten
3 tablespoons grated lemon rind
¾ cup orange juice
5 egg whites, at room
  temperature
½ teaspoon cream of tartar

Sift together flour, baking powder, salt and ⅔ cup sugar in a mixing bowl. Make a well in center of dry ingredients and add oil, egg yolks, lemon rind, and orange juice. Beat with an electric mixer on high for 5 minutes or until smooth. In a large mixing bowl beat egg whites and cream of tartar until soft peaks form. Add remaining ⅔ cup sugar a little at a time, beating until stiff peaks form. Pour yolk batter slowly over egg whites and then gently fold whites in. Pour into an ungreased 10-inch tube pan. Bake at 325° for 1 hour or until cake springs back to the touch. Invert pan on rack and allow to cool in pan 45 minutes. Loosen cake from pan by using a metal spatula or knife. Remove from pan and place on cake plate. Drizzle top with glaze.

GLAZE:
3 cups sifted confectioners'
  sugar
⅛ teaspoon salt
2¼ teaspoons grated lemon
  rind

¼ teaspoon lemon extract
3½–4 tablespoons fresh
  lemon juice

Mix all ingredients together and stir until smooth. Makes 1 (10-inch) cake.

Historic Lexington Cooks

Forest lands make up over sixty percent of Virginia's land area. There are two national forests and 23 recreational state parks. Wolf Trap Farm Park in Vienna is the only national park devoted to the performing arts.

Carrot Gold Cake

2 cups sugar
1½ cups vegetable oil
4 eggs, well beaten
2 cups flour
2 teaspoons baking powder
1½ teaspoons baking soda
1 teaspoon salt

2 teaspoons ground cinnamon
2 cups finely grated raw carrots
1 cup crushed pineapple, drained
1 cup angel flake coconut
½ cup chopped nuts

Beat sugar and oil together thoroughly. Add eggs, beating until fluffy. Sift next 5 ingredients together and blend in. Fold in remaining ingredients.

Pour into 3 greased and floured 8-inch layer pans and bake at 350° for 25–30 minutes. Or bake in a 9x13–inch pan for 40–45 minutes. Ice with cream cheese frosting. (If making sheet cake, use only half recipe of frosting.)

Variation: Omit crushed pineapple and add ¾ cup chopped dates instead.

CREAM CHEESE FROSTING:

1 (8-ounce) package cream cheese, softened
½ cup soft margarine

1 teaspoon vanilla
3 cups powdered sugar
Small amount of milk to mix

Combine all ingredients with 1 tablespoon milk or more and mix until smooth.

Mennonite Country-Style Recipes

Brandied Fresh Pear Cake

3 cups sifted cake flour
1 teaspoon baking soda
1 teaspoon salt
2 cups sugar
1½ cups cooking oil
⅓ cup brandy
1 teaspoon vanilla extract

3 jumbo eggs
3 cups chopped peeled firm
 ripe pears
1½ cups chopped English
 walnuts or pecans
Hot Buttered Brandy Sauce

Sift together the first 3 ingredients. In a large bowl, combine sugar, oil, brandy, and vanilla, beating at high speed of an electric mixer for 2–3 minutes. Add eggs, one at a time, beating well after each addition. Stir in dry ingredients. Fold in chopped pears and nuts, mixing well. Evenly spoon into a greased 10-inch tube pan. Bake in a moderate oven (350°) for 70–75 minutes or until a cake tester inserted in center comes out clean. Allow cake to cool in pan for 20 minutes, then turn out, top-side-up, onto a sheet of aluminum foil. Pour Hot Buttered Brandy Sauce over cake. Bring sides of foil up around cake. Allow cake to cool completely.

HOT BUTTERED BRANDY SAUCE:
½ cup butter or margarine   ⅓ cup brandy
1 cup sugar

In a small heavy saucepan, melt butter over low heat. Add sugar and brandy, mixing well. Bring mixture to a boil over moderate heat; reduce heat and simmer for 2–3 minutes. Yields one (10-inch) tube cake.

More Richmond Receipts

Blackberry Jam Cake with Caramel Icing

Mother's recipe for blackberry jam cake has always been particularly popular with the men.

1 cup butter	**1 teaspoon baking soda**
1 cup sugar	**1 teaspoon nutmeg**
4 eggs	**¼ cup buttermilk**
2½ cups flour	**1½ cups blackberry jam**

Cream butter and sugar. Add eggs one at a time, beating well after each addition. Sift flour, soda and nutmeg together and add to the batter, alternating with the buttermilk and the jam, beginning and ending with the flour mixture. Pour into 3 greased and lined 8- or 9-inch layer pans and bake at 375° for about 25 minutes or until done. When cool, spread with caramel icing.

CARAMEL ICING:

2 cups dark brown sugar	**1 teaspoon vanilla**
2 tablespoons butter	**¼ teaspoon cream of tartar**
½ cup rich milk	**Pinch of salt**

Mix sugar, butter and milk in a saucepan. Cook over medium heat, stirring constantly until mixture is dissolved. Cook 10 minutes more or until the soft-ball stage is reached. Remove from heat; add vanilla, cream of tartar and salt and beat until the icing begins to thicken. Spread on cake.

The Smithfield Cookbook

The world's largest musical instrument, the Great Stalacpipe Organ, creates haunting music from stone. It is in the Cathedral Room of the Luray Caverns.

Orange Juice Cupcakes

These were a specialty of Miss Huyetts' Tea Room, a popular gathering place in downtown Charlottesville in the 1920's.

½ cup shortening or butter
1 cup sugar
2 eggs
½ cup milk

1½ cups flour
2 scant teaspoons baking powder
½ teaspoon salt
1 teaspoon vanilla

SYRUP:
1 cup sugar
Juice and grated rind of 1
   lemon

Juice and grated rind of 1
   orange

Cream butter and sugar. Beat in eggs one at a time. Add milk alternately with mixture of flour, salt, and baking powder. Add vanilla. Bake at 425° until surface springs back to the touch (about 15 minutes).

While cupcakes are still warm, dip (do not soak) them in syrup. These keep well for several days. Yields 2 dozen.

The Best of the Bushel

Lemon Sponge Cups

2 tablespoons butter
1 cup sugar
4 tablespoons flour
¼ teaspoon salt

5 tablespoons lemon juice
Grated rind of 1 lemon
3 eggs
1½ cups milk

Cream butter; add sugar, flour, salt, lemon juice and rind. Add the well-beaten egg yolks which have been mixed with milk. Lastly, add the stiffly beaten egg whites. Pour into greased custard cups; set in a pan of water and bake 45 minutes at 350°. May be baked in a 2-quart dish also. There will be lemon custard at the bottom and sponge cake on top. Serves 6.

Spotsylvania Favorites

Applesauce Cake

½ cup shortening
1½ cups sugar
2 eggs, well beaten
2½ cups cake flour
½ teaspoon salt
1 teaspoon cinnamon
½ teaspoon cloves

1½ cups applesauce,
  unsweetened
1 teaspoon soda, dissolved in
  2 tablespoons hot water
1 cup chopped seedless raisins
½ cup chopped nuts (optional)

Cream shortening. Add sugar gradually and continue to beat until fluffy. Add well-beaten eggs and combine thoroughly. Sift flour, measure, and sift again with salt and spices. Add a third of the applesauce to creamed mixture and blend. Add dry ingredients alternately with remaining applesauce, beating thoroughly after each addition.

Dissolve soda in hot water and add to mixture. Mix thoroughly. Chop raisins and nuts on a board and flour lightly. Fold these into mixture. Pour into a large, greased loaf pan 5x9x4 inches. Bake at 350° for approximately 1 hour. Excellent flavor and keeps well.

Variation: Replace half of the applesauce with ¾ cup strained apricot pulp.

Mennonite Community Cookbook

Chilled Strawberry Meringue Cake

4 egg whites
1 cup sugar
1 pint fresh strawberries

4 tablespoons confectioners'
   sugar (divided)
1½ pints heavy cream

To prepare the meringue: Butter a sheet pan and dust it with flour. With a pointed instrument, mark 3 circles, each 6 inches in diameter, in the flour. Preheat the oven to 200°-250°. Beat the egg whites, adding the sugar a little at a time, until stiff. Fill a pastry bag, equipped with a half-inch plain tip, with the meringue. Dress a lattice pattern into 3 circles. Bake the meringue for about 2 hours, or until dry. Leave the oven door slightly ajar to allow steam to escape.

To prepare the cake: Wash the strawberries and remove the stems. Slice or cut the berries into small pieces. Whip the cream with 2 tablespoons of the confectioners' sugar. Carefully combine the strawberries, two-thirds of the whipped cream, and the remaining sugar. Place the strawberry mixture between layers of the meringue. Decorate the top with the remaining whipped cream and some nice strawberries.

The Great Chefs of Virginia Cookbook

Strawberry Angel Cake

½ angel food cake
1 (3–ounce) package strawberry
   gelatin, sugar free
1 cup water

1 (10-ounce) frozen strawberries
1 carton strawberry yogurt,
   low fat

Tear baked caked into ¾-inch pieces. Prepare gelatin using 1 cup water. When slightly thickened, stir in strawberries and yogurt. Pour over angel food cake pieces. Refrigerate. Serve as a healthful dessert when it is set.

The VIP Cookbook: A Potpourri of Virginia Cooking

Chocolate Roll

6 ounces dark, sweet chocolate
  (Baker's German sweet is
  good)
3 tablespoons cold water

5 large eggs
1 cup sugar
1 cup heavy cream
1 teaspoon vanilla

Break up the chocolate and put in a small pan with the water. Stir over a very low flame or heat in a double boiler until melted. Cool a little. Meanwhile separate the eggs. Beat the yolks with ¾ cup sugar until very light. Mix in the chocolate. Oil a jellyroll pan, line with aluminum foil, and oil again. Peanut oil is best. Don't use waxed paper or butter or you'll be sorry! Heat the oven to 375°. Beat the egg whites stiff and fold into the yolk and chocolate mixture. Spread in the prepared pan.

Bake 10 minutes at 375°, then 5 minutes with the oven set at 325°. Remove and cover with a cloth wrung out in cold water. Cool and refrigerate at least 1 hour. Remove cloth and dust cake heavily with cocoa. (Put in a small strainer and tap over the cake). Turn it over on wax paper, ease it out of the pan and remove foil carefully. Spread with stiffly whipped cream flavored with ¼ cup sugar and vanilla. Roll up lengthwise, using paper, ending upon a platter or board for serving.

The Foxcroft Cook Book

Mount Vernon Gingerbread

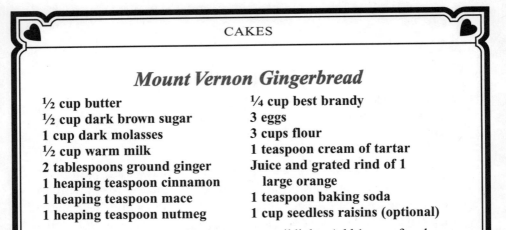

½ cup butter
½ cup dark brown sugar
1 cup dark molasses
½ cup warm milk
2 tablespoons ground ginger
1 heaping teaspoon cinnamon
1 heaping teaspoon mace
1 heaping teaspoon nutmeg

¼ cup best brandy
3 eggs
3 cups flour
1 teaspoon cream of tartar
Juice and grated rind of 1
  large orange
1 teaspoon baking soda
1 cup seedless raisins (optional)

Cream together butter and brown sugar until light. Add 1 cup of molasses and ½ cup warmed milk. Mix well. Mix separately the spices (ginger, cinnamon, mace and nutmeg) and stir into the batter. Add ¼ cup brandy. In a small bowl beat eggs until light and thick. Sift together flour and cream of tartar. Stir eggs and flour alternately into the batter. Stir in the juice and rind of the orange. Dissolve 1 teaspoon of soda in 1 teaspoon of warm water and add this to the batter. Beat batter until light. Add raisins, if desired, and pour into 2 greased and floured Pyrex baking dishes (8½x8½-inch size). Bake at 350° for 40–45 minutes. Let cool in pans. Turn out on a rack to cool completely before cutting into squares. This is a very dark and spicy gingerbread, not sweet. Mrs. Washington served it with a glass of madeira or rum or a mint julep. Yields 24 squares.

The Mount Vernon Cookbook

Fudge Frosting

2 cups granulated sugar   ¼ cup butter
2 squares chocolate   ⅔ cup evaporated milk

Combine all ingredients in saucepan. Bring to a full boil; cook for 2 minutes. Remove from heat and beat until thick enough to spread.

Cooking with Class

Caramel Frosting

2 cups light brown sugar   ½ teaspoon vanilla extract
½ cup butter or margarine   ½ teaspoon baking powder
5 tablespoons light cream

In medium saucepan, combine sugar, butter and cream. Bring to a boil over medium heat, stirring constantly. Boil gently while stirring for 2 minutes. Remove from heat. Add vanilla and baking powder. Beat until smooth and creamy, about 5 minutes. Makes enough to frost the tops of 2 (8-inch) layers.

Spotsylvania Favorites

Sherwood Forest Orange Cream Sauce

To serve on angel food cake. This always gets rave notices.

2 eggs (yolks)   1 cup cream (then whip)
½ cup sugar   1 angel food cake
½ cup orange juice

Put egg yolks, sugar and juice on stove. Cook until thick. When cooled, add 1 cup cream that has been whipped until stiff. Serve immediately on angel cake slices.

The Virginia Presidential Homes Cookbook

Dirt Cake

Use two new 8-inch plastic flower pots or three 6-inch pots.

2 (8-ounce) packages cream
  cheese
2 cups confectioners' sugar
3 cups milk
2 (6-serving) boxes instant
  vanilla pudding

1 teaspoon vanilla
1 (16-ounce) carton Cool Whip
2 (16-ounce) packages Double
  Stuff Oreo Cookies

Beat cream cheese and sugar until smooth. Beat milk and pudding until smooth and thick. Combine vanilla and Cool Whip. Blend into cream cheese and pudding mixture. Crush Oreo cookies in blender just a few at a time. Put waxed paper circles in bottom of pots to cover holes. Layer pudding into flower pots, ending with Oreos on top. Decorate with a few silk flowers.

WYVE's Cookbook/Photo Album

Cookies and Candies

New River, near Blacksburg, offers canoeing, tubing and fishing for outdoor lovers.

Jelly Topped Almond Bites

1 cup (2 sticks) butter, at
   room temperature
1 cup sugar
1 egg
1 teaspoon almond extract
2 cups flour
½ teaspoon baking soda

½ teaspoon salt
½ teaspoon nutmeg
1 cup quick-cooking or old-
   fashioned oatmeal, uncooked
1 jar cherry jelly (or other
   tart red jelly, such as currant)
1 package chopped almonds

Preheat oven to 375°. Beat butter and sugar together until light and fluffy. Add egg and almond extract and beat until blended. Sift together flour, soda, salt, and nutmeg. Gradually add to creamed mixture and beat well. Stir in oatmeal. Shape dough into 1¼-inch balls. Place on ungreased cookie sheets and make a hollow in each ball. Bake for about 12 minutes. Cool on racks. Then place a small amount of jelly in each hollow and sprinkle with chopped almonds. Yields about 3½ dozen.

Note: Any flavor jam or jelly you prefer can of course be used instead of cherry.

The Other Side of the House

Chocolate Crinkles Cookies

1 cup Bisquick mix
¾ cup sugar
⅔ cup nuts
⅓ cup cocoa

¼ cup salad dressing
1 teaspoon cinnamon
1 egg

Grease cookie sheet. Mix all ingredients till dough forms. Drop by rounded teaspoonfuls about 2 inches apart. Bake till set, at 375° for 8–10 minutes. Remove from sheet. Cool 2 minutes.

WYVE's Cookbook/Photo Album

The town of Lexington was destroyed by fire in 1796, and it was reconstructed with funds from a lottery.

Almond Cookies

½ pound butter
¼ cup granulated sugar
1 cup finely chopped almonds

2 cups all-purpose flour
½ teaspoon vanilla
Super fine granulated sugar

Cream butter and sugar. Add nuts, flour and flavoring. Form in small balls. Bake at 350° until light brown. Cool on brown paper and then roll in super fine granulated sugar. Excellent and great for a special gift in decorated tin. I usually decorate these with an almond or sometimes dip the cooled cookie in chocolate and then place almond on top.

The Candy Cookbook Plus

Raspberry-Orange Turnovers

½ cup butter, softened
1 (3–ounce) package cream
  cheese, softened
1 teaspoon finely grated
  orange peel

1 cup all-purpose flour
⅛ teaspoon salt
¼ cup raspberry preserves
Orange Glaze

Mix butter, cheese, orange peel, flour, and salt. Cover and refrigerate at least 1 hour.

Heat oven to 375°. Roll dough ⅛ inch thick on lightly floured cloth-covered board; cut into 2½-inch circles. Spoon about ½ teaspoon preserves onto each circle; moisten edge on half of each circle and fold dough over preserves. Press edges together. Place 1 inch apart on ungreased baking sheet.

Bake until edges are light brown, 8–10 minutes. Immediately remove from baking sheet; cool. Drizzle cookies with Orange Glaze. Makes about 2½ dozen cookies.

ORANGE GLAZE:

Mix until smooth and of desired consistency:

1 cup powdered sugar
About 2 tablespoons orange
  juice

1 teaspoon finely grated
  orange peel

Happy Times with Home Cooking

Aunt Lula's Mud Hen Cookies

My Great Aunt Lula Looper from Albany, Kentucky, was a wonderful cook. I enjoyed visiting my cousin, Susie Quails, her granddaughter, and eating at Great Aunt Lula's. We always thought these cookies had the funniest name. But they are good!

½ cup butter
1 cup sugar
3 eggs (reserve 2 egg whites)
1½ cups flour
1 teaspoon baking powder

1 teaspoon vanilla
½ teaspoon salt
1 cup nuts, chopped
1 cup brown sugar

Preheat oven to 350°. Mix first 7 ingredients together. Spread very thin in a greased 9x13–inch pan. Sprinkle with chopped nuts.

Beat egg whites stiff and add brown sugar. Spread over nuts and bake for 30 minutes. Cut into squares while hot. Makes 24 (2-inch) squares.

Cooking with Heart in Hand

Corn Flake Treats

1¼ cups white Karo syrup
1 cup sugar
1 cup peanut butter

4 cups cornflakes
2 cups peanuts

Bring syrup and sugar to a rolling boil. Then take off heat and add peanut butter. Mix well. Pour over cornflakes and peanuts. Mix well. Then pour into a 9x13–inch dish. Press smooth. Cut into squares.

Recipes from Jeffersonville Woman's Club

Taps was composed at Berkeley Plantation by General Daniel Butterfield when he was stationed there in 1862 with McClellan's Army of the Potomac. The General's bugler, O.W. Norton, left a remarkable account of this in his book *Army Letters*.

Pistachio Orange Drops

1 cup butter or margarine, room temperature
1 cup powdered sugar
1 teaspoon grated fresh orange peel
2 cups all-purpose flour

1 cup finely chopped pistachio nuts, divided use
1 cup semisweet chocolate chips
2 tablespoons vegetable shortening

Preheat oven to 375°. In a large bowl, beat butter, sugar and orange peel with electric mixer until fluffy. Stir in flour until well blended. Reserve 3 tablespoons pistachio nuts. Stir remainder into dough. Shape rounded teaspoonfuls into 1-inch balls. Arrange 1½ inches apart on cookie sheets. Bake 8–10 minutes until lightly browned. Remove to rack to cool. Melt chocolate and shortening in a small heavy saucepan over low heat; stir until smooth. Dip tops of cookies into chocolate mixture. Place cookies on rack; sprinkle with reserved nuts. Let stand until chocolate is set. Store in a cool place. Yields 72 cookies.

Cardinal Cuisine

Raisin Treasure Cookies

1 stick butter
2 cups whole-wheat pastry
　flour
½ teaspoon salt
½ teaspoon cinnamon
1 cup raw sugar
1 teaspoon Royal baking
　powder

1 teaspoon grated lemon rind
1 cup chopped pecans
1½ cups raisins
2 eggs, beaten
5 tablespoons milk

Cream butter. Stir flour, salt, cinnamon, sugar, and baking powder together. Blend butter and dry ingredients together until well blended. Add all remaining ingredients and mix thoroughly. Drop by spoonfuls onto a greased cookie sheet. Bake at 350°, about 15 minutes.

The New Life Cookbook

Esther's Flaky Pastries

1 cup sour cream
1 cup butter or margarine
  (soft)

2 cups sifted flour

Mix sour cream and butter thoroughly. Blend in flour and mix well. Refrigerate dough overnight.

Divide in 4 and roll each quarter on floured surface to a rectangle about 25x8 inches. Top with a fourth of filling. Roll up like jellyroll along the longer side. Place on ungreased cookie sheet. Make indentations with back of knife at 1-inch intervals. Bake at 350° for 50–60 minutes or until golden. Slice through indentations while still warm. May be frozen. Makes about 8 dozen.

FILLING:

1 large jar apricot preserves
1½ cups shredded coconut

2 cups chopped walnuts

Mix preserves with coconut and walnuts.

Could I Have Your Recipe?

Ellie's Grandma's Zucchini Cookies

As printed in Good Housekeeping.

¾ cup butter or margarine,
  softened
1½ cups sugar
1 egg
1 teaspoon vanilla
1½ cups grated zucchini
2½ cups flour
2 teaspoons baking powder

1 teaspoon cinnamon
½ teaspoon salt
½ cup almonds, coarsely
  chopped
1 (6-ounce) package chocolate
  chips
Powdered sugar

Cream butter and sugar. Beat in egg and vanilla; stir in zucchini. Stir in flour, baking powder, cinnamon and salt. Add almonds and chocolate chips. Drop by heaping teaspoons onto greased cookie sheet. Bake at 350° for 15 minutes or until lightly browned. Cool on wire rack. Sift powdered sugar over cookies. Yields 4–5 dozen.

Virginia Seasons

Lemon Bonbons

These would be very nice for a party because they are pretty as well as delicious.

1 cup butter	1¼ cups sifted flour
⅓ cup confectioners' sugar	½ cup finely chopped pecans
¾ cup cornstarch	

Mix butter with sugar until light and fluffy. Add cornstarch and flour, mixing well. Refrigerate until easy to handle. Start oven at 350°. Shape dough in 1-inch balls. Place balls on nuts scattered on waxed paper. Flatten with bottom of glass. Put cookies nut-side-up on ungreased cookie sheet. Bake 15 minutes. Frost with Bonbon Frosting. Makes 4 dozen.

BONBON FROSTING:

1 cup confectioners' sugar	2 tablespoons lemon juice
1 teaspoon soft butter	

Blend sugar, butter and lemon juice until smooth. Tint with desired food coloring.

Could I Have Your Recipe?

Chocolate Squares
A Chocolate Lover's Cookie

This is great to pass around at a cookout.

2 cups graham cracker crumbs	1 can sweetened condensed milk
12 ounces chocolate chips	

Mix all ingredients together. Place in a greased oblong pan. Bake at 350° for 20 minutes. Cool before cutting into squares.

THE What in the World Are We Going to Have for Dinner? COOKBOOK

Hermits

1 cup shortening (half butter)	1½ teaspoons cinnamon
2 cups brown sugar	½ teaspoon each of cloves
2 eggs	and nutmeg
2⅔ cups flour	⅓ cup milk
½ teaspoon salt	⅔ cup chopped raisins
2 teaspoons baking powder	⅔ cup chopped nuts
½ teaspoon baking soda	

Cream shortening and sugar together. Add eggs and beat until fluffy. Sift flour. Measure and add salt, soda, baking powder and spices. Sift again. Add sifted dry ingredients alternately with milk. Beat after each addition. Add chopped nuts and raisins and blend into mixture. Drop by teaspoonfuls onto greased baking sheet about 2 inches apart. Bake at 350° for 12–15 minutes. Makes about 5 dozen cookies.

Mennonite Community Cookbook

Spanish Gold Bricks

So easy and just delicious!

1 package graham crackers	½ cup butter
½ cup pecans, finely	½ cup margarine
chopped	½ cup sugar

Separate sections of graham crackers and line on ungreased jellyroll pan so that the sides of the graham crackers are touching. Finely chop pecans in the food processor, and sprinkle evenly over graham crackers. In a saucepan, melt together butter, margarine, and sugar. Boil and stir for 2 minutes. Pour slowly and evenly over the top of the graham crackers and nuts until all are covered. Bake at 325° for 8–10 minutes. Cool in the pan for about 10 minutes. Separate with a knife. Store in an airtight container. These can be frozen.

Gourmet by the Bay

Phyl's Gobs

4 cups flour
2 teaspoons baking soda
¾ teaspoon baking powder
1 teaspoon salt
½ cup cocoa
½ cup shortening

2 cups sugar
2 eggs
1 teaspoon vanilla
1 cup buttermilk
½ cup boiling water

Sift flour, soda, baking powder, salt and cocoa together. Cream shortening, sugar, eggs and vanilla together. Add buttermilk, alternately with the sifted ingredients. Add boiling water. Drop by teaspoon onto a greased baking sheet. Bake at 450° for 5–8 minutes.

FILLING:

5 tablespoons flour
1 cup milk
½ cup shortening
½ cup butter

1¼ cups sugar
2 teaspoons vanilla
Dash of salt

Measure flour in a saucepan. Make a paste from small amount of milk. Add rest of milk. Cook, stirring constantly, until thick. Cool. Cream shortening, butter, sugar, vanilla and salt. Beat well. Add the cooked mixture a tablespoon at a time. Keep beating until sugar granules disappear. Put cookies together with filling sandwich-style, and you will have 48 delicious "Gobs."

Recipes from Jeffersonville Woman's Club

Crème de Menthe Brownies

LAYER 1:

1 cup sugar
1 teaspoon vanilla
4 eggs, room temperature
1 cup flour
1 (16-ounce) can chocolate
   syrup

½ cup margarine, room
   temperature
½ cup chopped black walnuts
½ teaspoon salt

In large bowl of electric mixer, combine ingredients for Layer 1. Mix on very low speed but do not beat. Grease bottom of 8x13–inch pan. Spread mixture in pan and bake at 350° for 25–30 minutes. Let cool.

LAYER 2:

2 cups confectioners' sugar
3 tablespoons crème de menthe

½ cup margarine, room
   temperature

Blend all ingredients; spread on cooled cake and let sit a while.

LAYER 3:

6 ounces semisweet
   chocolate bits

6 tablespoons margarine

Melt together chocolate and margarine and spread evenly over mint layer. Chill thoroughly before cutting into small squares. Store in refrigerator.

Taste of Goodness

Arlington House, the Curtis-Lee Mansion built by Martha Washington's grandson and owned by General Robert E. Lee and his wife, overlooks the 612 acres of Arlington National Cemetery with its famous Tomb of the Unknown Soldier and the eternal flame of John F. Kennedy's grave. Nearby is the famous Marine Corps' Iwo Jima Memorial.

Brownies for a Crowd

½ cup margarine
1 cup sugar
4 eggs
1 teaspoon vanilla
1 (1-pound) can chocolate
  syrup

1 cup plus 1 tablespoon
  sifted flour
½ teaspoon baking powder
¼ teaspoon salt
½ cup walnuts or pecans,
  chopped

Beat margarine with sugar until light and fluffy. Beat in eggs, 2 at a time, then vanilla, and mix well. Stir in chocolate syrup. Sift flour, baking powder and salt together. Stir into chocolate mixture. Add nuts. Pour into well-greased 15½x10½x1-inch jellyroll or baking pan; spread evenly. Bake at 350° for 22–25 minutes, or until slight imprint remains when touched lightly. Remove pan to rack and let cool.

FROSTING:

6 tablespoons margarine
6 tablespoons milk
1 cup sugar

½ cup chocolate chips
1 teaspoon vanilla

Combine margarine, milk and sugar in saucepan; stir to mix. Bring to a boil and boil 30 seconds. Add chocolate chips; stir until mixture thickens slightly. Remove from heat and cool. Stir in vanilla; stir until ready to spread. Spread over cooled brownies. Cut in 2½x1-inch bars. Makes 5 dozen.

Spotsylvania Favorites

Bourbon Brownies

¾ cup sifted flour
¼ teaspoon baking soda
⅛ teaspoon salt
½ cup sugar
⅓ cup margarine or butter
2 tablespoons water

1 (6-ounce) package semisweet
  squares or chocolate morsels
1 teaspoon vanilla
2 eggs
1½ cups chopped walnuts
4 tablespoons bourbon

Preheat oven to 325°. Sift together flour, baking soda and salt and set aside. Combine sugar, margarine, and water. Bring to just a boil, stirring constantly. Remove from heat; stir in chocolate and vanilla until smooth. Beat in eggs, one at a time. Add flour mixture and nuts. Spread on greased 9-inch pan and bake for 25–30 minutes. (Better to undercook than cook too dry.) Remove from oven and sprinkle with bourbon and cool. Meanwhile prepare frosting; make glaze after frosting has been chilled.

WHITE FROSTING:

½ cup soft butter or
  margarine
1 teaspoon vanilla or rum
  extract

2 cups sifted confectioners'
  sugar

Combine butter and vanilla or rum extract and beat until creamy, gradually adding sugar. Beat until smooth after each addition. Spread White Frosting over cooled brownies and chill until firm. Cover frosting with glaze and chill. Cut in 1-inch squares with hot knife. Keep refrigerated until ready to serve. Yields 80 squares.

CHOCOLATE GLAZE:

1 (6-ounce) package semisweet
  chocolate morsels

1 tablespoon butter or
  margarine

Melt chocolate and margarine in double boiler.

The Best of the Bushel

Mansion Fudge Brownies

These tempting confections were a specialty served at the Virginia Executive Mansion while Eddy Dalton was First Lady of Virginia.

2 squares (ounces)
  unsweetened chocolate
½ cup butter or margarine
2 eggs, beaten
1 cup sugar
1 teaspoon vanilla extract
Pinch of salt

¼ cup sifted flour
⅔ cup chopped English or
  black walnuts, or pecans, or
  cashews, or peanuts (optional)
Sifted confectioners' sugar
  as needed

In a small heavy saucepan, melt chocolate and butter over low heat; cool. In a medium bowl, combine chocolate mixture, eggs, sugar, vanilla, and salt, beating well. Stir in flour, mixing well. Fold in nuts, if desired. Spoon into a lightly greased 9x9x2-inch baking pan, spreading evenly. Bake in a moderate oven (350°) for 25–30 minutes or until a cake tester inserted into the center of the brownies comes out clean. Do not overbake. Cool in pan 10 minutes; sprinkle top of brownies with confectioners' sugar and cut into squares. Yields about 16 brownies.

More Richmond Receipts

Choco-Chewies

FILLING:

1 (12-ounce) package
semisweet chocolate bits
1 (15-ounce) can sweetened
condensed milk

2 tablespoons butter

DOUGH:

1 cup butter, melted
1 pound brown sugar
½ cup chopped nuts
2 eggs

2 cups flour
1 teaspoon salt
1 teaspoon vanilla

Melt filling ingredients in the top of a double boiler. In a large bowl, mix remaining ingredients. Spread half the dough on a greased cookie sheet, 10x15x1 inches; drizzle filling over it, and top with the remaining dough. Bake at 350° for 30–35 minutes. Cut squares before cooling. May be frozen. Do not double.

The Belle Grove Plantation Cookbook

Lockness Bars

½ cup margarine
1 (6-ounce) package
chocolate chips
1 cup peanut butter

1 (10½-ounce) package
miniature marshmallows
4¼ cups crisp rice cereal
1 cup peanuts

FROSTING:

1 (6-ounce) package
chocolate chips

1 (6-ounce) package
butterscotch chips

Melt margarine, 1 package chocolate chips and peanut butter. Add marshmallows and stir until melted. Add cereal and nuts. Spread into 9x13-inch pan and refrigerate until set. Melt chocolate chips and butterscotch chips together and spread on top. Makes 60.

Children's Party Book

Chocolate Cherry Squares

1 cup unsifted all-purpose
  flour
½ cup packed light brown
  sugar
⅓ cup cold butter
½ cup chopped nuts
1 (8-ounce) package cream
  cheese, softened

½ cup sugar
⅓ cup Hershey's cocoa
¼ cup milk
1 egg
½ teaspoon vanilla
½ cup chopped red candied
  cherries
Red candied cherries, halved

Combine flour, brown sugar and butter or margarine (cut into chunks) in large mixer bowl. Blend on low speed to form fine crumbs, about 2–3 minutes. Stir in nuts. Reserve ¾ cup crumb mixture for topping; press remaining crumbs into ungreased 9-inch square pan. Bake at 350° for 10 minutes, or until lightly browned.

Meanwhile, combine cream cheese, sugar, cocoa, milk, egg, and vanilla in small mixer bowl; beat until smooth. Fold in cherries. Spread mixture over warm crust. Sprinkle reserved crumb mixture over top; garnish with cherry halves. Return to oven; continue to bake at 350° for 25 minutes, or until lightly browned and filling is set. Cool; cut into squares. Store in refrigerator. Makes about 3 dozen squares.

Happy Times with Home Cooking

Caramel Chocolate Squares

1 (14-ounce) bag caramel
candy
²/₃ cup evaporated milk,
divided
1 box German chocolate cake
mix

¾ cup butter, softened
1 cup chopped pecans
1 (6-ounce) package chocolate
chips

Combine caramels and ⅓ cup evaporated milk in top of double boiler to melt. In the meantime, combine the cake mix, butter, remaining ⅓ cup evaporated milk and pecans. Press half of this mixture into a greased sheet cake pan. Bake at 350° for 6–10 minutes until firm. Sprinkle chocolate chips on top then pour on melted caramels. Crumble remaining cake mixture on top of this. Return to oven and bake 20–25 minutes. Cool slightly, then chill in the refrigerator about 30 minutes before cutting into squares.

THE What in the World Are We Going to Have for Dinner? COOKBOOK

Pecan Pie Squares

3 cups flour
¼ cup plus 2 tablespoons
sugar

¾ cup margarine, softened
Dash of salt

Heat oven to 350°. Grease a jellyroll pan. Combine ingredients until crumbly. Press firmly in pan. Bake 20 minutes. Pour filling over baked layer; spread evenly. Bake 25 minutes. Cool. Cut in 1½-inch squares.

FILLING:

4 eggs, slight beaten
1½ cups sugar
1½ cups Karo syrup

2½ cups chopped pecans
3 tablespoons margarine, melted
1½ teaspoons vanilla

Mix all ingredients until well blended. Stir in pecans. Makes 36 squares.

Think Healthy

Chocolate Buttercream Squares

These absolutely devine squares remind you of a brownie combined with buttercream candy. Cut into very small pieces since they are very rich.

COOKIE LAYER:

¼ cup butter
½ cup sugar
1 egg, beaten
1 ounce unsweetened
   chocolate, melted

½ cup flour
¼ cup nuts (optional)

Preheat oven to 350°. Grease and flour an 8x8-inch pan. Cream butter, sugar, and egg. Add melted chocolate, flour, and nuts. Put in prepared pan and place in oven. Check after 10 minutes; it should be cooked. *Do not overbake.* Cool.

FILLING LAYER:

2 tablespoons margarine,
   softened
1 cup confectioners' sugar

1 tablespoon cream
½ teaspoon vanilla

Blend ingredients. Chill 10 minutes and spread over cookie layer.

ICING:

1 ounce unsweetened
   chocolate

1 tablespoons butter or
   margarine

Melt ingredients together and pour over filling. Chill in refrigerator. Cut into 24 small bars.

Virginia Hospitality

Deluxe Chocolate Marshmallow Bars
A Family Favorite

¾ cup margarine	½ teaspoon baking powder
1½ cups sugar	½ teaspoon salt
3 eggs	3 tablespoons cocoa powder
1 teaspoon vanilla	½ cup chopped nuts (optional)
1⅓ cups flour	4 cups miniature marshmallows

Cream margarine and sugar together thoroughly. Add eggs and vanilla, beating until fluffy. Sift dry ingredients together and add. Fold in nuts. Spread in greased 11x15-inch pan. Bake at 350° for 15–18 minutes. Sprinkle marshmallows evenly over chocolate layer as soon as you remove it from oven. Return to oven for 2 minutes to slightly melt. Use knife to spread evenly. Cool.

DELUXE TOPPING:

1⅓ cups chocolate chips	1 cup peanut butter
3 tablespoons butter or margarine	2 cups Rice Krispies cereal

Combine chocolate chips, butter and peanut butter in saucepan. Stir constantly over low heat until melted. Remove from heat. Stir in Rice Krispies. Spread over top of bars.

OPTIONAL CHOCOLATE TOPPING:

2 cups powdered sugar	3 or 4 tablespoons hot coffee to
3 tablespoons cocoa powder	mix
3 tablespoons soft margarine	¼ teaspoon vanilla

Beat together until smooth. Spread over bars.
    Dip knife in water occasionally to aid in spreading if necessary.

Mennonite Country-Style Recipes

 Trinity Church served as the state capitol during the Revolutionary War.

All-Time Favorite Lemon Squares

Taste like little lemon pies—a tart-like cookie that is a real favorite.

CRUST:

½ cup butter or margarine   ¼ cup confectioners' sugar
1 cup flour

Combine butter, flour and confectioners' sugar; blend together until mixture clings together (I use pastry blender). Pat evenly into a 9x9-inch pan. Bake at 350° for 20 minutes or until edges begin to brown.

FILLING:

2 eggs   1 teaspoon grated lemon rind
1 cup sugar   Dash of salt
1 tablespoon flour   Confectioners' sugar
2 tablespoons lemon juice

Beat together eggs, sugar, flour, lemon juice, lemon rind (if you don't use rind, add an extra tablespoon lemon juice), and salt. Pour over partially baked crust. Return to oven and bake 20 minutes longer or until set. Sprinkle with confectioners' sugar. Cool. Cut into squares (small ones for a tea).

Tip: Garnish tray with lemon twist and a sprig of mint. Cool looking.

Variation: To make Apricot-Lemon Squares, add ¾ cup finely chopped dried apricots (soaked in boiling water and drained) to filling above. Delightful.

Holiday Treats

Little Chess Cakes

As a child at Capshaw Elementary School, I would swap food at lunch for these! We had terrific Southern cooks at school who made homemade breads and desserts each day. These taste like little chess pies.

¾ cup butter   3 egg yolks
1½ cups sifted flour   1 cup chopped pecans
3 teaspoons granulated sugar   ½ teaspoon vanilla
2¼ cups dark brown sugar   3 egg whites

Cream butter. Add slowly the sifted flour and granulated sugar. Pat into a 9x13–inch pan with 1½-inch sides. Bake 20–30 minutes in a 375° oven, or cook until the crust is golden brown. Meanwhile, make the filling by mixing the dark brown sugar with the beaten egg yolks.

CONTINUED

When thick and spongy, add the pecans. Add vanilla and fold in the stiffly beaten whites. Spread filling evenly over the crust. Return pan to oven and cook 25–30 minutes longer, or until the filling sets. Do not cook too long, as the filling should be transparent and semi-soft, never hard or chewy. Dust with powdered sugar and when cool, cut into squares. Makes 4 dozen.

Cooking with Heart in Hand

Martha's Rum Soaked Chocolate Truffles

7 ounces semisweet baking chocolate
1 ounce (square) unsweetened baking chocolate
¼ cup dark rum
2 tablespoons strong liquid coffee
½ cup unsalted butter or margarine, cut in 1-inch pieces
¾–1 cup gingersnap crumbs
½ cup sifted cocoa
¼ cup instant coffee crystals

Break chocolate into small pieces. In the top of a double boiler, combine chocolate, rum, and liquid coffee. Cover and place over bottom of double boiler containing boiling water. Remove double boiler from heat. When chocolate has melted, beat in butter, a small amount at a time. Blend in gingersnap crumbs. Chill mixture for several hours. Combine cocoa and instant coffee crystals; spread chocolate on a plate. With a tablespoon or teaspoon, shape chilled chocolate mixture into rough shaped balls. Roll each ball in cocoa-coffee mixture. Place each truffle on a paper candy cup and refrigerate until ready to serve. Truffles may be stored in an airtight container in the refrigerator for several weeks. Yields 12–18 large or 40–50 small truffles.

More Richmond Receipts

Christmas Cheer Fudge

Superb! A must for Christmas, but you do not have to wait until Christmas to make this fudge, just omit the candied fruit.

2 cups sugar
1 cup half-and-half cream
⅓ cup white corn syrup
⅓ cup butter
¼ teaspoon salt
1 teaspoon vanilla

½ cup candied red cherries, halved
½ cup candied green pineapple, diced
1 cup broken walnuts
1 cup halved pecans

Combine sugar, cream, corn syrup, butter and salt in heavy saucepan. Cook and stir over medium heat until sugar is dissolved. Cover saucepan and boil 1 minute (this helps prevent sugar crystals from forming). Uncover; cook at medium steady boil to the soft-ball stage (236°) or until a soft ball forms in cold water. Remove from heat. Add vanilla and immediately beat with electric mixer at medium speed. Beat until mixture is creamy and begins to hold shape, about 10 minutes. Thoroughly mix in fruits and nuts. Pour into a greased 9-inch square pan. When firm enough, cut into squares. Let stand for 24 hours.

Tip: Great for gifts, but give it to your best friends, as it is expensive.

Holiday Treats

Caramel Fudge Balls

1 cup walnuts
¼ cup butter
1 cup brown sugar, packed
1 cup granulated sugar
¼ teaspoon salt
¾ cup dairy sour cream
1 teaspoon vanilla

Chop ½ cup of walnuts to medium-size pieces. Chop remaining walnuts into fine pieces for coating.

Fudge Balls: Melt butter in heavy 2-quart saucepan. Add sugars, salt and sour cream. Cook over low heat, stirring until sugars dissolve. Cover; boil slowly 5 minutes. Uncover; cook rapidly without stirring to 236° (soft-ball stage). Remove from heat; cool to lukewarm. Add vanilla; beat until mixture is creamy and begins to hold its shape. Stir in medium-size walnut pieces. Drop by rounded teaspoonfuls onto waxed paper. Quickly shape into balls. Roll in finely chopped walnuts. Let stand until firm. Makes 24 balls.

Dan River Family Cookbook

Dad's Peanut Butter Delights

2 cups peanut butter, room
   temperature
1 cup white chocolate, melted
1 pound semisweet chocolate,
   (put in crockpot on low heat
   and melt)

Blend peanut butter and melted white chocolate together and pour in a squeeze bottle. Melt and pour dark chocolate in a separate bottle. Start with dark chocolate for bottom layer, let set for couple of minutes, then squeeze peanut butter mixture. Let set up same time. Add dark chocolate to cover peanut butter layer. Freeze for 10 minutes, then turn pan upside down and they will be ready to eat! Very rich!

Note: I have used this recipe for 10 years and have a board with 48 miniature holes that you put mini liners in and squirt your chocolate "assembly line style," takes 5 minutes and "48" delightful candies later! So good, just ask Dad!

The Candy Cookbook Plus

Baked Caramel Corn

Tastes like Cracker Jacks.

5 quarts popped corn (1¼
  cup unpopped)
1 can peanuts (optional)
2 cups brown sugar
½ cup white corn syrup (or
  ½ molasses)

2 sticks butter or margarine
1 teaspoon salt
½ teaspoon baking soda

Spread popped corn and peanuts in large shallow sheet pan. Keep warm in a 250° oven. Combine brown sugar, corn syrup, butter, and salt in a heavy saucepan. Place on medium heat; bring to a boil and boil 5 minutes. Remove from heat and stir in baking soda (syrup will foam). Pour syrup over popped corn and peanuts in a fine stream. Stir and mix well. Return to oven and bake 45 minutes to 1 hour, stirring every 15 minutes. Cool and serve or store in airtight containers; keep in a cool place. Makes about 5 quarts.

Granny's Kitchen

Pies and Other Desserts

The Shenandoah Valley is one of the nation's most historic and scenic areas, and is home to many Mennonite families.

Christiana Campbell's Tavern Rum Cream Pie

1 Crumb Crust
1 envelope unflavored gelatin
½ cup cold water
5 egg yolks

1 cup sugar
⅓ cup dark rum
1½ cups whipping cream
Unsweetened chocolate

Prepare a Crumb Crust (below). Soften the gelatin in ½ cup cold water. Place over low heat and bring almost to a boil, stirring to dissolve.

Beat the egg yolks and sugar until very light. Stir the gelatin into the egg mixture; cool. Gradually add the rum, beating constantly.

Whip the cream until it stands in soft peaks and fold it into the gelatin mixture. Cool until the mixture begins to set, then spoon it into the Crumb Crust and chill until firm enough to cut. Grate the unsweetened chocolate over the top before serving.

CRUMB CRUST:
2¼ cups graham cracker
    crumbs
½ cup butter, melted

2 tablespoons sugar
½ teaspoon cinnamon

Combine the ingredients and press into a 9-inch pie pan. Chill.

The Williamsburg Cookbook

Simple Sweet Potato Pie

2 large sweet potatoes (1
    pound), baked or boiled
1 can condensed milk
2 eggs

1 tablespoon vanilla
Pinch of salt
½ cup white chocolate, melted
1 unbaked pie shell

Mash potatoes with mixer and add condensed milk, eggs, vanilla, salt and white chocolate. If needed, I add ½ cup evaporated milk. Pour into unbaked pie shell and bake for 35 minutes at 350° or until pie doesn't jiggle in the middle.

Note: One half cup flaked coconut and ½ cup chopped pecans may be added if desired. This gives you the most delicious pie you have ever put in your mouth!

Note: Canned sweet potatoes can also be used.

The Candy Cookbook Plus

Geba's Iron Skillet Chocolate Pie

This is my mother's (Geneva Winningham) chocolate pie recipe. As a child this was our everyday favorite pie. Now at the restaurant it is the number one dessert sold!

2 cups sugar (see Note)
4 rounded tablespoons flour
4 rounded tablespoons dry
  cocoa
½ cup butter or margarine

5 eggs, separated
2¼ cups milk
1 teaspoon real vanilla
1 (9-inch) pie shell (deep-dish)

Mix all dry ingredients. Melt butter or margarine in 10-inch iron skillet (or Teflon-lined skillet). Add dry mixture; mix lightly. Combine beaten egg yolks with milk; add to mixture, stirring constantly. Cook slowly until really thick. Remove from heat, add vanilla, blend well and pour into baked pie shell.

Cool and serve with sweetened whip cream. Serves 6 chocoholics or 8 smaller servings.

Note: The sugar mixture can be cut by ¼–½ if you desire a less sweet chocolate.

Also you can make a meringue of the 5 egg whites (room temperature) to which a pinch of salt, pinch of cream of tartar and ¼ teaspoon vinegar have been added. Beat until stiff and add 10 tablespoons of sugar until well blended. Put on pie; pile high with uneven finish. Bake at 350° for 10–12 minutes.

Cooking with Heart in Hand

Best Pumpkin Pie

1½ cups pumpkin
1 cup brown sugar
3 eggs, separated
½ teaspoon salt

1 tablespoon cornstarch
1–1½ teaspoons pumpkin pie
  spice
1½ cups scalded milk

Mix pumpkin, sugar, egg yolks, salt, cornstarch and spice. Gradually add scalded milk and mix thoroughly. Fold in stiffly beaten egg whites. Pour mixture into an unbaked crust. Bake at 425° for 10 minutes, then reduce heat to 350° and bake for 30 additional minutes.

Happy Times with Home Cooking

Holly's "Best" Apple Pie

The best apple pie that you will ever eat. The secret is soaking the apples in the melted butter. Serve warm to get the best rich butter flavor.

4 cups sliced apples
½ cup butter or margarine, melted
⅔ cup sugar

2 tablespoons flour
¾ teaspoon ground cinnamon
¼ teaspoon nutmeg
1 (9-inch) unbaked pastry shell

TOPPING:
½ cup flour
¼ cup brown sugar

¼ cup butter or margarine
½ cup chopped pecans (optional)

Pour melted butter over sliced apples and soak a few minutes. Combine sugar, flour, and spices. Remove apples from butter (reserve any that is left and use in topping). Coat apples with sugar mixture; pour into pastry shell. Combine topping ingredients and crumble over apples. Bake at 400° for 40–45 minutes, or until brown and apples are tender. Serve warm with a scoop of vanilla ice cream.

Holiday Treats

Kiss Froth

Beat the white of an egg to a stiff froth. Sift on a very little sugar and set in the oven to brown slightly. It makes a very pretty garnishing for sweet dishes.

Thomas Jefferson's Cook Book

Martha Washington Damson Pie

3 eggs, separated
1 cup sugar
2 tablespoons flour
½ cup butter

¼ cup milk
1 teaspoon vaniila
1 cup damson preserves

Beat egg yolks. Add sugar and flour, then mix in butter, milk and flavoring. Spread preserves on unbaked crust. Pour on custard mixture. Bake at 350° for 45 minutes. When done cover with meringue (beaten egg whites with a little sugar) and brown.

Dan River Family Cookbook

Cranberry Pie

2 cups fresh cranberries
1½ cups sugar
½ cup walnuts or pecans,
  chopped
2 eggs

1 cup flour
½ cup butter or margarine,
  melted
¼ cup shortening, melted

Preheat oven to 325°. Spread cranberries in well-greased 10-inch pie plate. Sprinkle cranberries with ½ cup sugar and nuts. In a bowl beat eggs, adding 1 cup sugar gradually. Add flour, butter, shortening, and beat well. Pour mixture over cranberries and bake at 325° for 1 hour. Serve warm or cold with vanilla ice cream or whipped cream.

Tip: Freeze fresh cranberries and prepare this pie out of season.

Command Performances

Southern Nut Pie

2 (9-inch) unbaked pie shells
6 eggs
1¼ cups light brown sugar
2¼ cups light corn syrup
2 teaspoons vanilla, divided
3 tablespoons butter, melted

1½ cups finely ground
  peanuts
2 cups seedless raisins (optional)
1 cup whipping cream
¼ cup confectioners' sugar

Preheat the oven to 350° for 10 minutes before the pies are ready to be baked. Do not bake the shells.

Beat the eggs well. Add the brown sugar, corn syrup, and 1½ teaspoons of vanilla. Mix well. Add the melted butter and peanuts. Add the raisins, if desired. Pour the mixture into the pie crust shells. Bake at 350° for 40 minutes. Cool on a rack.

Whip the cream until stiff. Add the confectioners' sugar and ½ teaspoon of vanilla. Garnish the pies with the sweetened whipped cream. Makes 2 pies.

Favorite Meals from Williamsburg

"The Groaning Board" was a board so heavy with food that the weight of it would make the board groan.

Peanut Pie

From the heart of the peanut country.

1 (3–ounce) package cream
  cheese, softened
½ cup creamy peanut butter
1 cup confectioners' sugar
½ cup milk

1 (9-ounce) carton whipped
  topping
Crushed peanuts, garnish,
1 (1-inch deep) graham cracker
  crust shell

Beat all ingredients except whipped topping. Add whipped topping and pour mixture into pie shell and place in freezer until ready to serve. Crushed peanuts may be sprinkled on top. Serves 6–8.

The VIP Cookbook: A Potpourri of Virginia Cooking

Bourbon Pecan Butterscotch Pie

A different version of the Southern favorite pecan pie.

1 (9-inch) unbaked pie shell
Butterscotch chips for
  bottom of the pie shell
3 eggs
½ cup sour cream
½ cup dark corn syrup

1 cup sugar
⅛ teaspoon salt
1 teaspoon vanilla
2 ounces bourbon
1¾ cups chopped pecans

Preheat oven to 400°. Cover bottom of pie shell with butterscotch chips. In a medium-size mixing bowl combine eggs, sour cream, corn syrup, sugar, salt, vanilla and bourbon. Mix well to blend ingredients and until mixture is smooth. Add pecans. Pour into the pie shell with chips. Place in oven and immediately turn down temperature to 350°. Bake for 50 minutes or until firm and a knife comes out clean when inserted in the center.

Note: If using extra large or jumbo eggs, use a 10-inch pie plate. If a less sweet pie is desired, sugar may be reduced to ¾ cup.

Virginia Wine Country

Pecan Tassies
(or Lemon Tassies)

"Nutty" rich—a real favorite.

PASTRY:

1 (3–ounce) package cream
   cheese, softened
1 stick margarine, softened

1 cup flour
Dash of salt

Blend together cream cheese, margarine, flour, and salt. Shape into 24 balls; press each ball into 1¾-inch muffin tins (press dough in bottom and sides with fingers, do not leave any holes).

FILLING:

2 eggs, beaten
1 cup brown sugar
2 tablespoons margarine,
   melted

1 teaspoon vanilla
Dash of salt
1 cup pecans, chopped

Combine eggs, brown sugar, margarine, vanilla, and salt. Mix well (do not beat with beater, or tops will be crusty instead of nutty). Divide pecans evenly in pastry shells. Pour filling in shells, filling two-thirds full. Bake at 350° for 20–25 minutes. Cool slightly before removing from pans. Cool on wire rack. Makes 24.

Variation: Lemon Tassies, substitute white sugar for brown; omit pecans and add 2 tablespoons lemon juice and 1 teaspoon lemon rind.

Granny's Kitchen

Colonial Innkeeper's Pecan Pie

3 eggs
½ cup sugar
¼ teaspoon salt
1 teaspoon vanilla

1 cup dark corn syrup
¼ cup melted butter
1 cup whole pecan halves
1 unbaked pie shell

Beat eggs; add sugar, salt and vanilla and beat lightly. Add syrup and butter. Place pecans in bottom of unbaked pie shell and pour filling over. Bake at 350° for 50–60 minutes.

Variation: Substitute white corn syrup or use two tablespoons flour and one less egg.

Dan River Family Cookbook

Toll House Cookie Pie

5 eggs
1 cup flour
l cup sugar
½ teaspoon salt
1 cup brown sugar
2 cups butter, melted
2 teaspoons vanilla extract

2 cups pecans
12 ounces semisweet chocolate
   morsels (I prefer Nestle's)
1 (10-inch) pie crust (use a
   deep pan, and flute the crust
   high around the edges)

Preheat oven to 325°. In a large bowl, beat the eggs until light. Blend in the dry ingredients, then add butter and vanilla. Stir in the pecans and chocolate bits, then pour the mixture into the pie shell. Bake on the lower shelf of the oven for 1¼ hours, or until the crust is golden brown and the filling is firm. This can be served hot or cold, but it's easier if it has been cooled to room temperature. This is very rich, so you will want to make the pieces small. Yields 8–10 servings.

The Other Side of the House

Coconut Pie

¼ cup butter, softened
1¾ cups sugar
3 eggs
1 cup sweet milk

1 can flaked coconut
1 tablespoon flour
1 teaspoon vanilla

Mix all ingredients and bake in unbaked crust, 15 minutes at 400°. Then decrease heat to 300° and bake until done.

More Than a Cookbook

Annie Hill Carter and Governor Harry "Light Horse" Lee were married at Shirley Plantation (circa 1613). It is still owned and occupied by 9th- and 10th-generation Hills and Carters. Sherwood Forest Plantation was owned by two presidents, John Tyler and William Henry Harrison. Tyler's descendents still live there.

Whole Lemon–Lemon Pie

1 (9-inch) pie shell, pierced
  and baked
1 stick butter, softened
1 cup sugar
4 large eggs

1 whole lemon, cut in sections
  (remove seeds and stem ends)
Kiwi fruit and strawberries
  for garnish

Bake the pie shell for 5 minutes at 400°. Remove from oven. Turn oven down to 325°. Place all ingredients in blender or food processor, except lemon sections and garnish. Process. Continue processing, adding lemon sections 1 at a time. Blend until smooth.

    Pour into crust and bake for 35 minutes or until set. Cool on rack. Garnish with fresh kiwi fruit and strawberries.

Keeping the Feast

Inverted Lemon Pie

This is a fabulous dessert, light but rich.

4 eggs separated
Pinch of salt
¼ teaspoon cream of tartar
1½ cups sugar, divided

1 lemon
1 cup heavy cream
Mint leaves

Crust: Beat 4 egg whites with a pinch of salt and ¼ teaspoon cream of tartar until stiff. Add 1 cup sugar, a little at a time, and continue beating until mixture is glossy and sugar is melted. Spread in a well-buttered 9-inch pie plate. Bake in a very slow oven (275°) for 25 minutes. Then raise the heat to 300° for 25 minutes or until a faint brown tinge has appeared.

    Filling: Beat 4 egg yolks until thick. Add ½ cup sugar, ¼ cup lemon juice and rind of lemon. Stir and cook in the top of a double boiler until mixture thickens. Use a whisk or spoon. Remove from heat and cool. Whip cream. Fold it into the cooled filling and turn it into the crust. Wrap well and keep in refrigerator. Garnish with mint leaves.

Could I Have Your Recipe?

Clifton Cherry Cobbler

As a child in Tennessee, Mrs. Bice, my next door neighbor, would let me climb her sour cherry trees and pick for pies. Mother would make fresh cobblers and package the remaining cherries in the freezer. When fall and winter rolled around, I would "sneak" the sugared frozen cherries, a few at a time, out of each container, thinking they wouldn't be missed. I thought wrong!

Today, I have a wonderful sour cherry tree in my yard which produces enough cherries for real Clifton Cherry Cobbler to serve at the restaurant (Heart in Hand).

1 cup butter (no substitute)	**4–6 cups red sour cherries**
2 cups self-rising flour	**(fresh or frozen)**
1½ cups sugar	**¼–½ cup sugar**
2 cups milk	**¼ cup butter**
½ teaspoon almond extract	**¼ cup sliced almonds**

Preheat oven to 350°. Put butter in oven-proof roaster-size pan (11 x16½ inches) and melt in oven. Whisk flour, sugar (1½ cups), milk, and almond extract to make a batter. Remove pan from oven, add batter, and sprinkle cherries on top. Scatter extra sugar (¼–½ cup), dots of butter, and almonds on top. Return to oven and bake until batter is golden brown and puffed around the fruit. Takes 30–40 minutes. Delicious with homemade vanilla ice cream. Serves 12.

This recipe can be halved. This is a basic recipe to make apple, peach, blueberry or blackberry cobblers.

Apple: Use 4 cups homemade applesauce or 4–6 cups sliced apples, cinnamon and nutmeg for flavoring, with pecans on top.

Peach: Use 4–6 cups peeled sliced peaches (fresh or frozen). Add almond flavoring and nutmeg. Almonds on top.

Blueberry: Use 4–6 cups berries with mace as flavoring. Sprinkle brown sugar on top.

Blackberry: Use 4–6 cups berries; add extra sugar on top if berries are real tart.

If a more moist cobbler is desired, add 1 cup liquid to each fruit, i.e. orange juice, water, or with 2 or 3 tablespoons liqueur mixed into batter. Crème de cassis for blueberry or blackberry. Peach or apricot brandy or peaches. Applejack for apples or kirsch in cherries.

Cooking with Heart in Hand

Apple Blueberry Crisp

3 cups sliced tart apples
3 cups blueberries
Brown sugar, to taste
1 cup flour
¾ cup sugar

1 teaspoon baking powder
¾ teaspoon salt
1 egg
⅓ cup butter, melted
½ teaspoon cinnamon

Grease baking dish and add apples and blueberries, brown sugar to taste. Mix flour, sugar, baking powder, salt, and unbeaten egg with fork until mixture becomes crumbly. Sprinkle over fruit. Top with cooled, melted butter and sprinkle with cinnamon. Bake at 350° for ½ hour or until top is golden brown. Serve warm with cream. Serves 8.

Culinary Contentment

Apple Crisp with Orange Juice

4 cups sliced pared tart apples
¼ cup orange juice
1 cup sugar
¾ cup flour, sifted

½ teaspoon ground cinnamon
¼ teaspoon ground nutmeg
Dash of salt
⅓ cup butter

Mound apples in buttered pie plate and pour orange juice over them. In separate bowl, combine sugar, flour, spices, and salt. Cut in butter until mixture is crumbly. Sprinkle over apples. Bake at 375° for 45 minutes or until apples are tender and topping is crisp. Serve warm with cream.

Mrs. Barbara Bush, The White House, Washington, DC

The VIP Cookbook: A Potpourri of Virginia Cooking

Trifle

Tipsy cake or English Trifle has been popular with Virginians for 200 years. It is served today most often during the Christmas season. The ingredients have been traditionally ladyfingers, fruit, custard and sherry.

4 eggs	1 cup apricot jam
½ cup sugar	½ cup muscatel
2 cups milk	½ pint heavy cream, whipped
⅛ teaspoon salt	and sweetened
24 ladyfingers	½ cup sliced almonds, toasted

Beat eggs slightly; combine with sugar, milk and salt in double boiler. Cook over hot, not boiling, water, stirring constantly until mixture thickens slightly and coats spoon. Cool. Split ladyfingers and sandwich together with apricot jam. Place in serving dish, making 2 layers; sprinkle each layer with muscatel. Pour custard over and chill several hours or overnight. Before serving, top with cream; sprinkle with almonds. Serves 8–10.

Virginia Hospitality

Snow Eggs

Separate 5 eggs and beat the whites until you can turn the vessel bottom upwards without their leaving it. Gradually add 1 tablespoonful of powdered sugar and ½ teaspoonful of any desired flavoring (Jefferson used orange flower or rose water).

Put 2 cups of milk into a saucepan, add 3 tablespoonfuls of sugar, flavoring, and bring slowly to a boil. Drop the first mixture into the milk poach until well set. Lay them on a wire drainer to drain.

Beat the yolk of 1 egg until thick, stir gradually into the milk. Add a pinch of salt. As soon as the custard thickens pour through a sieve. Put your whites in a serving dish and pour the custard over them. A little wine stirred in is a great improvement.

Thomas Jefferson's Cook Book

Ladyfinger Layer Cake

1 cup butter or margarine,
  softened
2 cups powdered sugar
4 eggs
1 (13¼-ounce) can crushed
  pineapple, drained

1 cup chopped pecans
2 dozen ladyfingers, split
½ pint whipped cream or
  frozen whipped topping

Cream butter and sugar until light and fluffy. Beat in eggs one at a time. Add pineapple and nuts. Mix well. Line a loaf pan with waxed paper. Pack the bottom of the pan with split ladyfingers; fill in the "holes" with broken pieces. Make a layer of the pineapple filling. Continue until pan is full. Cover and refrigerate 6–8 hours or overnight.

Unmold on cake plate and ice with whipped cream or thawed topping. Garnish with mint leaves and additional chopped pecans. Serves 8.

THE What in the World Are We Going
to Have for Dinner? COOKBOOK

Martha's Ladyfinger Delight

1½ envelopes gelatin
⅓ cup cold water
6 eggs, separated
¾ cup lemon juice
1½ cups sugar
1 tablespoon lemon rind

½ tablespoon salt
24 ladyfingers
2 cups whipped cream or
  Dream Whip
½ cup flaked coconut

Soften gelatin in cold water. Put beaten egg yolks and lemon juice in double boiler; stir in ¾ cup sugar. Cook over hot but not boiling water until mixture will coat a spoon. Remove from heat and stir in gelatin and lemon rind until gelatin is dissolved.

Beat egg whites and salt until it forms soft peaks. Slowly add ¾ cup sugar and beat until stiff. Fold in lemon mixture. Line sides and bottom of torte pan with split ladyfingers. Pour half of mixture in prepared pan; arrange rest of split ladyfingers on top, then cover with rest of mixture. Chill. Just before serving, turn out of pan and spread whipped cream on top and sides of cake. Garnish with coconut.

Note: Make at least 1 day before serving.

Kitchen Keys

Four Layer Cherry Pie

Preheat oven to 350°. Spread the following layers in a 9x13–inch pan.

FIRST LAYER:

1 stick margarine, melted   ¾ cup finely chopped nuts
1 cup flour

Mix margarine and flour together. Use a spoon to press the mixture in the pan. Sprinkle nuts on top. Bake for 15 minutes. Chill well.

SECOND LAYER:

1 (8-ounce) package cream   1 cup confectioners' sugar
  cheese, softened   1 cup Cool Whip

Mix well, cream cheese and sugar, then fold in 1 cup Cool Whip (from large container). Pour and spread over the first layer. Chill.

THIRD LAYER:

1 large can cherry pie filling

Pour and spread over second layer. Chill.

FOURTH LAYER:

Cool Whip (remainder of large container)

Spread over third layer. Chill.

WYVE's Cookbook/Photo Album

Cold Lemon Soufflé

1 tablespoon gelatin
¼ cup cold water
3 eggs, separated
1 cup sugar

2 cups heavy cream
⅓ cup lemon juice (not strained)
  and grated rind of 1 lemon
1 teaspoon vanilla

Dissolve gelatin in cold water; dissolve over hot water. Beat yolks until light; add sugar and beat well until smooth and pale. Add lemon juice, vanilla and rind. Add melted gelatin to yolks. Beat whites stiff and fold yolks into them. Fold this into stiffly beaten cream. Chill 2 or 3 hours. Serves 6.

Note: This should be chilled in a regular souffle dish and piled very high. (May be decorated with rosettes of sweetened whipped cream and grated lemon peel, although not necessary.)

The Hunt Country Cookbook

Crème Brûlée

An easy gourmet dessert!

2 cups light cream
5 egg yolks
3½ tablespoons sugar

2 tablespoons vanilla
¼ cup dark brown sugar

Preheat oven to 325°. Heat cream in top of a double boiler until warm. Do not allow water in bottom of double boiler or the cream to boil!

Use electric mixer to beat egg yolks; gradually add sugar. Very slowly add the warm cream to the egg yolk mixture. Allow mixer to run slowly while adding cream; add vanilla and pour into an uncovered 1½-quart oven-proof dish. (Do not use a flat dish since the custard will be too thin.) Place dish in a pan of hot water and bake 40–45 minutes or until set. Remove baking dish and pan of water from the oven and sift the brown sugar over the custard immediately; place custard under broiler for one or two minutes or until the sugar melts. Do not scorch! Chill until very cold! Easy—yet sensational! Serves 6.

Note: Do not allow sugar to be thicker in some places than in others or it won't melt completely.

Words Worth Eating

Easy-Do Fresh Strawberry Mousse

1 pint (about 1½ cups
  mashed) ripe strawberries,
  hulled, cleaned, and dried
1 (3–ounce) package
  strawberry-flavored gelatin
1 cup boiling water
½ tablespoon lemon juice
¼ cup sugar
Pinch of salt

¼ cup strawberry liqueur or
  brandy (optional)
1 cup heavy cream
Additional sweetened-flavored
  whipped cream for garnish
Additional whole strawberries
  for garnish
Fresh mint sprigs for garnish
  (optional)

Slice strawberries and then coarsely mash with a potato masher; set aside. In a small bowl, dissolve gelatin in boiling water. In a large bowl, combine strawberries, lemon juice, sugar, and salt. Add dissolved gelatin and strawberry liqueur, if desired, mixing well. Chill in the refrigerator until mixture is the consistency of unbeaten egg whites.

In a chilled small heavy bowl, beat cream with chilled beaters until stiff peaks are formed. Fold whipped cream into chilled gelatin mixture. Spoon mousse into individual sherbet glasses or dishes or a 1-quart mold; chill in the refrigerator for several hours until mousse is set. Garnish each serving with additional sweetened-flavored whipped cream, if desired, a whole strawberry, and a fresh mint sprig, if desired.

Variation: One pint fresh raspberries may be substituted. Purée and strain berries. Raspberry liqueur may be used. Yields 4 servings.

More Richmond Receipts

Strawberry Soufflé

Take one quart of fresh strawberries, mash them through a colander, add one cup sugar and the beaten whites of five eggs; place in buttered dish; sprinkle sugar over top; bake slowly half hour. Serve with cream sauce.

Chesapeake Bay Country

Mousse in a Minute

1 (6-ounce) package
  chocolate chips
¾ cup scalded milk
2 tablespoons strong coffee
	2 eggs
	4 teaspoons dark rum or
	  (sherry, Grand Marnier, or
	  Crème de Menthe)

Put all ingredients in blender. Whirl for 1½ minutes. Pour into 4–6 serving dishes. Refrigerate at least 2 hours. Top with whipped cream and serve.

Culinary Contentment

Cream Puffs

Take one and a half pints water and put into a porcelain kettle, let it come to a boil; add quarter pound butter and let it melt; then stir in quickly three-quarters pound flour, and three teaspoonfuls Royal baking powder (sifted into the flour three or four times), this forms a stiff dough; take from fire, let cool, then beat in six eggs (two at a time); stir to a smooth paste; have baking pan greased, take one large tablespoonful at a time and lay in the pan, a little space between each; bake about twenty minutes, in hot oven, to a delicate brown.

FILLING:

Take one pint fresh milk, two tablespoonfuls corn starch, mixed with a little milk, quarter pound pulverized sugar and two eggs; stir well together, and cook until it thickens, stirring all the time; flavor with vanilla, or any seasoning you prefer; split the cake at one side, and fill with this cream.

The Old Virginia Cook Book

Old recipes called for many eggs because the hens were not as richly fed, and the eggs were smaller.

Baked Apple Pudding with Sauce

A delicious harvest dessert.

⅓ cup butter or margarine
1 cup sugar
1 large egg (or 2 small)
1 cup flour
1 teaspoon baking soda
¼ teaspoon salt

1 teaspoon cinnamon
½ teaspoon nutmeg
1 teaspoon vanilla
2 cups grated or finely
  chopped apples
½ cup chopped nuts

Cream butter and sugar. Add egg and beat until light. Sift together dry ingredients; add to creamed mixture. Stir in vanilla, apples, and nuts. Turn into a greased 8- or 9-inch square pan. Bake at 350° for 35–45 minutes or until tests done. Serve warm with sauce or whipped cream (or both).

SAUCE:

1 stick butter or margarine
½ cup granulated sugar
½ cup brown sugar

2 tablespoons light corn syrup
6 tablespoons cream
1 teaspoon vanilla

Combine butter, sugars, corn syrup, and cream in small saucepan. Bring to a boil, stirring constantly. Boil 1 minute. Remove from heat and add vanilla. Serve warm over Baked Apple Pudding.

Granny's Kitchen

Mary Baldwin Apple Nut Pudding

1 egg
¾ cup brown sugar
1 teaspoon vanilla
3 tablespoons (heaping) flour
1½ teaspoons baking powder
¼ teaspoon salt

½ teaspoon nutmeg
½ cup chopped nuts (walnuts
  or pecans)
2 medium apples, pared and
  chopped fine

Break egg into bowl; beat with sugar and vanilla. Add flour, baking powder, salt, nutmeg, and blend well. Stir in nuts and chopped apple. Bake in greased and floured 9-inch square pan in moderate oven (350°) for 30 minutes. Serves 4–6.

From Ham to Jam

Toasted Pecan Pudding

½ cup margarine
1 cup flour
1½ cups flaked coconut

½–1 cup chopped pecans
¼ cup brown sugar

Microwave margarine on HIGH for 45 seconds until melted. Mix next 4 ingredients in until crumbly. Brown half of crumbs at a time in flat dish for 6–7 minutes, stirring frequently to brown evenly. Cool.

PUDDING:

2 (3½-ounce) packages
  instant vanilla pudding

3 cups milk
1 (9-inch) container Cool Whip

Beat pudding and milk together on low for 2 minutes. Chill 5 minutes until set. Fold in Cool Whip. Spread half of crumbs in bottom of 8x12-inch dish. Spread pudding over crumbs. Sprinkle remaining crumbs over the top. Chill and serve the same day made. Yields 8 servings.

Mennonite Country-Style Recipes

Date Pudding (II)

SYRUP:

1 cup brown sugar
1 cup water

1 tablespoon butter

BATTER:

½ cup brown sugar
1 cup flour
2 teaspoons baking powder
¼ teaspoon salt

½ cup milk
1 cup dates, chopped
½ cup chopped nuts

Combine 1 cup brown sugar and water; cook together 3 minutes to make syrup. Remove from heat and add butter. To make batter: Sift sugar, flour, baking powder and salt together. Add milk and stir until smooth. Fold in chopped dates and nuts, blending well into mixture. Pour syrup in a greased baking dish. Pour batter on top of hot syrup and bake at 350° for 35–40 minutes. Serve plain or with whipped cream. Makes 6 servings.

Mennonite Community Cookbook

Chocolate Chestnut Pudding

6 ounces semisweet chocolate
1¾ cups milk
½ cup sugar
⅛ teaspoon salt
2 teaspoons vanilla
2 eggs
2 egg yolks

1 (15½-ounce) can chestnut
  purée
1 cup whipping cream
2 tablespoons confectioners'
  sugar
Candied violets (optional)

Preheat the oven to 350°. Butter a 1½-quart soufflé dish. Combine the chocolate, milk, sugar, and salt in the top of a double boiler. Mix well. Cook over hot water until the chocolate melts. Remove from the heat. Add the vanilla.

Beat the eggs and egg yolks well. Gradually add the chestnut purée, beating until the mixture is smooth. Gradually add the chocolate mixture to the chestnut mixture, beating constantly. Pour the pudding into the prepared dish and place it in a pan of hot water on the middle shelf of the oven. Bake for 60–65 minutes. Cool completely. Refrigerate overnight. Whip the cream until stiff. Add the confectioners' sugar. Garnish with the whipped cream and candied violets, if desired. Serves 8.

Note: This pudding is very rich—servings should be small.

Favorite Meals from Williamsburg

Chocolate Pizza

In medium pizza pan, pour 2 cups semisweet melted chocolate. Place miniature pretzels all around with maraschino red and green cherries with stems, miniature marshmallows, toasted coconut, pecan halves and cashews. You must work fast as chocolate will harden and then "Pizza Fixins" will not stick! After all ingredients are in place, draw slices with cake icing in decorator tube. This is a great treat for an 8- to 10-year-old group get-together!

Let your imagination run wild!

The Candy Cookbook Plus

Chocolate Intemperance

1 (19.8-ounce) package Duncan
 Hines Fudge Brownie Mix
2 tablespoons water
3 eggs
1 pound semisweet chocolate
 bits
½ cup strong coffee
3 eggs, separated
½ cup Kahlúa (or less)
2 tablespoons sugar
1 cup whipped cream

Mix brownie mix with water and 3 eggs. Bake in 2 foil-lined 9-inch cake pans until done, 350° about 15–18 minutes. Set aside to cool. Melt chocolate with coffee in top of double boiler. Remove from heat. Beat 3 egg yolks until pale yellow. Stir into cooled chocolate mixture. Gradually stir in Kahlúa.

In separate bowl beat whites, gradually adding sugar until stiff. Whip cream. Gently fold whipped cream into cooled chocolate and then fold in egg whites. Place one brownie layer in springform pan. Pour chocolate mixture over. Top with remaining brownie layer. Chill. This dessert serves about 20 people and freezes nicely.

Culinary Contentment

Peanut Chocolate Dessert

½ cup butter, softened
1 cup flour
⅔ cup finely chopped dry
 roasted peanuts
1 (8-ounce) package cream
 cheese, softened
⅓ cup peanut butter
1 cup powdered sugar
1 (12-ounce) carton Cool
 Whip, thawed and divided
1 small package vanilla instant
 pudding
1 small package chocolate
 instant pudding
2¾ cups milk
1 small bar chocolate, shaved
½ cup chopped dry roasted
 peanuts

Cut butter into flour till mixture resembles coarse meal. Stir ⅔ cup of peanuts into flour. Press into 9x13x2-inch pan. Bake at 350° for 20 minutes or until lightly browned. Cool. Combine cream cheese, peanut butter, and powdered sugar. Beat until fluffy. Stir in 1 cup whipped topping; spread over crust. Chill. Combine puddings and milk; beat 2 minutes at medium speed. Spread over cream cheese mixture. Spread remaining Cool Whip over pudding layer. Garnish with shaved chocolate and roasted peanuts.

Cooking with Class

Angel Food Dessert

Use whole cake or the interior of one that is to be stuffed. Pluck into small pieces.

⅔ cups chopped nuts
  (optional)
½ cup brandy or bourbon,
  or more

1 pint whipped cream

Mix well. Place in serving dish. Mixture must be moist enough to stick together. Refrigerate at least 6 hours. Serve with Hot Chocolate Sauce and whipped cream.

HOT CHOCOLATE SAUCE (MRS. WHITE'S):

4 squares baking chocolate
3 tablespoons butter
2 cups sugar

2 (5-ounce) cans Pet Milk
1 teaspoon vanilla
Pinch of salt

Melt chocolate and butter over low heat. Mix sugar, milk, vanilla, and salt to start dissolving. Add sugar mixture to chocolate. Stir constantly until sugar is melted. Turn up heat, bring to good boil and cook for 3 minutes, stirring constantly to keep from sticking. Keeps indefinitely in ice box.

More Than a Cookbook

French Mint Patties

1 cup margarine
2 cups powdered sugar
4 ounces baking chocolate
4 eggs, beaten
1 teaspoon peppermint flavor

2 cups graham cracker crumbs
2 teaspoons vanilla
½ pint whipping cream,
  whipped

Beat margarine and sugar until light. Add baking chocolate, melted and cooled. Beat! Beat! Beat! Add eggs and beat. Add peppermint and vanilla. Beat!

Line 18 muffin cups with paper cups. Sprinkle bottom of each with graham cracker crumbs. Fill with custard. Sprinkle crumbs on top. Freeze. Just before serving add whipped cream.

Command Performances

Silver Bowl Macaroons

4 eggs, separated
1 cup sugar
1 pint milk
2 or more tablespoons sweet
  sherry

1 envelope gelatin
2 dozen almond macaroons
1 pint heavy cream, whipped

Make custard sauce as follows: Beat yolks of eggs in double boiler. Add ½ cup sugar and milk and cook over hot water till mixture thickens. Remove custard and add sherry. Soften gelatin in a little cold water and add to hot sauce. Cool and fold in beaten egg whites. In a silver bowl, place crushed macaroons, then sauce. Alternate layers until bowl is almost full. Chill several hours. Top with cream sweetened with ½ cup sugar. Serves 10.

More Delectable Cookery of Alexandria

Macaroon Ice Cream Dessert

½ gallon coffee ice cream
½ pound almond macaroons
Rum or sherry (Taylor's
  Golden)

½ pint whipped cream or
  frozen whipped topping
1 package slivered almonds,
  toasted

Remove ice cream from freezer to soften. Crumble macaroons in a 3-quart bowl. Sprinkle rum or sherry over macaroons. Spread softened ice cream over macaroons, then cover with whipped cream. Sprinkle with toasted almonds. Toast almonds by placing them in a flat pan under the broiler for a few minutes until they have browned—watch closely. Place dessert in freezer until firm. Remove from freezer a short while before serving. Serves 8.

*THE What in the World Are We Going
to Have for Dinner? COOKBOOK*

Norfolk Naval Base is the largest in the nation, as well as the largest employer in Norfolk.

Tangy Fruit Combo

Quick and Easy! Serve as a dessert with Cool Whip on top, a snack, or any time.

2 tablespoons Tang
1 (3-ounce) package vanilia
  pudding (instant)
2 cans pineapple tidbits,
  not drained

1 can sliced peaches
Fruits–kiwi (sliced), strawberries,
  oranges, bananas (sliced),
  grapes, cherries

Sprinkle Tang and pudding mix (less if desired) over sliced fruit. Stir and refrigerate.

Taste of Goodness

Charlotte

Stew any desired fruit until soft. Sweeten to taste and put in any spices you may wish. There should be 2 cups. Trim the crusts of slices of bread and cut bread to about the width of two fingers. Dip in butter and fry until a golden brown. Powder with sugar. Butter a round baking pan or Pyrex dish and line with the fingers of fried bread. Pour the fruit in and set in a moderate oven for half an hour. Turn out on a platter. Set under the broiler a moment to glaze the sugar.

Thomas Jefferson's Cook Book

Catalog of Contributing Cookbooks

PHOTO COURTESY OF VIRGINIA TOURISM CORPORATION

Virginia Beach is a stretch of sand 28 miles long. Near the entrance to Hampton Roads, two lighthouses—one old, one new—are in command.

Catalog of Contributing Cookbooks

All recipes in this book have been selected from the cookbooks shown on the following pages. Individuals who wish to obtain a copy of any particular book may do so by sending a check or money order to the address listed by each cookbook. Please note the postage and handling charges that may be required. State residents add tax only when requested. Prices and addresses are subject to change, and the books may sell out and become unavailable. Retailers are invited to call or write to same address for discount information. Some of the contributing cookbooks have gone out of print since the original publication of this book. See pages 289–290 for a listing of out-of-print cookbooks.

THE BELLE GROVE PLANTATION COOKBOOK

Belle Grove, Inc.
P. O. Box 537   540-869-2028
Middletown, VA 22645

This is a collection of recipes from the Belle Grove, Inc. Board of Trustees, Docents Guild, community members, and the descendants of Jost Hite, the builder of Belle Grove, and other Hite family members. We hope the users of this collection of recipes from the Shenandoah Valley will enjoy them. We have shared with you something of the spirit that still pervades this venerable mansion. The book has 246 pages and 400 recipes.

$12.50   (Includes postage and handling)   ISBN 0-9616530-0-0

Make check payable to Belle Grove, Inc.

CHILDREN'S PARTY BOOK

Junior League of Hampton Roads   Phone 757-873-0281
729 Thimble Shoals Boulevard, Suite 4-D   Fax 757-873-8747
Newport News, VA 23606   www.jlhr.org-volunteer@jlhr.org

Children's Party Book contains over 25 preplanned children's parties, complete with invitations, menus, activities, decorations, and games. A unique gift for teachers, care-givers, and new or expecting parents. First published in 1984, it was updated in 1996 to include multi-cultural holidays such as Hanukkah and Kwanzaa.

$13.95   Retail price   Visa/MC accepted
  .70   Tax for Virginia residents   ISBN 0-9613600-3-8
 3.50   Postage and handling

Make check payable to Junior League of Hampton Roads

COMMAND PERFORMANCES

Opera Roanoke
The Dumas Center, 108 First Street   Phone 540-982-2742
Roanoke, VA 24016   www.operaroanoke.org

This book will delight gourmet cooks and music lovers alike! The format features an operatic theme, from "Curtain's Up," to "Encores." Divider pages depict various operas produced by the Southwest Virginia Opera–a young professional company in Roanoke. The more than 400 recipes were contributed by board members, performers and friends. 248 pages, over 400 recipes.

$10.00   Retail price
 3.00   Postage and handling

Make check payable to Opera Roanoke

COOKING WITH HEART IN HAND

by Suzanne W. Worsham
P. O. Box 170 Main Street
Clifton, VA 20124   Phone 703-830-4111

Down home southern cooking with original family and friends recipes. Included in the 231-page cookbook are many favorite recipes served and enjoyed at the Heart in Hand restaurant.

$16.95   Retail price   ISBN 0-9619445-0-1
   .85   Tax for Virginia residents
  3.45   Postage and handling

Make check payable to *Cooking with Heart in Hand*

COULD I HAVE YOUR RECIPE?

by Janice Porter
2104 Lirio Court   Phone 703-620-2383
Reston, VA 20191   porterwj@comcast.net

Could I Have Your Recipe? is a 114-page, indexed, charmingly illustrated collection of favorite recipes of the author. She started cooking and collecting recipes as a child and has never stopped. This book contains her favorites of 40 years.

$10.95   Retail price   ISBN 0-96076700-2
  2.50   Postage and handling

Make check payable to Janice Porter Books

CULINARY CONTENTMENT

Virginia Tech Faculty Women's Club
P. O. Box 10252   mjs8439@aol.com
Blacksburg, VA 24060

A 256-page collection of over 600 favorite recipes of the members of the Virginia Tech Faculty Women's Club. The "Entertaining" section features recipes for multi-course dinner parties and brunches and for international dinners. Proceeds from sales are used to provide scholarships for outstanding students at Virginia Tech.

$8.00   Retail price
  .36   Tax for Virginia residents
 2.00   Postage and handling

Make check payable to Virginia Tech Faculty Women's Club

GRANNY'S KITCHEN

by Theone L. Neel
6983 Clearfork Road   Phone 276-988-6472
Bastian, VA 24314-4532

Granny's Kitchen was written as a labor of love, which was a gift to the author's grandchildren. The simple kitchen-tested recipes call for ingredients that most cooks have on hand. Over 800 recipes, plus menu ideas and cooking tips sprinkled throughout. Index. 409 pages.

$12.00   Retail price
 3.00   Postage and handling

Make check payable to Theone L. Neel

THE GREAT CHEFS OF VIRGINIA COOKBOOK

The Donning Company
c/o Schiffer Publishing Ltd.
4880 Lower Valley Road   Phone 610-593-1777
Atglen, PA 19310

Virginia Chefs Association President, Marcel Desaulniers, collected almost 200 delicious recipes from 35 members. Short biographies of each contributor and mouthwatering illustrations. You'll find some of the freshest, most creative recipes available not just in Virginia, but in America.

$10.95   Retail price   ISBN 0-89865-242-1
  .49   Tax for Virginia residents
 3.95   Postage and handling

Make check payable to The Donning Company Publishers

THE GREAT TASTE OF VIRGINIA SEAFOOD COOKBOOK

by Mary Reid Barrow with Robin Browder
The Donning Company Publishers, c/o Schiffer Publishing Ltd.
4880 Lower Valley Road   Phone 610-593-1777
Atglen, PA 19310

Containing over 300 of the best seafood recipes in the state, this book includes gourmet recipes from celebrated Virginia chefs, prize-winning recipes from the Annual Virginia Seafood Contest, tips on ways to buy and prepare seafood, fun facts about fish and shellfish, historical tidbits, and color photographs.

$12.95   Retail price   ISBN 0-89865-323-1
  .58   Tax for Virginia residents
 3.95   Postage and handling

Make check payable to The Donning Company Publishers

THE HAM BOOK

by Robert W. Harrell, Jr. and Monette R. Harrell
Harrell Hams
407 W. Riverview Drive   Phone 757-539-2447
Suffolk, VA 23434   ham5ham5@yahoo.com

This historical cookbook about ham has over 350 of the most delicious recipes using ham of all types, and includes accompanying delights from appetizers to desserts. Was selected as one of the Top Fifteen Virginia Cookbooks by *Virginia Living Magazine*.

$14.95   Retail price   ISBN 0-915442-14-0
  .67   Tax for VA residents
 2.00   Postage and handling

Make check payable to Harrell Hams

KITCHEN KEYS

Episcopal Churchwomen of St. Peter's Parish Church
8400 St. Peters Lane   Phone 804-932-4846
New Kent, VA 23124

St. Peter's Episcopal Churchwomen chose this project to finance their missionary budget and support the operation of their small historic church. Some members, descendants of Martha Dandridge Curtis who married George Washington, have included old family recipes besides more contemporary versions from other members.

$15.00   Retail price
  .68   Tax for Virginia residents
 2.95   Postage and handling

Make check payable to E.C.W. St. Peter's Church

MENNONITE COMMUNITY COOKBOOK

by Mary Emma Showalter
Herald Press   Phone 724-887-8500 or 800-245-7894
616 Walnut Avenue   Fax 724-887-3111
Scottdale, PA 15683-1999   www.heraldpress.com • hp@mph.org

Here's 1,100 mouthwatering recipes from old Mennonite cookbooks, brought up to date with standard measures and directions. Simple but wonderful country cookery contributed by Mennonite women and families noted for their excellent cooking.

$19.99   Retail price   Visa/MC accepted
  $2.50   Postage and handling   ISBN 0-8361-3625-X
Make check payable to Herald Press

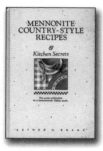

MENNONITE COUNTRY-STYLE RECIPES AND KITCHEN SECRETS

by Esther H. Shank
Herald Press   Phone 724-887-8500 or 800-245-7894
616 Walnut Avenue   Fax 724-887-3111
Scottdale, PA 15683-1999   www.heraldpress.com • hp@mph.org

Mennonite homemaker Esther H. Shank, from Harrisonburg, Virginia, has collected and perfected good recipes and food preparation tips for 25 years. In this remarkable collection of more than 1,000 recipes and hundreds of hints for success, she shares her legacy of kitchen know-how.

$21.99   Retail price   Visa/MC accepted
  $2.50   Postage and handling   ISBN 0-8361-3697-7
Make check payable to Herald Press

THE MICROWAVE AFFAIR: SINGLE SERVINGS

by Paula J. Smith
Serenity's Edge
4404 Murray Hollow road   Phone 540-947-2468
Thaxton, VA 24174

This neat "single serving" cookbook is perfect for people who want to eat well but spend little time in the kitchen and have no wasted ingredients or leftovers. It is easy to read with instructions in 1, 2, 3 steps. Includes 208 carefully tested recipes and 2 weeks of menus for easy meal planning. It sports a red vinyl loose-leaf binder for easy viewing.

$14.95   Retail price   ISBN 0-914749-00-5
  3.00   Postage and handling
Make check payable to Serenity's Edge

MORE THAN A COOKBOOK: A FLAVORFUL HERITAGE

Stafford County Historical Society
P. O. Box 1664   Phone 540-752-9339
Stafford, VA 22555-1664

This cookbook contains recipes from appetizers to charts on weights and measures and charts on herbs and spices. In addition to the delicious recipes, the book contains a wealth of Stafford County history.

$12.50   Retail price
  3.00   Postage and handling
Make check payable to Stafford County Historical Society

THE MOUNT VERNON COOKBOOK

Mount Vernon Ladies' Association
P. O. Box 110   Phone 703-799-8691
Mount Vernon, VA 22121

This colorful publication includes a fascinating introduction describing life in the 18th century and the Washington's special style of living and entertaining. Sparkling laminated cover, spiral-bound, 400 time-tested recipes, enhanced by color photographs of the Mount Vernon estate. A fully cross-referenced index, 256 pages, 34 line drawings, 10 color illustrations.

$15.95   Retail price
.72   Tax for VA residents
Call for postage and handling charges
Make check payable to The Mount Vernon Ladies' Assn.

RICHMOND RECEIPTS

by Jan Carlton
12066 Foxfield Circle   Phone 804-364-5120
Richmond, VA 23233   janetcarlton8!@aol.com

Culled from the recipes of a variety of local residents, *Richmond Receipts* is a smorgasbord of regional cuisine, local culture, and treasured history. Over 600 recipes are nestled among interesting tidbits of Richmond folklore, and garnished with handsome illustrations and fascinating anecdotes. Recommended by *Bon Apetite* magazine.

$17.00   Retail price (includes postage and handling)
Make check payable to Jan Carlton

THE SMITHFIELD COOKBOOK

The Woman's Club of Smithfield
P. O. Box 754   Phone 757-357-3063
Smithfield, VA 23431   sgewell@charter.net

This collection of traditional local recipes and stories of historical significance define the town of Smithfield and Isle of Wight County. The customs and traditions of the area are reflected in the food and dining practices of past generations, and the cookbook is a record of such to be handed down and preserved.

$15.00   Retail price
$.75   Tax for VA residents
$2.00   Postage and handling
Make check payable to The Woman's Club of Smithfield

A SOUTHERN LADY'S SPIRIT

Riddicks Folly
P. O. Box 1722   Phone 757-934-1390
Suffolk, VA 23439

The book is prefaced by a fictional diary of a Suffolk resident during the Civil War (based on actual events). Recipes feature local favorites including seafood and peanuts, spiced with lines of homespun advice and common sense, with occasional recipes for historical favorites thrown in.

$6.50   Retail price
.29   Tax for VA residents
2.00   Postage and handling
Make check payable to Riddick's Folly

SPOTSYLVANIA FAVORITES COOKBOOK

The Spotsylvania County Woman's Club
4116 Redwood Circle   Phone 540-898-0175
Fredericksburg, VA 22408

The *Spotsylvania Favorites Cookbook* was first published in 1985 and had its third printing in 1988. Not only does it contain delicious recipes, it has information and sketches of old homes in Spotsylvania County, Virginia. This book was compiled by members of the county's Woman's Club as a fundraising project.

$10.00   Retail price (includes postage and handling)
Make check payable to The Spotsylvania County Woman's Club

THE STUFFED COUGAR

The Patrons Association of the Collegiate Schools
103 N. Mooreland Road   Phone 804-740-7077
Richmond, VA 23229

The Stuffed Cougar is 375 pages of tested recipes. First printed in 1973, it is still a very popular cookbook. Many people who collect cookbooks insist *The Stuffed Cougar* is their favorite!

$14.95   Retail price   ISBN 0-681217-0-30
  .67   Tax for VA residents
3.00   Postage and handling
Make check payable to The Collegiate Schools

THOMAS JEFFERSON'S COOK BOOK

by Marie Kimball
The University Press of Virginia
Box 400318   Phone 800-831-3406
Charlottesville, VA 22903

Out of print for several years, this delightful cookbook has been reprinted in response to popular demand. Marie Kimball has fully adapted Thomas Jefferson's cuisine to practical modern use by reducing the enormous proportions of the 18th century to the familiar measures of the present. Features an essay by Helen D. Bullock, entitled, "Thomas Jefferson . . . Gourmet."

$12.95   Retail price   ISBN 0-8139-0706-3
  .58   Tax for VA residents
4.00   Postage and handling
Make check payable to The University Press of Virginia

TIDEWATER ON THE HALF SHELL

The Junior League of Norfolk-Virginia Beach, Inc.   Phone 757-623-7270
P. O. Box 956   Fax 757-623-3932
Norfolk, VA 23501   www.jlnvb.org • info@jlnvb.org

Since its first printing in 1985, *Tidewater on the Half Shell* has sold over 150,000 copies. This cookbook of casual elegance captures the classic yet contemporary flavor of Hampton Roads' distinctive cuisine with 566 fine Virginia recipes.

$18.95   Retail price   Visa/MC accepted
 $.95   Tax for VA residents   ISBN 0-9614767-0-2
$5.00   Postage and handling
Make check payable to JLNVB

VIRGINIA HOSPITALITY

Junior League of Hampton Roads
729 Thimble Shoals Boulevard, Suite 4-D
Newport News, VA 23606

Phone 757-873-0281
Fax 757-873-8747
volunteer@jlhr.org • ww.jlhr.org

Virginia Hospitality is a 300-page community cookbook first published in 1975. It features 600 triple-tested recipes, sketches, and histories of famous Virginia houses and discussions of cooking and entertaining. This cookbook is in its 19th printing. Inducted into the McIllhenney Tabasco Community Cookbook Hall of Fame in 1991.

$17.95   Retail price
  $.90   Tax for VA residents
 $3.50   postage and handling

Visa/MC accepted
ISBN 0-9613600-1-1

Make check payable to Junior League of Hampton Roads

THE VIRGINIA HOUSE-WIFE

by Mary Randolph/edited by Karen Hess
University of South Carolina Press
718 Devine Street
Columbia, SC 29208

Phone 800-768-2500
www.sc.edu/uscpress/

This book is part of the University of South Carolina Press's First Cookbooks in America Series designed as facsimile editions of 1800's cookbooks. Contains recipes which reflect the social commentaries of the early 19th century, considered to be the "golden age of cooking" in America. It is believed that *The Virginia House-wife* (1824) is indeed THE oldest cookbook in America.

$29.95   Retail price
  5.00   Postage and handling

Visa/MC/Disc
ISBN 0-87249-423-3

Make check payable to USC Press

THE VIRGINIA PRESIDENTIAL HOMES COOKBOOK

by Payne Bouknight Tyler
P. O. Box 8, Sherwood Forest Plantation
Charles City, VA 23030

Phone 804-829-5377

President Tyler's granddaughter writes lovely descriptions of the homes of eight Virginia presidents. These memories, manuscripts and recipes, present some of the social and cultural influences of these presidents. Includes 64 pages, full color, interior and exterior of presidential houses and the White House.

$15.00   Retail price
  .75   Tax for VA residents
 3.00   Postage and handling

Make check payable to Sherwood Forest Plantation

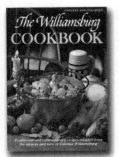

THE WILLIAMSBURG COOKBOOK

by Letha Booth and the staff of the Colonial Williamsburg Foundation
c/o *Williamsburg Catalog*
P. O. Box 3532
Williamsburg, VA 23187

Phone 800-446-9240

Visitors return again and again for the delicious dishes served at Colonial Williamsburg's famed taverns and restaurants. In this best-selling book, the authors have adapted for the home kitchen 193 traditional and contemporary recipes from Colonial Williamsburg's dining places. Wonderfully fascinating historical tales.

$16.95   Retail price
  .76   Tax for VA residents
 5.00   Postage and handling

(Item #2881)
ISBN 0-910412-91-X

Make check payable to *Williamsburg Catalog*

The cookbooks listed below are out of print and may no longer be available for purchase. Quail Ridge Press is pleased to offer a selection of the most popular recipes from these cookbooks in fulfillment of our mission of

Preserving America's Food Heritage.

Apron Strings
The Women's Committee of the Richmond
  Symphony
Richmond, VA

The Best of The Bushel
Junior League of Charlottesville, Inc.
Charlottesville, VA

The Boar's Head Cookbook
Boar's Head Inn/Compiled by Felicia Rogan
Charlottesville, VA

The Candy Cookbook Plus
Bobbie S. Ellis
Chester, VA

Cardinal Cuisine
Mount Vernon Hospital Auxiliary
Alexandria, VA

**Chesapeake Bay Country: Nature Notes
  and Country Cooking**
The Donning Company Publishers
Virginia Beach, VA

Cooking with Class, Volume II
Ruth Bible Class
Chincoteague, VA

Dan River Family Cookbook
Dan River Inc.
Danville, VA

Delectable Cookery of Alexandria
by Polly Norment Burke and
  Anne Mudd Cabaniss
Alexandria, VA

Dining at the Homestead
by Albert Schnarwyler/Eleanor and James
  Ferguson
The Homestead
Hot Springs, VA

The Enlightened Titan
The Patrons Association of Trinity Episcopal
  School
Richmond, VA

**Favorite Meals from Williamsburg:
  A Menu Cookbook**
The Colonial Williamsburg Foundation
Williamsburg, VA

The Foxcroft Cook Book
Foxcroft School
Middleburg, VA

From Ham to Jam
Mary Baldwin Alumnae Association
Staunton, VA

Gourmet by the Bay
Dolphin Circle of The King's Daughters
Virginia Beach, VA

Happy Times with Home Cooking
Barbara Easter's Shenandoah Valley Recipes
Mt. Airy, NC

Hearthside Cookbook
by Nancy Carter Crump
Howell Press
Charlottesville, VA

A Heritage of Good Tastes
TWIG, Junior Auxiliary of Alexandria
  Hospital
Alexandria, VA 22302

**Historic Lexington Cooks: Rockbridge
  Regional Recipes**
Historic Lexington Foundation
Lexington, VA

Holiday Treats from Granny's Kitchen
by Theone L. Neel
Bastian, VA

The Hunt Country Cook Book
Warrenton Antiquarian Society
Warrenton, VA

Keeping the Feast
Women of St. Thomas Episcopal Church
Abingdon, VA

More Delectable Cookery of Alexandria
by Polly Norment Burke and
    Anne Mudd Cabaniss
Alexandria, VA

More Richmond Receipts
by Jan Carlton
Norfolk, VA

A Neapolitan Peasant's Cookbook
by John J. Scialdone
The Donnine Company Publishers
Virginia Beach, VA

The New Life Cookbook
by Marceline A. Newton
The Donning Company Publishers
Virginia Beach, VA

Of Pots and Pipkins
The Junior League of Roanoke Valley
Roanoke, VA

The Old Virginia Cook Book
Petersburg Department of Tourism
Petersburg, VA

*The Other Side of the House: A
    Cookbook and Survival Manual*
by Janie Whitehurst
Virginia Beach, VA

The Rappahannock Seafood Cookbook
Rappahannock Community College
    Educational Foundation, Inc.
Warsaw, VA

*Recipes from Jeffersonville Woman's
    Club*
Jeffersonville Woman's Club
Tazewell, VA

*Smyth County Extension Homemakers
    Cookbook Volume II*
Smyth County Extension Homemakers
Marion, VA

Taste of Goodness
United Methodist Women
Farmville, VA

Think Healthy
Fairfax County Department of Extension
Fairfax, VA

The Trellis Cookbook
by Marcel Desaulniers
Williamsburg, VA

*The VIP Cookbook: A Potpourri of
    Virginia Cooking, Volume VII*
American Cancer Society
Glen Allen, VA

Virginia Seasons
Junior League of Richmond
Richmond, VA

Virginia Wine Country
by Hilde Gabriel Lee and Allan E. Lee
Charlottesville, VA

*Virginia's Historic Restaurants and
    Their Recipes*
by Dawn O'Brien
John F. Blair, Publisher
Winston-Salem, NC

*THE What in the World are We Going to
    Have for Dinner? COOKBOOK*
by Sarah E. Drummond
Richmond, VA

The Words Worth Eating Cookbook
by Jacquelyn G. Legg
Newport News, VA

WYVE's Bicentennial Cookbook
WYVE Radio Station
Wytheville, VA

WYVE's Cookbook/Photo Album
WYVE Radio Station
Wytheville, VA

Index

This statue in Richmond of the famous Civil War general has the shortest inscription of all the world's monuments—"Lee."

BEST OF THE BEST STATE COOKBOOK SERIES

ALABAMA
(all-new edition)
(original edition)*

ALASKA

ARIZONA

ARKANSAS

BIG SKY
Includes Montana and
Wyoming

CALIFORNIA

COLORADO

FLORIDA
(all-new edition)
(original edition)*

GEORGIA
(all-new edition)
(original edition)*

GREAT PLAINS
Includes North and South
Dakota, Nebraska, and
Kansas

HAWAII

IDAHO

ILLINOIS

INDIANA

IOWA

KENTUCKY
(all-new edition)
(original edition)*

LOUISIANA

LOUISIANA II

MICHIGAN

MID-ATLANTIC
Includes Maryland,
Delaware, New Jersey, and
Washington, D.C.

MINNESOTA

MISSISSIPPI
(all-new edition)
(original edition)*

MISSOURI

NEVADA

NEW ENGLAND
Includes Rhode Island,
Connecticut, Massachusetts,
Vermont, New Hampshire,
and Maine

NEW MEXICO

NEW YORK

NO. CAROLINA
(all-new edition)
(original edition)*

OHIO
(all-new edition)
(original edition is out-of-
print)

OKLAHOMA

OREGON

PENNSYLVANIA
(revised edition)

SO. CAROLINA
(all-new edition)
(original edition)*

TENNESSEE
(all-new edition)
(original edition)*

TEXAS

TEXAS II

UTAH

VIRGINIA

VIRGINIA II

WASHINGTON

WEST VIRGINIA

WISCONSIN

*Original editions only available while current
supplies last.

All BEST OF THE BEST STATE COOKBOOKS are 6x9 inches
and comb-bound with illustrations, photographs, and
an index. They range in size from 288 to 352 pages
and each contains over 300 recipes.

Retail price per copy $16.95.

To order by credit card, call toll-free
1-800-343-1583, visit **www.quailridge.com**,
or use the order form shown below.

Order Form

Send check, money order, or credit card info to:
QUAIL RIDGE PRESS • P. O. Box 123 • Brandon, MS 39043

Name _____

Address _____

City_____

State/Zip _____

Phone # _____

Email Address _____

❏ Check enclosed

Charge to: ❏ Visa ❏ MC ❏ AmEx ❏ Disc

Card # _____

Expiration Date _____

Signature _____

Qty.	Title of Book (State) or HOF set	Total

Subtotal _____

Mississippi residents add 7% sales tax _____

Postage ($4.00 any number of books) + $4.00

TOTAL _____